Life in a
RAILWAY
FACTORY

Alfred Williams, known as 'The Hammerman Poet', standing by his steam drop-hammer. He was a skilled craftsman fascinated by all the smith's techniques

Life in a
RAILWAY
FACTORY

Alfred Williams

With an introduction and
commentary to illustrations by
Michael Justin Davis

WRENS
PARK

This edition is for Kaye and Graeme

A Sutton Publishing Book

This illustrated edition first published in 1984 by Alan Sutton Publishing
Limited, an imprint of Sutton Publishing Limited
Phoenix Mill · Thrupp · Stroud · Gloucestershire · GL5 2BU

This edition published in 1999 by Wrens Park Publishing, an imprint of
W.J. Williams & Son Ltd

A catalogue record for this book is available from the British Library

ISBN 0-905-778-316

Typeset in Bembo 11/13.5pt
Typesetting and origination by
Sutton Publishing Limited.
Printed in Great Britain by
Redwood Books Limited,
Trowbridge, Wiltshire.

ACKNOWLEDGEMENTS

The editor is indebted to many people for encouragement, advice and help. He wishes to express his thanks to all, especially to Roger Trayhurn and his colleagues at the Swindon Reference Library; to 'Friends of Alfred Williams', particularly Jack Maisey, JP; to Sue Joslin at 'Railprint'; to Paul Plowman; to Robert Avery; to the Marlborough Branch of the Wiltshire County Library; and to Alan Peck, both for his suggestions and for the information conveyed by his masterly book, *The Great Western at Swindon Works*.

Denis Bird has been extremely generous, and so has Robert Dickinson of the Swindon Museum and Art Gallery, in giving their time, knowledge and skills to finding and providing photographs. The editor is deeply grateful to those experts, and to his wife for her unfailing support and help. To all these kind people, deepest thanks.

Leonard Clark's edition of *Life in a Railway Factory* and his biography, *Alfred Williams, His Life and Work*, have been essential aids for which the editor is grateful. He has also been much helped by the 1911 and 1912 editions of the *Great Western Railway Magazine*.

He wishes to thank Carol Smith, Edward Cowley and Kevin Chan for their typing and their cheerful willingness to help.

For permission to reproduce photographs, acknowledgement is gratefully made as follows: to the Denis Bird Collection, for those on pages xi, xii, xiii, xiv (from the original owned by Mrs Joan Jefferies), xvii (from the *Daily Mirror*), xviii, 12, 13, 26, 27, 28, 29, 34, 48, 49, 50, 51, 60, 61, 62, 63, 64, 65, 72, 78, 94, 95, 110, 111, 115, 118, 119, 206, 207, 209, 212, 213, 234, 235, 245 (bottom), 246, 247, 248 (top), 250 (bottom), 251, 260, 262, 263, 270, 271, 274, 275; to the Borough of Thamesdown (Swindon Museum and Art Gallery) for the frontispiece and those photographs on pages 17, 19, 24, 25, 106, 126, 133, 134, 205, 208, 211, 214, 220, 221, 223, 224, 225, 226, 230, 245 (top), 248 (bottom), 250 (top), 258 (top), 258 (bottom), 259, 261, 272, 280; to British Rail (Western) for those on pages xxxiv, xxxv, 10, 11, 73, 218, 219, 241, 282.

Michael Justin Davis

INTRODUCTION

Life in a Railway Factory is a book that needed to be written. Shortly before the First World War, in the vast and important Swindon Works of the Great Western Railway, the fundamental problems of men in industry were apparent but unsolved. Those problems were, and still are, crucial to the twentieth century. They concern human individuality in an industrial world.

South Marston Village, four miles east of Swindon, about 1900. On right, Dryden Cottage, Alfred and Mary's home for fifteen years after their marriage. On left, village shop

Alfred Williams needed to write the book because he felt passionately about all that he had done and witnessed during his 23 years as a workman in the factory. Himself a skilful, dedicated factory-hand, he was nevertheless by temperament and background an outsider. He was also, by virtue of his exceptional talent and self-education, a dedicated author. The factory both enthralled and repelled him.

He was born in 1877 in the Wiltshire village of South Marston, near Swindon. His father, of Welsh stock, was a carpenter, a fine craftsman; and his mother was a farmer's daughter. The marriage was unhappy: after ten years Alfred's father left her, and she had eight children to bring

White Hart Crossroads, close to South Marston. Alfred passed here to work at Swindon, off left. The horse is coming along Ermine Street from Stratton St Margaret

up. She sold sweets and delivered newspapers to pay for their schooling, and took the older ones gleaning at harvest-time. Despite her poverty she was a fine mother. Alfred, the fifth child, became a 'half-timer' when he was eight, spending only part of the day at school and the rest working for a farmer. He loved his mother's story-telling and the folk-songs that he heard at the farm: and he was an active, adventurous boy who enjoyed games and was fascinated by trains and machinery. Several engine-drivers gave him short rides on the nearby Great Western Railway line to London. For a dare, when he was ten, he lay down between the metals of the track and stayed there while a long train rumbled over him.

At the age of eleven he left school to work full-time on the farm. His delight in country life and its physical activity equipped him to enjoy his job as a farm-labourer, but the pay was wretched. The G.W.R. works in Swindon offered much higher wages, and when he was fifteen he already had marriage in mind. Two of his elder brothers were employed at the G.W.R. works. He decided to leave the farm and join them. Their daily walk from South Marston to Swindon (about four miles) took them to the centre of a thriving community.

White Hart inn, Stratton St Margaret. A photographer standing at the corner could have taken the previous picture. Many villagers kept a barrel of beer at home, according to Alfred

Swindon had been chosen by the G.W.R. as the site of its large central repair depot for the maintenance of locomotive stock when, in 1841, the railway line from London to Bristol was completed. Two years later the works were in regular operation. To accommodate the workers who flocked to the new, expanding industry, the railway-company built a model village of substantial houses, a church, a shopping centre, gardens, a cricket ground, a Mechanics' Institute (for education, social gatherings and concerts), a hostel and other amenities. New Swindon, built on the plain to the north of the old town, grew fast. Railway sidings and workshops developed until they covered 326 acres. When employ-

Alfred and Mary on their wedding day, 21 October 1903. She was three years
his junior. Their honeymoon at Torquay was their first experience
of a seaside holiday

ment reached its peak, 12,000 men were occupied in building and maintaining locomotives, carriages and waggons. Craftsmanship was of the highest order. Apprenticeships served in the railway workshops came to be highly valued as a passport to jobs elsewhere. The company formed a medical fund for railway employees as early as 1847, built a hospital and, as enlightened pioneers, established a health service. Swimming-baths were opened in the year Alfred went to work at the factory, 1892.

He began as a rivet hotter and soon after that he became a furnace boy in the stamping shop, where metal articles were stamped out between dies under steam-hammers. He enjoyed the arduous physical challenge of heavy factory work with its violent processes, and he was completely dependable. In 1893 he became a drop-stamper. Although he accepted the responsibility of being chargeman of his gang, twice he refused further promotion. He would not become foreman, because he did not wish to give orders to others or sacrifice any of his individuality.

Harry Byett, who knew Alfred well, described his appearance as a young man: 'He was well over medium height, spare of flesh, had squarish, angular features, powerful lower jaw; dry, wrinkled and almost colourless lips generally parted in a pleasing smile, revealing pale gums and a perfect set of well-tended, gleaming white teeth. Blue-grey, far-seeing eyes which looked straight into yours, proclaiming sincerity, and forbidding aught else. . . . Light brown hair cropped from time to time, as necessitated by his hot, sweating work as hammerman. Fair complexion; perfectly upright figure, head erect whether walking, standing or sitting, imparting a military bearing and a sense of invincibility when confronted with obstacles.'

In his spare time, Alfred continued to roam the countryside, and he gained a local reputation for knowledge of nearby sites and customs. He took up painting: some of his pictures he sold in the neighbourhood. He also showed an interest in politics, at first as a Liberal. His thirst for knowledge and for self-expression was remarkable. In 1897 he began reading English literature in earnest during his spare time, and would not waste a minute of his dinner hour.

Despite the exhausting demands of full-time factory work and his long daily walk, Alfred began a four year course in English Literature with Ruskin Hall, Oxford, in 1900. Baffled by the numerous Latin quotations in the books he had to study, he determined to teach himself Latin and soon learned much of the *Aeneid* by heart.

When he was 26 he married Mary Peck, a moulder's daughter from

Eddington. They lived at Dryden Cottage, South Marston. At the railway factory he continued to work as a hammerman, rising at 4.00 a m to teach himself Greek and French before walking to Swindon. He rapidly mastered the languages and he read avidly, filling the cottage with books. Mary dedicated her life entirely to him and his needs. On Sundays, they walked in the country. He was a good naturalist, and shared his knowledge with the village children. He and Mary never had children of their own. Among adults he was solitary and an egoist.

His political views moved towards progressive Conservatism. At the factory, as chargeman of his gang he was responsible for six men and three steam-hammers and he worked with masochistic fervour. To help him learn languages, he chalked words on the back of his sooty furnace. An official objected: Alfred refused to obliterate them and antagonism developed.

He translated Ovid, wrote a verse play, and in 1907 and 1909 received praise from the critics for poems published in anthologies. Lord Edmund Fitzmaurice, a member of the Government and an eminent man in Wiltshire, became his patron. When Alfred was 32 he read Richard Jefferies for the first time. Both writers suffered agonies of doubt, but Alfred had come to believe in the Christian God.

Songs in Wiltshire, a book of love songs and nature poems, was published in 1909. It was well received but sold slowly, except among his few friends. He travelled the country at weekends, trying to sell copies, and he lectured at the Mechanics' Institute. He began to be known in Swindon. His health became poor because of overwork, but he refused to give up either his factory work or his writing.

In 1910 he went to a poets' dinner in London. A reporter there advised him to write an account of his experience in the Swindon factory, a suggestion which sowed the seeds of this book. Next day, Alfred was mentioned in the *Daily Mail* as a 'young man who works a steam hammer in the locomotive shop at Swindon in the week and muses with nature on the "Wiltshire Downs" on Sunday'.

Songs in Wiltshire received enthusiastic revues in Berlin, and sales of the book eventually covered all expenses. Alfred worked intensively on its successor, *Poems in Wiltshire*, despite Mary's attempts to persuade him to ease up, and his health deteriorated further. His dependence on her is apparent in these lines he wrote for her thirty-first birthday in 1910, in which he declares that they are one in heart and soul:

> "For thou hast been my loving wife,
>   My father, mother, kindred, all;
>   My comfort of a weary life,
>   My tower, my fortress, and my wall."

This is no empty birthday compliment, because, as Leonard Clark, Alfred's biographer, points out, Mary guarded her husband jealously against all disturbances and devoted her whole life to him. When he

POETIC BLACKSMITH.

Mr. Alfred Williams, Swindon's poetic blacksmith, composing a sonnet during his dinner-hour. Among his admirers was Mr. Swinburne.—(*Daily Mirror* photograph.)

Cutting from *Daily Mirror*, about 1910

wrote he needed her company, so she sat up with him far into the night. 'She was no scholar herself, but sympathetic to all he undertook: her nature was so finely drawn that she understood the nature of all his strivings.' A self-effacing, devoted wife, 'she looked upon her task as a privilege.' *Poems in Wiltshire* was published in 1911. It includes nature poems, autobiographical work and translations.

Realising that ill health might force him to give up factory work and turn to writing for a living, Alfred decided that his next book was to be in prose: 'a record of my experience in the workshop, strong, faithful pictures of the industrial life, rough and vigorous.' He wrote it in twelve weeks 'at night, after leaving the forge'. In the autumn of 1911, he could declare: 'I have written a prose book this summer entitled *Life in the Factory*, about 250pp which greatly pleases me. I have the confidence to hope that it will be of interest to a great many when I have the opportunity of printing it, which will not be yet, however.' It was

WEA ramble, Bassett Down House, late 1920s. Back row: Alfred (left),
Reuben George (centre). Middle row: Mrs Reuben George (left),
Mary (next), Misses E. Alley and W. Davis, milliners

obvious to Alfred that he could not publish his outspoken account of life in the railway factory without losing his job there. He had, though, tried 'to give a faithful picture of the *life* of the place. Not of localities and machinery. Neither is it of an aggressive kind, but moderate in tone, though sufficiently sympathetic with the people, I hope.'

Alfred acknowledged that the question of Capital and Labour was a delicate one. What he experienced, in his own workshop, summed up his grievance: 'There is a total lack of tact in dealing with the workmen; it is the haughty and autocratic spirit of the staff generally which drives men to extreme views.' He confessed that his own position was 'somewhat illogical. Frankly, I cannot subscribe to the extreme views held by the Socialist-Labour people. Of late years I have inclined to the moderate view, though this again is not compatible with true progress.' Alfred's passionate concern for the individual made 'the moderate view' uncomfortable to maintain. Through the Workers' Educational Association, which he had belonged to for a number of years, he was in touch with powerful thinkers such as Alfred Zimmern, Albert Mansbridge (founder of the W.E.A.) and Reuben George (Secretary of the Swindon Branch).

While Alfred's account of factory life awaited publication, more of his poetry appeared, and so did two prose books: *A Wiltshire Village* and *Villages of the White Horse*. These are loving, detailed, vivid portrayals of local people and places. By 1912, Williams had spent all his life savings on the publication of his poetry, and considered emigrating to Canada. Outside Wiltshire he was regarded as a genuine poet.

A Wiltshire Village sold well and *Cor Cordium*, Alfred's most intense book of poetry, was published in 1913. Its tone is philosophical and religious. *Villages of the White Horse,* published in the same year, contains some of his most evocative prose.

In February, 1914, Alfred was forced by 'violent pains below the heart' to take his bed and 'lie up for a week or two'. Smoke from the furnaces had, his doctor told him, destroyed the whole of Alfred's digestive system. His body could no longer bear the double burden of factory work and writing. In his early days, he had welcomed heavy manual toil as a relief from literary work. Now he had come to hate everything connected with the factory. On 3rd September, 1914, he left the railway works for ever, having chalked on the plate above his furnace the single Latin word *VICI*: 'I have conquered'. Perhaps he *had* conquered; but he left in a mood of bitterness.

He was, however, a resilient man with very wide interests. He began collecting the words of local folk-songs, from singers in the villages, and took up market-gardening. His condemnation of factory life was published in 1915. The book abounds in portraits of characters, and the degradation to which they are subjected is unflinchingly described. *Life in a Railway Factory* created a dramatic stir and received exciting reviews.

The Daily Chronicle hailed it as 'a book of revelation', *The Globe* said it deserved to stand beside the sociological works of Prince Kropotkin and *The Yorkshire Post* regarded it as 'literature in the Carlylean sense, being an actual transcription of life as lived by the writer.' *The Times Literary Supplement* considered it at length, in the following review:

THE WORKSHOP FROM WITHIN

LIFE IN A RAILWAY FACTORY BY ALFRED WILLIAMS (Duckworth, 5s. net)

This book may be read either as pure literature or as a social study; it is both. The author is a workman who has already achieved a recognized literary standing in poetry and prose. He is best known as a lover of nature and an observer of country life, gifted with the poet's dower of insight, sympathy, passion, and musical expression. He has here turned his gifts on to the factory in which he has worked for twenty-three years. He describes it faithfully. He gives us a picture of the workshops and the men in them, not with any ulterior purpose, but as a study of life. He tells us what the place is like, what the men are like, what work they do, how they do it, how they behave, how they are treated. All this is described quite simply and directly, without any straining after effect, but with the vividness of intimate knowledge and genuine feeling. There is neither 'word-painting' on the one hand, nor an affected dryness on the other. Mr. Williams puts into words what he sees as well as he can, and since he is a born observer with a gift of words and a love of truth, and since his subject is real life, the result is admirable.

The book has a special interest, merely as description, just now, when such works as those described have been raised by the war into a novel position and have become objects of universal attention. The particular works described are those of the Great Western Railway at Swindon; and they are what we call in this country 'engineering' works, though a great many things beside engines are made there. The railway works are among those which have been converted, more or less completely, to war purposes, because they are equipped for making many of the things required; and the appliances and processes described by Mr. Williams are now being used, with qualifications, for war work. Anyone who wishes to know what these places are like and what is done in them will get a better general idea from his book than from any other source that we know. Its value for the general public is not appreciably lessened by a certain weakness on the technical side, provided that readers do not rely too much on detailed accuracy. For instance, Mr. Williams says that 'very little iron ore is now manufactured on the premises.' He does not mean ore, which is not manufactured at all on the premises, or, indeed, anywhere else; it is smelted in blast furnaces. He means pig iron. There are sundry little slips of this kind, and some of the things he describes are antiquated. But the general view of the works and the descriptions of particular shops are perfectly true to life. His own work was stamping; but all the processes with hot metal evidently attract him, and his account of the forge, the smiths, and the hammermen, is the best in the book. For the delicate work of the moulders and the skilled engineers he has less sympathy.

Upon what are called 'social questions' the book throws a very instructive light for those who read it with understanding. Hardly anything is said about trade unions and Socialism, but there is a good deal about 'unrest'; and the first chapter contains a strong indictment of the treatment of workmen by 'the capitalist and his agents'. Two things are emphasized. One is the lack of personal recognition and consideration, the other is the speeding up of machinery and driving of the men without any corresponding recompense. Both charges are well founded; but to understand them fully it is necessary to note carefully what he says and to remember what manner of man he is. He evidently feels the first grievance most keenly himself, no doubt because he has suffered from it. This is how he puts it:–

> One thing is specially to be deplored in the factory, and that is the serious lack of recognition and appreciation of the skilful and conscientious workman; there is very little inducement for anyone to make efforts in order to obtain better results at the steam hammer or other machine. If a workman proves himself to be possessed of unusual skill and originality, instead of being rewarded for it, he is boycotted and held in check. Even the managers are not above exhibiting the same petty feeling where they find their ideas have been eclipsed by those of less authority.

And again:–

> If any sharp and enterprising workman sees the possibility of improvement anywhere and makes a suggestion he is soundly snubbed for his pains. . . . But those

ideas which are most valuable, provided they are not complex and the simple-minded official can readily grasp them, he secretly cherishes and stealthily develops, and afterwards parades them to his superior with swaggering pride as his own inventions. . . . Meanwhile the very workman whose idea has been purloined and exploited is treated as a danger by the foreman; henceforth he must be watched and kept well in subjection. The cowardly overseer sees in him a possible rival and is fearful for his own credit.

This is the grievance of a superior man and the result of personal experience. It does not touch the bulk of the men, who are truthfully described as apathetic, fond of the factory and the town, given to artless merriment, and on the whole enjoying life more than those who pity them. They take the work as it comes and do not notice things which distress a man of refined nature like Mr. Williams. It is the superior and intellectual man of his type who suffers in the factory; and the reason is that he is a fish out of water. Such men are not common, but are becoming more numerous. The most irksome thing to them is the degrading treatment they receive from their factory superiors, who are their intellectual inferiors and hate them for it. They are kept down and bullied, and live in a state of mental suffocation from which they feel impotent to escape. The second grievance affects a far larger number of men, and especially the best and hardest workers. The reward they get for speeding up is having the price cut. It is utterly foolish and stupid from the employer's own point of view; but he can no more be moved from the belief that it is advantageous to him to pay low wages than the workman can from the corresponding belief that there is only a fixed quantity of work, which must be spun out in order to 'go round.'

The persons most responsible for both the grievances denounced by Mr. Williams are the minor officials immediately over the men – the foremen and overseers. The book is full of the foremen and their ways. And who are they? Ex-workmen and trade unionists, generally members of that exclusive caste – the engineers. Nearly all the foremen of the different sheds, says Mr. Williams, are appointed from among the fitters; anyone else has very little chance. Simple folk who talk about giving labour 'a share in the management' – they are talking about it now – are recommended to study this passage.

Before a fitter has been promoted to the position of foreman he is a bold champion of the rights of labour, one loud in the expression of his sympathy with his fellow-men, a staunch believer in the liberty of the individual and a hearty condemner of the factory system. If he has been appointed overseer, however, there is a considerable change in his manner and attitude towards all these and kindred subjects. A great modification of his personal views and opinions soon follows; he begins to look at things from the official standpoint. He is now fond of telling you that 'things are not as they used to be.' . . . At the same time he will be fairly loyal to his old mates, the journeyman fitters, and treat them with superior respect. To the labourers, however, he will not be so disposed. He will ignore their interests and rule them with a rod of iron.

Mr. Williams urges, and looks forward confidently to, shorter hours, better wages, and more freedom for workmen; and we believe that he is perfectly right. The speeding up of machinery must be accompanied by a shortening of hours. It is plain common sense and sound economy. But if any should wish to appeal to humanity too, the pathetic picture of Pinnell and the Yankee hammers will give them material.

Very different from that sympathetic appreciation of Alfred's work was the hostile and damning review printed in the G.W.R. magazine in January, 1916:

A POET'S LIFE IN A RAILWAY FACTORY

'A chiel's amang ye takin' notes,
And, faith, he'll prent it.'
                                        – *Burns*

Mr Alfred Williams, 'the Wiltshire Poet,' who worked for over twenty years at the forge in the Great Western Railway Works at Swindon, is the author of a recently-published book entitled 'Life in a Railway Factory.' The book is of interest in more than one respect. Firstly, it describes graphically the workshop from within – the worker's life from his own outlook, or rather, as we shall endeavour to shew, from this particular worker's own point of view, amid the furnaces, smoke, steam and din of machinery, and in his contact with the living organisation of foremen, supervisors, managers, and 'the firm.' Secondly, it has merits from a purely literary point of view. Its style is natural and pleasing, the author's studies of various types of workmen and his vivid descriptions of things and tasks are strikingly good, while the liveliness that runs through every page maintains interest, induces sympathy, and compels reflection. On account of both these aspects the book has attracted considerable notice and not a few commendations.

In the Magazine for October last was given a brief sketch of Mr. Williams's remarkable career and an appreciation of some of his poetical works. The emergence from obscurity of a man of high literary attainments and the revelation of a character which, considering its persistent struggle against adverse circumstances, smacks of genius, are matters of uncommon interest; and there is a third aspect of the book before us – an aspect that will gain in interest as the author continues to rise, as he seems destined to do, in the literary world – namely, that it affords a study of the poet's mind in prosaic surroundings, where poesy is of small account compared with brawn, and where the poet's temperament must have received many a rude shock.

The description of life in a railway factory is such as to represent that the general conditions were almost unendurable. Had the book not been written by a man of abnormal susceptibilities whose heart was in hedgerows, flowers, and streamlets, its lurid descriptions would cause one to wonder that the earth had not long ago opened and swallowed up the Swindon Works, with all that appertained unto them.

At the forge Mr. Williams was utterly out of his element; the work, surroundings, and general conditions were all and always bitter to his taste; while at his work his mind was roaming in the fields, on the hills, among the flowers of the countryside, or straying to the books of his beloved library. He used the tarred surface of his boiler for marking thereon extracts from Greek authors, which he was bent on memorising, and felt pain and mortification when his less classical mates poked fun at these exercises or put a fresh coat of tar on the boiler.

Would it not be expecting too much to look for an uncoloured description from one endowed with these attributes – to suppose that there could be, in such a case, straight vision?

In fairness to all concerned at the Swindon Works – and from the highest to the lowest no one escapes more or less castigation – it is well to bear in mind the oblique mentality of the writer, due so largely to the uncongenial environment.

He detested the factory simply because it *was* a factory. To him the buildings, because they shut out views of hills and fields, were like fortresses or prisons. Here is his description:–

'Southward the shed faces a yard of about ten acres in extent. This is bounded on
every side by other workshops and premises, all built of the same dingy materials –
brick, slate, and iron – blackened with smoke, dust, and steam, surmounted with tall
chimneys, innumerable ventilators, and poles for the telephone wires, which effectively
block out all perspective. To view it from the interior is like looking around the inner
walls of a fortress. There is no escape for the eye; nothing but bricks and mortar, iron
and steel, smoke and steam arising. It is ugly; and the sense of confinement within the
prison-like walls of the factory renders it still more dismal to those who have any
thought of the hills and fields beyond. . . . The sky, roofs, walls, the engines moving to
and fro, the rolling stock, the stacks of plates and ingots of iron and steel, the sleepers for
the rails, the ground underneath – everything is dark, sombre, and repellent. Not a glint
upon the steel lines! Not a refraction of light from the slates on the roof! Everything is
dingy, dirty, and drab. And drab is the mind of the toiler all this time, drab as the skies
above and the walls beneath. Doomed to the confinement from which there is no
escape, he accepts the conditions and is swallowed up in his environment.'

What man in a normal state of mind would bemoan that the
workshops were not situated in a flower garden? Drabness and sombre-
ness are unavoidable – if regrettable – attributes of smoking furnaces,
machinery, and vast manufacturing premises; unfortunately, we 'have
need of all these things' – and Swindon possesses no monopoly in them.

The man is a Nature-lover, and no blame to himself; but were our
author travelled, what might he not say of perspective in relation to the
flat iron buildings of New York, of the infernos of the Black Country, of
the industrial surroundings on the Clyde, the Mersey, the Logan, or the
Liffey – of the æsthetic aspect of the Lancashire mill, or the Glamorgan
iron-works? There should be more to come. We are not sure that
inspiration might not be sought in a printing house office.

'Dark, sombre and repellent!' If a *miner* had said it, we could understand.

He hated the factory and all its associations, with the possible
exception of a fence and a hedgerow on the northern boundary of the
works' yard, where some wild flowers bloomed; here

'the rosebay climbed up the ash bank and ran among the metals, growing and thriving
high among the iron wheels and frames of carriages, and revelling in the soft ashes and
cinders of the track. Blooming side by side with it were the delicate toadflax, bright
golden ragwort, wild mignonette, ox-eye daisies, meadow-sweet, ladies' bedstraw,
and other flowers; the wild rose bloomed to perfection and the bank was richly draped
with a vigorous growth of dewberry, laden with blossoms and fruit. In a corner,
beside a streamlet, was a patch of cats'-tails and a magnificent mass of butter-bur.'

Alas! the patch of cats'-tails and butter-bur was denied. This fairest
piece
of the premises was forbidden ground. The soul-less 'management'

placed it under the eye of watchmen, who ordered the men away. And why? He supplies the reason, although far from having any sympathy with it. It was that a number of slackers had been known to go that way, not to gaze on the flowers, but to jump over the fence and decamp from the factory while booked at their machines!

He is severe upon many of the workmen. In fact, he is down upon everybody and everything. 'The workmen do not think for themselves; and if you should be at the pains of pointing out anything for their benefit, they will tell you that you are mad, or curse you for a Socialist. It would need an earthquake to rouse many of the men out of their apathy and indifference. . . . The whole system of life requires overhauling and revolutionising; the national character is become flat and stale.'

He speaks thus of the unsympathetic nature of the workmen:

'One has to die before his mates in the shed think there is anything the matter with him. Then, in nine cases out of ten – especially if he happens to be one of the poorest and most unfortunate – he is mercilessly sneered over. Probably that was his own fault. They even blame him for dying; in three days he is almost totally forgotten. Cruel hearts and feelings are bred in the atmosphere of the factory.'

And out of it, Mr. Williams; remember Belgium and Serbia!

The author's bitter spirit against the management gave him an ungovernable disposition to credit the most uncharitable rumours or idle tittle-tattle about them. He says, for example:

'I remember once, when the work was slack in the shed, the day overseer left orders for the night boss to send the men outside in the yard and keep them there for two or three hours shifting scrap iron, in order that they might "catch cold and stop at home, and give the others a chance." After the last great discharge of hands at the factory, in the year 1909, when a thousand men were dismissed, in order to "reduce expenses", it was reported that every manager at the works was granted a substantial increase in salary.'

We happen to be in a position to know that there was absolutely no foundation for this statement.

He preached unconditional discontent:

'When I hear of a man's being satisfied I know that he is done for; he might as well be dead.'

It is fortunate for the industrial welfare of the nation that workers of this type are rare, and that the men usually take a commendable interest

in the vast and important activities that they carry on within factory walls.
It seems that all the while the author was at his work he was longing for
finishing time, and he condemned wholesale every workman who was not
as eager as himself to get away.

'Every hour spent outside the factory walls is a precious addition to life; whoever
willingly throws away the opportunity of enjoying it is guilty of the highest folly and
negligence. He is the curtailer of his dearest rights and liberties, the forger of fetters for
himself and his children after him, and the sooner the working classes can be brought to
see this, the better it will be for them.'

The spirit in which he entered upon his duties day by day may be gauged
from the following description of the morning start:

'As for a smile! A morning smile on the way to work is indeed a rarity. . . . There is
the day's work to be faced, the smoke and heat, the long stand at the machine, the
tedious confinement, the hard work and bitter speech, the daily anxiety, the unnatural
combat for the necessaries of life, and it all looms big on the horizon. . . . A terrible din,
that could be heard in the yard long before you came to the doors of the shed, is already
awaiting. . . . The morning freshness, the bloom, vigour, the hopeful spirit, the whole
natural man will be entirely quelled and subdued after the first few moments of this
living pandemonium. Wife and children, friends and home, town and village, green
fields and blue skies, the whole outside world will have been left far behind. There is no
opportunity to think of anything but iron and steel, furnaces and hammers, the coming
race and battle for existence.

We might recall, in this connection, that the author elsewhere acknowledges that he found opportunities while at his work to think about his
Greek and other studies, and to mark his exercises on the boiler's surface.
So much for day work. What of the night shift? Here is his description
of it:

'Whatever the trials of the day shift at the forge may be, those of the night turn are
sure to be far greater. . . . There is a poignancy in preparing for the night shift, the
feeling is really one of tragedy. . . . You are off to sweat and slave in a modern inferno,
in the Cyclops' den, with the everlasting wheels, the smoke and steam, the flaring
furnace and piles of blazing hot metal all around you. . . . Arrived at the shed, you are
greeted with the familiar and dreadful din of the boilers priming, the loud roar of the
blast and the whirl of the wheels. . . . There are many things to keep you alive, and
always the fear of not earning your money for the turn and having to be jeered at and
bullied by the chargeman or overseer, and so have your life made miserable. . . . The
greatest weariness assails you about midnight, and continues to possess you till towards
three o'clock. Then Nature struggles violently, demanding her rights, twitching,
clutching, and tugging at your eyelids and striving in a thousand ways to bring you into

submission and force her rule upon you, but the iron laws of necessity, circumstance, and system prevail; you must battle the power within you and repel the sweet soother, struggling on in the unnatural combat. . . .

A few minutes before six o'clock the engines slow down and stop, and the roar of the blast ceases. The mighty toil is over, for this turn, at any rate. The forgers, stampers, and smiths file out of the shed. Not for them the joy of morning, the vigour, freshness and bloom, the keen delight in the open air, the happy heart and elevated spirit. They slouch away, half-blinded with the bright daylight, blinking and sighing, feeling unutterably and unnaturally tired, out of sorts and out of place, too, and crawl home like rats to their holes.'

Or, in some cases, to study Nature and rhythm!

With remarkable inconsistency, however, when it suited Mr. Williams to criticise the management in regard to the working of overtime, he advocated an extension of night working! 'The putting on of a few new hands,' he says, '*and the addition of a night shift* would obviate much overtime and give the unemployed a chance.'

One may reasonably question why, if he found the employment so unendurable as depicted, he clung to it for upwards of twenty years. It was open to him to put in his notice at any time and leave. If, to be charitable to his views, we assume that in his particular case there were peculiar circumstances that compelled him to endure for these long years the tortures of 'a modern inferno,' surely other workmen would have shown greater independence and shaken the dust of the Swindon Works from off their feet.

Other portions of the book show that the author's soured view of life in the railway factory was not shared by the other men who worked there. The following are examples:–

'Once a man becomes settled in the factory he is very reluctant to leave it. Notwithstanding the rigour of the system imposed, he usually remains there till the end of his working days, unless he happens to meet with an accident or dismissal.'

'As soon as it becomes known that it is intended to discharge a number of hands considerable anxiety is evidenced by the rank and file, and especially by the unskilled of the shed. They begin to quake and tremble and to be full of apprehension.'

'I know of several cases in which workmen have been offered financial help in order to instal them in small-holdings, and they have refused point-blank.'

'Men with families take great care to get their sons started in the shed at the very earliest opportunity. As soon as they leave school they are brought along in knickerbockers and presented to the overseer, with the earnest hope of a speedy admission to work on the premises.'

We have no desire to detract from the author's reputation. As a literary man, and more so as a poet, we hold him in high esteem. With the beauties of Nature – which his soul loves – he is at home, and his passion intensifies the charm of his poetical utterances. His service in the Swindon factory yielded as much satisfaction to him – and as little – as an artist would derive from a machine-made daub. To this, no doubt, is to be ascribed the tone of reproach and bitterness that runs through the book. In the preface he acknowledges failings and prejudices. We cannot help feeling it to be regrettable that he allowed them to dominate him.

> All seems infected that th' infected spy,
> As all looks yellow to a jaundic'd eye.
> – Pope

It is not pleasant to discover that a mind capable, on the one hand, of sweet conceptions and sublime expressions, on the other can be moved to bitter prejudices and unwholesome gibes.

If one of the objects of the book is to gird at labour because it *is* labour, we can only say that, after all, labour is honest and manly – since man was born to it; and it is to be hoped that until we reach the millennium there will be plenty of it. In the past, the lack of it has given great trouble.

But Mr. Williams is a good writer, and we recommend his book to impartial perusal. If he labours at making some more, they will be welcome.

Distressed by these criticisms, Alfred asked the editor of the G.W.R. magazine to allow him to reply. The editor refused, on the grounds that space was short in wartime: but, when pressed, he grudgingly consented and in March, 1916, the following letter from Alfred Williams appeared in the G.W.R. magazine:

Dear Sir, I shall not attempt to plead extenuation nor seek to justify myself in relation to anything I wrote in my book, 'Life in a Railway Factory,' for I assume there is no need of either. To me the things of which I wrote were so simple and so unavoidably obvious that I could not possibly escape mentioning them, if I wrote at all. I said many serious things, and I knew they were serious things. I wrote the book in twelve weeks, in summer, at night, after leaving the forge, but I held it for three years before publication. In that interval I read it many times, and inquired of myself whether or not I might tone down the materials and admit modifications. In the meantime, matters at the factory developed upon such a line that it would have been utterly impossible for me to alter what I had penned without being guilty of misrepresentation and personal timidity. The opportunity occurred to me; I made use of it.

Your reviewer says many pleasant things of myself and of my work, and I thank him for his sincerity, and for his generosity. I am candid, and he is candid. I admire a brave man, and I do not object to criticism when I perceive that the critic has studied his subject. I can drink my medicine cheerfully and go on my way strengthened and refreshed. I may here confess that I do not make a practice of replying indiscriminately to reviews of my books. If an author should be induced to do that he might obtain a little self-advertisement, but he would certainly deteriorate in mental strength and composure. But since your article touches me somewhat nearly and has been read by many of my old personal mates in the factory, who know me well, and by thousands of thoughtful and intelligent persons elsewhere employed on the Great Western Railway, who do not know me, and since, if I do not explain away several of the misconceptions entertained by your reviewer, they may come to be believed and accepted as matters of fact by those who could have no opportunities of forming an accurate and independent estimation of my writings and of my character, I should like to be allowed to say a few words in my own behalf.

First, as to my 'abnormal sensibilities' and my 'oblique mentality.' These are indeed hard words, and would cut like knives to the heart of more than one writer of my acquaintance. And they would undoubtedly sear me, too, if I were half as tender and exquisite as the reviewer imagines me to be. It may well be that the poets Keats and Kirke White were done to death by the pens of their reviewers. For myself, I am in no such danger. If I had been excessively sensitive I should have been stifled long ago. The man of abnormal sensibilities never finally succeeds anywhere; it is the choice spirit contained in the tough, rude casket that survives and eventually triumphs. My 'oblique mentality' may be a matter of taste or opinion. The same might also be said of my point of view, which is of rather slight importance. To my mind the thing that matters is not whether my point of view is that of the average individual or not, but whether what I have written is accurate or inaccurate. The average working man has no very precise point of view. It is certain that my own does not fully coincide with that ordinarily expressed. What seems to have embarrassed your reviewer was the fact that I am both independent in outlook and unconventional in behaviour. From this independence and unconventionality I derive satisfaction; they are my stronghold, from which I am not to be too easily driven or expelled.

One of the most obvious, and perhaps the most pardonable, mistakes your reviewer commits is that of supposing that I was possessed of a continual and bitter hatred of the factory, and of everything that pertained to it, and he quotes several passages from my book which, because they embody a little nature description, he considers explanatory of my attitude and proof positive that my thoughts and interests were on the hills and about the meadows and countryside. The real truth is that those passages are among the weakest in the book, and their presence in it could not be defended if it were not that they are there for a purpose, which is merely to describe the immediate environment of the works and give to the stamping shed its local setting; they have no other significance whatever. The pity is that description is mistaken for condemnation. I describe, not condemn. The scheme is the same throughout the book. I have depicted; appreciation or condemnation may be expressed at pleasure, and in whatever degree appears most fitting to the reader. I never hated the factory. As a matter of fact, many of my most happy days were spent there. It was there I found contact with the soul of the world. There I learned the lessons of life. There I became linked with humanity. There, also, I consolidated my studies, and, while working at my steam-hammer, peered through the world and out into the universe beyond. I consider the best gifts I possess I owe to my connection with the factory, always excepting that inestimable one – the original spirit within me, and the determination never to be beaten, to master my conditions, and not to let them master me. I had many true friends in the factory; I have them still. Some of them I criticised, and, as your reviewer puts it, castigated; I am happy to know that they accepted my criticism generously, and our friendship is unimpaired.

As, when a boy, I embraced the cattle in the field, so I afterwards embraced my steam-hammer, and rejoiced in striking the perfect blow, and in evolving new ideas as to dies and processes. As time went on, however, and the studied cruelty of those in authority became more and more manifest, I became a little sick at heart, not on my own account – for I knew my strength – but on that of those around me, who had not the means of escape, which were always open to me, when I felt inclined to make use of them. And this I will say here: the most cruel and bitter torture I suffered at any time in the factory proceeded not from any sense of isolation, as your reviewer suggests, but from a knowledge of the deliberate and systematic smothering of my original and inventive faculty by the shed foreman, and from the certainty that whatever suggestions I might make for the good of the work were doomed to be frustrated; that I could not improve and simplify a forging, lessen the toil and expenses of production, and assist manufacture in what I considered to be the only real and vital direction. My workmates never derided me, or made fun of my studiousness. On the other hand, they were proud of me, and of my attainments. We agreed well together, and to them I was no mystery. It was the foreman who wickedly assailed and humiliated me, who obliterated my beautiful Greek and Latin words, and periodically smeared my furnace and tool chests with grease and tar, using the pretext that he had instructions from the manager of the department to do so, though we knew that was absolutely false. And I believe most, if not all, in the shed remember when word was left for men of the night turn to be sent into the yard shifting scrap-iron, so that they might 'catch cold and stop at home, and give the others a chance.' It was an outrageous proposition, but I am confident that it was made. With regard to the discharge of hands in 1909, and the matter of the managers' salaries, you will note that I merely said 'it was reported,' as it most certainly was, and very freely, too, as has been confirmed to me within these last few days.

When your reviewer goes on to say that all the while I was at the factory I was longing for finishing time, that I had no interest in my work, that I am dominated by bitter prejudices, and so on, he is labouring his case, and committing an injustice rather against himself than against me. I am aware that I have been subjected to a certain amount of slanderous abuse by those who were anxious to prove my uselessness and general incompetence – to use no worse terms – both in and out of the shed. This affects me but little, however. The folly is theirs, and not mine. In respect to this I might point out that at the age of fourteen I left the farm for the factory; at seventeen I was made chargeman over three steam-hammers and six men; for the following twenty years I was head drop-stamper, and I held every record on the ground for speed stamping in heavy or light materials, for producing bright and clean work, and for the greatest length of life of the dies used in the steam-hammer. The many extracts taken from my book and printed with the review do not faithfully represent the general tone,

scheme, and argument of the chapters. A paragraph taken from its context and placed side by side with another passage similarly detached from its original position might easily appear negative and directly contradictory, whereas, considered in the order and sequence of the whole, it is perfectly correct and admissible.

There is much more I could say and many points are raised by the reviewer which might be elucidated by a little brief comment, but I fear that I have already trespassed at too great a length upon your time and space. I would, however, like this to be borne in mind. I am out to depict real life. Three volumes I have penned on that of the countryside; the fourth deals with that of the factory. The basis and point of view in all these are identical; everywhere I have employed the same method, and observed with the same eye. It is illogical, because the scene was different, to say that here or there my vision was distorted. If it is distorted in one case it is so in all, and if it is once correct then it is everywhere correct. The life of the factory is forced, artificial, and unnatural, to a greater degree, in my opinion, than it has need to be. What I have shown of it is literal and reliable, and it must stand in contrast with my picture of that other life outside, which is fresher, simpler, purer more beautiful, and the more abiding.

Faithfully yours,

ALFRED WILLIAMS

South Marston, Swindon,
February 14th, 1916.

Although *Life in a Railway Factory* was praised by unbiased reviewers, the book sold badly. During its first year, only about a dozen copies were bought in Swindon, to Alfred's bitter disappointment. He and Mary somehow managed to live on next to nothing at this time. His gardening yielded little, but he persisted in cycling long distances to collect folk-songs.

In 1916, worried by not fighting for his country, he volunteered for military service. To his surprise, doctors passed him as fit and he became a gunner in the Royal Field Artillery. He was a keen and effective one.

Overleaf: GWR men photographed in September 1915, for identification in respect of government work in wartime

While stationed in Fermoy Barracks, Co. Cork, he injured his back lifting a gun trailer. He became friendly with Ida Levinge, a nurse who loved poetry. Mary, living at home in extreme poverty, was hurt, but he tried to reassure her in his letters. His correspondents at this time included the Poet Laureate, Robert Bridges.

The battery left for India in 1917. Conditions for the troops aboard were wretched: the food was inadequate and the squalor appalling. He wrote a book about the soldiers. Three days in Capetown provided some relief, but while crossing the Indian Ocean he burned his feet badly in the sun.

From Bombay, the battery moved to Roorkee. India disappointed Alfred at first: it seemed dull, dirty and unapproachable. He was worried about the health of his mother, whom he had left sick: now he heard that she was dead.

The soldiers' pay was delayed, and Mary's rheumatism and poverty brought him additional anxiety. India, however, soon began to fascinate Alfred, who defied convention and mixed with the Indians as much as he could. He showed great interest in all aspects of Indian life, and travelled whenever possible. The battery moved to Cawnpore and to Ranikhet, within sight of Mount Everest. He loved the landscapes, trees, flowers and animals. The battery did not go into action and he made time to write two more prose books: one about the voyage out and one about his experiences in India. These manuscripts, like *Boys of the Battery*, were rejected by publishers and remain unpublished.

In India, his philosophical and religious ideas were challenged by a great alien culture: he rejected formal Christianity and came to believe in the unity of all spiritual insight. He considered settling in India with Mary, but the lure of his own plot of soil in England, with his own fruit trees on it, proved strong enough to bring him home to be demobilised in 1919 and to settle down with Mary in South Marston again. He found himself virtually forgotten as a writer, but a grant from the Royal Literary Fund helped him when he was desperately poor.

With their own hands, he and Mary built themselves a house, 'Ranikhet', using old bricks from the lock walls of a disused canal. The work was physically agonising: but in 1921 they moved in, and this house in South Marston remains. There, Alfred completed his attractive prose book *Round about the Upper Thames* (1922), compiled *Folk Songs of the Upper Thames* (1923), and embarked on his most amazing project: he taught himself Sanskrit. He also continued to write poetry, newspaper articles and a novel, and to struggle with market gardening. His poverty was dire, but somehow he and Mary survived. Having mastered Sanskrit, he translated *Tales from the Panchatantra*. Basil Blackwell agreed to publish these.

Eventually Mary fell ill. When Alfred visited her in hospital and realised that she had cancer, the news proved mortal to him. He died at 'Ranikhet' in April, 1930. Mary was brought home from hospital and watched his funeral from their upstairs window. She died in a few weeks.

Tales from the Panchatantra was published posthumously, some months later. It is a rich but virtually unknown memorial to Alfred Williams, for whom a Civil List Pension arrived too late.

Of Alfred's many and varied works, the one which perhaps most urgently demands attention now is *Life in a Railway Factory*. It is a deeply human, richly detailed book, appreciative of man's generosity, strength, skill, devotion and sense of fair-play: but intensely scornful of man's inhumanity, selfishness, arrogance and ruthlessness. The outraged author is warm in his sympathy for those who are young, unfortunate, wronged or weak. He loves the country, loathes industrial ugliness, but grapples with the human problems that modern life imposes. An idealist with his feet on the ground, Alfred has much to say to all of us who, in our imperfect world, need to work harmoniously together.

Michael Justin Davis
June, 1984

Life in a
RAILWAY
FACTORY

Life in a
Railway Factory

PREFACE

My object in penning 'Life in a Railway Factory' was to take advantage of the opportunities I have had as a workman, during twenty-three years' continuous service in the sheds, of setting down what I have seen and known for the interest and education of others, who might like to be informed as to what is the actual life of the factory, but who have no means of ascertaining it from the generality of literature published upon the matter.

The book opens with a short survey of several causes of labour unrest and suggestions as to its remedy. Then follows a brief description of the stamping shed, which is the principal scene and theatre of the drama of life exhibited in the pages, the central point from which our observations were made and where the chief of our knowledge and experience was acquired. After a glance into the interior we explore the surroundings and pay a visit to the rolling mills, and watch the men shingling and rolling the iron and forging wheels for the locomotives. Continuing our perambulation of the yard we encounter the shunters, watchmen, carriage finishers, painters, washers-down, and cushion-beaters. The old canal claims a moment's attention, then we pass on to the ash-wheelers, bricklayers, road-waggon builders, and the wheel-turning shed. Leaving them behind we come to the 'field,' where the old broadgauge vehicles were broken up or converted, and proceed thence into the din of the frame-building shed and study some portion of its life. Next follows an exploration of the smithy and a consideration of the smith at work and at home, his superior skill and characteristics. From our study of the smiths we pass to that of the fitters, forgemen, and boilermakers, and complete our tour of the premises by visiting the foundry and viewing the operations of the moulders.

The early morning stir in the town and country around the sheds, the preparations for work, the manner in which the toilers arrive at the factory, and the composition of the crowd are next described, after which we enter the stamping shed and witness the initial toils of the forgemen and stampers, view the oil furnace and admire the prowess of 'Ajax' and his companions. The drop-hammers and their staff receive proportionate attention; then follows a comparison of forging and smithing, a study of several personalities, and an inspection of the plant known as the Yankee Hammers. Chapter XI is a description of the first quarter at the forge expressed entirely by means of actual conversations, ejaculations, commands, and repartees, overheard and faithfully recorded. Following that is a first-hand account of how the night shift is worked, giving one entire night at the forge and noting the various physical phases through which the workman passes and indicating the effects produced upon the body by the inversion of the natural order of things. The remainder of the chapters is devoted to the description and explanation of a variety of matters, including the manner of putting on and discharging hands, methods of administration, intimidating and terrorising, the interpretation of moods and feelings during the passage of the day, week and year, holidays, the effects of cold and heat, causes of sickness and accidents, the psychology of fat and lean workmen, comedy, tragedy, short time and overtime, the advantages – or disadvantages – of education and intelligence, ending up with a review of the industrial situation as it was before the war and remarks upon the future outlook. A table of wages paid at the works is added as an appendix.

The site of the factory is the Wiltshire town of Swindon. This stands at the extremity of the Upper Thames Valley, in the centre of a vast agricultural tract, and is seventy-seven miles from London and about forty from Bristol. Its population numbers approximately fifty thousand, all largely dependent upon the railway sheds for subsistence. The inhabitants generally are a heterogeneous people. The majority of the works' officials, the clerical staff, journeymen, and the highly skilled workers have been imported from other industrial centres; the labourers and the less highly trained have been recruited wholesale from the villages and hamlets surrounding the town. About twelve thousand men, including clerks, are normally employed at the factory. A knowledge of the composition of the inhabitants of the town is important, otherwise one might be at a loss to account for the low rate of wages paid, the lack of spirited effort and efficient organisation among the workers, and other conditions peculiar to the place.

The book was never intended to be an expression of patriotism or unpatriotism, for it was written before the commencement of the European conflict. It consequently has nothing directly to do with the war, nor with the manufacture of munitions, any more than it incidentally discovers the nature of the toils, exertions, and sacrifices demanded of those who must slave at furnace, mill, steam-hammer, anvil, and lathe producing supplies for our armies and for those of our Allies in the field. It is not a treatise on economics, for I have never studied the science. If I had set out with the intention of theoretically slaughtering every official responsible for the administration of the factory I should have failed signally. I never contemplated such a course. Instead I wished to write out my own experiences and observations simply and from my own point of view, mistaken or otherwise, without fear or favour to any. I have my failings and prejudices. What they are is very well known to me, and I have no intention of disavowing them. Whoever disagrees with me is fully entitled to his opinion. I shall not question his judgment, though I shall not easily surrender my own. I am not anxious to quarrel with any man; at the same time I am not disposed to be fettered, smothered, gagged or silenced, to cower and tremble, or to shrink from uttering what I believe to be the truth in deference to the most formidable despot living.

A. W.

24th July 1915.

A portion of Chapter XIII has appeared in the *English Review*. My thanks are due to the Editor for his courteous permission to reproduce it in the volume.

CHAPTER I

LABOUR UNREST

Someone once asked the Greek Thales how he might best bear misfortune and he replied – 'By seeing your enemy in a worse condition than yourself.' He would have been as near the truth if he had said 'friend' instead of 'enemy.' Everyone appears to desire to see every other one worse off than himself. He is not content with doing well; he must do better, and if his success happens to be at the expense of one less fortunate he will be the more highly gratified. This lust of dominion and possession dates from the very foundation of human society. It is a feature of barbarism, and one that the wisest teaching and the most civilising influences at work in the world have failed to remove or even very materially to modify. The idea behind the *Sic vos non vobis* of Virgil has always been uppermost in the minds of the powerful. This it was that doomed the captives of the Greeks and Romans to a life of wretchedness and misery in the mines. This was responsible for the subjugation of the English peasants, and their reduction to the order of serfs in feudal times. And this is what would enslave the labouring classes in mine, field, and factory today. It must not be permitted. There is a way to defeat it. That is by law. Not a law made by the depredators but by the workers themselves. They have the means at their disposal. If they would summon up the courage to make use of them they might shatter the power of the capitalist at a stroke and free themselves from his domination for ever.

A principal cause of trouble everywhere between the employer and the employed is the lack of recognition of the worker. I mean this in its broadest sense. I do not mean merely that great and powerful combinations do not want to recognise Trade Unions. We all know that. It is a part of their policy and is dictated by pride and the spirit of intolerance. But they make a much more serious and fatal mistake. They refuse to recognise a man. All kinds of employers are guilty of this. The mineowner, the trading syndicate, the railway or steamship company, municipal authorities, the large and small manufacturer, the farmer and shopkeeper are equally to blame. If they would recognise the man they might be led to a consideration of his legitimate needs. They must first admit him to be equally a member of the human family and then recognise that, as such, he has claims as righteous and sacred as they. That is where the representative of capital invariably fails. He will not admit that the one under his authority has any rights of his own. To him the worker is as much a slave as ever he was, only he is conscious that his treatment of him must be subject to the limitations imposed by the modern laws of the land. And as he flouts the individual so he contemns the collective organisations of the men. He is determined not to recognise them. He considers this to be a proof of his strength. In reality it is a badge of his weakness. Sooner or later it will prove his undoing.

I will give an illustration. Several years ago, working in the same shed as myself, was a grey-headed furnaceman. He was not an old man; he could have been no more than fifty. One day he met with a serious accident. While attending to his furnace, in a stooping position, someone in passing accidentally pushed him. This caused him to lose his balance and he slipped on the plate and fell head-first into a boshful of boiling water underneath the fire hole. His head and shoulders were severely scalded, and he was absent on the sick list for two months. When he came in again he was not allowed to resume work at the furnace but was put wheeling out ashes from the smiths' fires. To my steam-hammer an oil furnace had recently been attached and several managers came daily to experiment with it. One morning, while they were present, the ex-furnaceman came to wheel away the debris. Then a manager turned to me and said –

'Who's that? What's he doing here?'

I explained who the man was and what he was doing.

'Pooh! What's the good of *that thing!* He ought to be shifted outside,' replied he.

In a short while afterwards the furnaceman was discharged.

There is something even worse than this and much more serious in effect. That is a result of too great recognition. I am referring to the common fault of interfering with and penalising men of superior mental and intellectual powers. There is even a certain advantage in a man's ability to escape attention. Especially if he is of a courageous turn of mind, has views and ideas of his own, and is able to influence others. He will live the more easy for it. Left to himself he can work away quietly, informing the minds and leavening the opinions of those round about him. If he can escape recognition. But he cannot. He is soon discovered, gagged, smothered, or got rid of. The safest way to strengthen a flame is to fan it. And if you want to intensify a man's dissatisfaction with a thing attempt to prevent him by force from giving expression to it. That is a sure means of provocation and will bear fruit a hundredfold.

We hear a great deal about the 'discontent' of the workers, and a degree of censure and reproach is usually conveyed with the expression. It is not half general enough. The average working man is too content. He is often lazily apathetic. Is the mineowner, the manufacturer, or the railway magnate content? Of course he is not. Strength is in action. When I hear of a man's being satisfied I know that he is done for. He might as well be dead. I wish the workers were more discontented, though I should in every case like to see their discontent rationally expressed and all their efforts intelligently directed. They waste a fearful amount of time and energy through irresolution and uncertainty of objective.

The selfishness, cruelty, and arrogance of the capitalist and his agents force the workers into rebellion. The swaggering pomposity and fantastic ceremony of officials fill them with deserving contempt. Their impudence is amazing. I have known a foreman of the shed to attack a man by reason of the decent clothes he had on and forbid him to wear a bowler hat. Not only in the workshop but even at home in his private life and dealings he is under the eye of his employer. His liberty is tyrannically restricted. In the town he is not allowed to supplement his earnings by any activity except such as has the favour of the works' officials. He must not keep a coffee-shop or an inn, or be engaged in any trading whatever. He may not even sell apples or gooseberries. And if he happens to be the spokesman of a labourers' union or to be connected with any other independent organisation, woe betide him! The older established association – such as that of the engineers – is not interfered with. It is the unprotected unskilled workman that must chiefly be terrorised and subjugated.

The worker is everywhere exploited. The speeding-up of late years has been general and insistent. New machinery is continually being installed in the sheds. This is driven at a high rate and the workman must keep pace with it. The toil in many cases is painfully exacting. There may be a less amount of violent physical exertion required here and there, though much more concentration of mind and attention will be needed. The

---

Overleaf: Group of engineers at the Mechanics' Institute, 31 July, 1908: success-ful people in a world remote from that of Alfred!

output, in some instances, has been increased tenfold. I am not exaggerating when I say that the actual exertions of the workman have often been doubled or trebled, yet he receives scarcely anything more in wages. In some cases he does not receive as much. He may have obtained a couple of shillings more in day wages and at the same time have lost double the amount in piecework balance. Occasionally, when the foreman of a shed has mercilessly cut a man's prices, he offers him a sop in the shape of a rise of one or two shillings. On the hammers under my

'B2' Shed, 1907, equipped with steam traverser and overhead electric cranes to build and repair tenders. Formerly, narrow gauge engines and boilers were repaired here

charge during the last ten years the day wages of assistants – owing to their being retained on the job up to a greater age – had doubled, and the piecework prices had been cut by one half. As a result the gang lost about £80 in a year. A mate of mine, whose prices had been cut to the lowest fraction, though offered a rise, steadily refused it on the ground that he would be worse off than before. Though slaving from morning till night he could not earn his percentage of profit. In many cases where the workman was formerly allowed to earn a profit of 33 per cent. on his day wages he is now restricted to 25 per cent., and the prices have been correspondingly reduced. Even now the foreman is not satisfied. He will still contrive to keep the percentage earned below the official figure in order to ingratiate himself with the managers and to give them the impression that he is still engaged in paring the prices.

At the same time, a marvellous lack of real initiative is discovered by the factory staff. Things that have been so are so, and if any sharp and enterprising workman sees the possibility of improvement anywhere and makes a suggestion he is soundly snubbed for his pains. In their

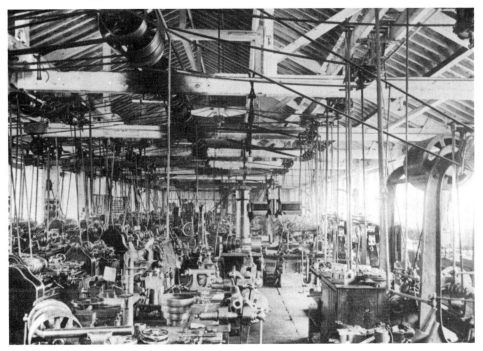

'O' Shop, 1907, for making and repairing tools: dies, milling cutters, taps, gear wheels, gauges, etc. By 1911, making and repairing equipment for GWR motor-cars had become important here

particular anxiety to exact the last ounce from the workman in the matter of labour the managers overlook multitudes of important details connected with their own administration, but which the workman sees as plainly as he does the nose on his face. They often spend pounds to effect the saving of a few pence. They lavish vast sums on experiments that the most ordinary man perceives have no possible chance of being successful, or even useful if they should succeed. Men's opinions upon a point are rarely solicited; if offered, they are belittled and rejected. Where an opinion is asked for it is usually intended as a bait for a trap, the answer is carefully recorded and afterwards used to prove something to the other's disadvantage.

But those ideas which are most valuable, provided they are not complex and the simple-minded official can readily grasp them – which is not always the case – he secretly cherishes and stealthily develops and afterwards parades them to his superior with swaggering pride as his own inventions. It is thus Mr So-and-so becomes a smart man in the eyes of the firm, while, as a matter of fact, he is a perfect blockhead and an ignoramus. Meanwhile, the very workman whose idea has been purloined and exploited is treated as a danger by the foreman; henceforth he must be watched and kept well in subjection. The cowardly overseer sees in him a possible rival, and is fearful for his own credit. This is one of the worst ills of the manufacturing life, and has crushed many a brave, good spirit, and smothered many a rising genius. The disadvantage is twofold. There is a loss to manufacture in not being assisted with new and bright ideas, and another to the individual, who is not only deprived of the fruits of his inventive faculty but is systematically punished for the possession of an original mind. In a word, officialism at the works is continually straining at the gnat and swallowing the camel.

What means are to be adopted in order to do away with the anomaly? One of the first things to do would be to recognise the individual. We want a better understanding and a new feeling altogether. The worker does not need a profusion of sentiment; he claims justice. He is willing to give and take. He knows that enormous profits are made out of his efforts and it is but natural that he should demand to receive a fair amount of remuneration and equitable conditions. My companion of the next steam-hammer, by means of a new process, in one week saved the company £20 in the execution of a single order. He had to work doubly hard to do it but he received not a penny extra himself. The piecework system as it stands is grossly unfair. All the profits accrue to one side and when the worker demands what is, after all, an insignificant participation in them he is described as being unreasonable and discontented. Where day wages have risen all round on piecework jobs the prices should be increased in proportion, otherwise the workman is simply paying himself for his additional efforts out of his own pocket.

Better wages and shorter hours are desired in every sphere of labour and especially in factories. The worker is not greatly concerned as to whether he is employed by the State or by a syndicate as long as he obtains justice. It is no more trouble for Parliament to formulate a law for a private concern than for a Government department. Forty-eight hours a week is long enough for any man to work. I would have the factory week completed in five turns. There is no need for the half-day Saturdays. It is a waste of time. It is expensive for the employers and unprofitable for the men. They can neither work nor play. If forty-eight hours were divided out into five turns the expense of steaming for the half-turn on Saturday would be saved. The amount of work produced would not fall very far below that made at present, and the men would be better satisfied. They would at least be able to have a clear rest and come to work fresh and fit on the Monday. I would even go further and suggest forty-five hours – that is, five turns of nine hours each – as a working week for factories in the future. This is not so impossible nor yet as unreasonable as it may appear. The proposal will doubtless strike some as being amazing. Nevertheless, I recommend it to them for their leisurely consideration. By aiming high we shall hit something. But there are obstacles to remove and difficulties to overcome.

CHAPTER II

THE STAMPING SHOP – GENERAL ENVIRONMENT – THE 'COALIES' –
THE ROLLING MILLS – PUDDLING AND SHINGLING – ACCIDENTS AT
THE ROLLS – THE SCRAP WAGGONS – WASTE

The Stamping Shop is square, or nearly so, each lateral corresponding to a cardinal point of the compass – north, south, east, and west, the whole comprising about an acre and a quarter. That is not an extensive building for a railway manufactory. There are some shops with an area of not less than five, six, and even seven acres – a prodigious size! They are used for purposes of construction, for carriages, waggons, locomotives, and also for repairs. The premises used for purely manufacturing purposes, such as those I am now speaking of, are generally much smaller in extent.

The workshop is modern in structure and has not stood for more than fifteen years. Before that time the work proceeded on a much smaller scale, and was carried on in a shed built almost entirely of wood and corrugated iron – a dark, wretched place, without light or ventilation, save for the broken windows and rents in the low, depressed roof. With the development of the industry and general expansion of trade this became altogether inadequate to cope with the requirements of the other sheds, and a move had to be made to larger and more commodious premises. Thereupon a site was chosen and a new shop erected about a quarter of a mile distant. The walls of this are of brick, built with 'piers' and 'panels,' thirty feet high, solid, massive, and substantial, with no pretence to show of any kind. The roof is constructed in bays running north and south, according to the disposition of the long walls, and presents a serrated appearance, like the teeth of a huge saw. Of these bays the slopes towards sunrise are filled in with stout panes of glass; the opposite sides are of strong boards covered with slates, the whole supported by massive sectional principals and a network of stout iron girders.

The roof is studded with hundreds of wooden ventilators intended to carry off the smoke and fumes from the forges. Above them tower numerous furnace stacks and chimneys from the boilers, with the exhaust pipes of the engines and steam-hammers. Towards summer, when the days lengthen and the sun pours down interminable volumes of light and heat from a cloudless sky, or when the air without is charged with electricity and the thunder bellows and rolls over the hills and downs to the south, and the forked lightning flashes reveal every corner

Carriage and Wagon Stamping (No. 18) Shop, 1907, during the twenty years when Alfred was head drop-stamper here, chargeman over three steam-hammers and six men

of the dark smithy so that the heat becomes almost unbearable, a large quantity of the glass is removed to aid ventilation; the heat, assisted by the ground current, rises and escapes through the roof. But when the rain comes and the heavy showers, driven at an angle by the wind, beat furiously through upon the half-naked workmen beneath, even this is not an unmixed blessing. Or when the sun shoots his hot arrows down through the openings upon the toilers at the steam-hammers and forges, as he always does twice during the morning – once before breakfast, and again at about eleven o'clock – it is productive of increased discomfort;

the sweat flows faster and the work flags. This does not last long, however. Southward goes the sun, and shade succeeds.

The eastern and western ends of the shed are almost half taken up with large sliding doors, that reach as high as to the roof. These rest on wheels which are superimposed upon iron rails, so that a child might push them backwards and forwards. Through several of the doors rails are laid to permit of engines and waggons entering with loads of material – iron and steel for the furnaces – and also for conveying away the manufactures. A narrow bogie line runs round the shed and is used for transferring materials from one part to another and to the various hydraulic presses and forges. Here and there are fixed small turn-tables to enable the bogies to negotiate the angles and move from track to track.

Southward the shed faces a yard of about ten acres in extent. This is bounded on every side by other workshops and premises, all built of the same dingy materials – brick, slate and iron – blackened with smoke, dust, and steam, surmounted with tall chimneys, innumerable ventilators, and poles for the telephone wires, which effectually block out all perspective. To view it from the interior is like looking around the inner walls of a fortress. There is no escape for the eye; nothing but bricks and mortar, iron and steel, smoke and steam arising. It is ugly; and the sense of confinement within the prison-like walls of the factory renders it still more dismal to those who have any thought of the hills and fields beyond. Only in summer does it assume a brighter aspect. Then the sun scalds down on the network of rails and ashen ground with deadly intensity; the atmosphere quivers and trembles; the fine dust burns under your feet, and the steel tracks glitter under the blinding rays. The clouds of dazzling steam from the engines are no longer visible – the air being too hot to admit of condensation – and the black smoke from the furnaces and boilers hangs in the air, lifeless and motionless, like a pall, for hours and hours together.

But when the summer is over, when the majesty of July and August is past and gone and golden September gives place to rainy October, or, most of all, when dull, gloomy November covers the skies with its impenetrable veil of drab cloud and mist day after day and week after week, with scarcely an hour of sunshine, the utter dismalness and ugliness of the place is appalling. Then there is not a vestige of colour. The sky, roofs, walls, the engines moving to and fro, the rolling stock, the stacks of plates and ingots of iron and steel, the sleepers for the rails, the ground beneath – everything is dark, sombre, and repellant. Not a glint upon the steel lines! Not a refraction of light from the slates on the roof! Everything is dingy, dirty, and drab. And drab is the mind of the toiler all this time, drab as the skies above and the walls beneath. Doomed to the confinement from which there is no escape, he accepts the condition and is swallowed up in his environment.

There is one point, and only one, a few paces west of the shed, from which an inspiriting view may be had. There, on a fine day, from between two towering walls, in the little distance, blue almost as the sky and yet distinct and well-defined, may be seen a great part of Liddington

Richard Jefferies Festival, Chiseldon, 1913. The man top right, in cart, resembles Alfred, who is now commemorated in part of the Jefferies Museum at Coate

Hill, crowned with the *castellum*, the scene of many a lively contest in prehistoric days, and the holy of holies of Richard Jefferies, who spent days and nights there trying to fathom the supreme mystery that has baffled so many great and ardent souls. When the sky is clear and the air free from mist and haze – especially as it appears sometimes in the summer months, under a southern wind, or before or after rain – so distinct does the sloping line of the hill show, with its broad front towards you, that you may even perceive the common features and details of it. Then you may plainly view the disposition of the stone walls running from top to base, with the white chalk-pits gleaming like snow in the distance, and tell the outer wall of the entrenchment. In short, you might imagine yourself to be standing within the mound and looking out over the magnificent valley – north, east, and west; towards Bristol, over Cirencester, and beyond Witney and Oxford. But in the winter even this is denied. Then the dark lowering clouds sweep along the downs and shut them out of view, or grey mist fills the intervening valley, or the rain, falling in torrents or driving in the furious south-west gale, hides it completely; or if it is at all visible under the cold sky, it seems so far removed and the distance so intensified as to lose all resemblance to a hill and to look like a dim blue cloud faintly seen on the horizon, and which is no more than a suggestion, a shape phantasmal.

Everywhere about the yard is evidence of industry and activity; there all is suggestive of toil, labour, and power. On the right, stretching for a quarter of a mile, are hundreds upon hundreds of wheels, tyres, and axles for carriages and waggons, in every phase and degree of fitness; some fresh from the rolling mills – from Sheffield and Scotland – some turned and fitted in the lathe, huge jointless tyres newly unladen waiting to take their turn in the operation of fitting them to the wheels, and others finished, wheels, tyres, and axle compact, dipped in tar – except the journals – to prevent them from rusting, and all ready to be placed underneath the waggons. There are wheels of solid steel, wheels with spokes, and wheels of oak, teak, and even of paper composition, of many sorts and sizes, for smooth-running carriages. One would think there were enough of them to stock the whole railway system, but a few weeks of steady consumption would thin them down, and the yard would soon be bare and empty if fresh consignments were not every day arriving.

In front of the wheels, in rows and lines, are the huge cast-iron blocks and dies used for punching and pressing by the hydraulic machines. They are of all shapes and dimensions, puzzling to the eye of the stranger, but easily identified by those who are accustomed to use them, and who have been acquainted with them perhaps from boyhood. There are sets for 'joggling' and 'up-setting,' and others for shaping and levelling. In the midst of them stands a stout, three-legged machine called a 'sheer legs.' To this is attached strong pulley blocks for lifting the sets from the ground – many of them weigh considerably more than a ton; afterwards a stout bogie is run underneath and the blocks are lowered and so carried off to the field of operations.

Many an accident has happened in the conveyance of blocks and dies to and from their destination; many a bruised foot or broken limb has resulted from a lack of carefulness and attention on the part of the workmen. The slightest disregard may lead to injury. The bogie may slip, or the block slide, and woe be to the individual who chances to be in the way of the falling mass. Unassuming, and even valueless as the collection of dies may appear to the uninitiated, it is really worth a huge sum, for manufacturing tools are of a very expensive character.

Close on the left is a long line of waggons laden with coal fresh from the Welsh pits, and nearby is a large bunk into which it is emptied to allow of the speedy return of the vehicles – an important item in railway administration. Here the dark and grimy coal heavers, with faces as black as the mineral they are handling, grunt and sweat, their eyes obtaining peculiar prominence from being inset in a ground of ebony, and their teeth glistening pearly white through the blackened lips, appearing the more remarkable if they should smile at you. For even they will brighten up sometimes. Hard and laborious as their toil is, they will now and then relax into pleasantry and relieve the tedium of work with a snatch of song and hilarity.

The coalies are not highly paid. Their day wages are eighteen shillings or a pound a week, but, as all the work of the shed is done at the piece rate, they are enabled to earn a few shillings above that sum. The dullest men – those whose misfortune it is to have missed the right education, or those who are naturally slow and awkward – are usually selected for coal-heaving. Very often, however, shrewd and capable, smart and intelligent men, who might be more profitably employed than in shovelling coal from the truck to the bunk or wheel-barrow, are put at the task. Perhaps this is the result of carelessness on the part of the overseer, or it may be dearth of hands, and very likely it is intentional. The man is out of favour and has been clapped there as a punishment.

Near the coal station stand piles upon piles of iron and steel, in plates, bars, and ingots, some six and some ten feet high, in large square stacks, and the long bars disposed between uprights to keep them together and separate those of different lengths and sizes. The chief part of this comes in from 'abroad,' that is, from the midlands and the north of England, for very little iron ore is now manufactured on the premises. A small amount of pig iron is imported and worked up at the local rolling mills, but the greater part of the metal is purchased of the big firms and dealers away from the town.

The chief occupation of the factory rolling mills now is to receive the iron scrap from the various workshops, such as clippings, shearings, punchings, and drillings, with all the old iron proceeding from the breaking up of worn-out engines and vehicles. This is first of all reduced to convenient shape and then set up in 'piles' on thin pieces of wood to enable of its being placed in the furnace on the peels used for the purpose. In the making of piles the flat pieces of metal are placed around the outside, leaving a hollow within, which is filled up with punchings and drillings, old rivets, nuts, bolts, and other similar scrap. The pile is set in the furnace and heated, when it coalesces into a mass; afterwards it is brought out to the heavy steam-hammer and beaten into rough bars or slabs, several feet in length. This process is called 'shingling.' When the iron has become fairly solid and of convenient length, the bars, still spluttering and fizzing – for they have not been under the hammer for more than two or three minutes – are hurried off to the rolls. There they are received by the men in charge, who stand stripped to the waist, with tongs in hand, and dexterously guide the rough ingots into the ponderous rollers that revolve at speeds suited to the size and weight of the bars, and always with a loud clanking noise.

As soon as the bar is rolled through – already drawn out to two or three times its original length – the rolls stop and instantly revolve in the other direction. The bar is again guided into the channel of the rollers and emerges on the other side, longer and smoother. This process is continued four or five times until the bars are finished; then other small rollers in the floor are set in motion and the bars travel along the ground to the steam saws, where they are cut up into the lengths required. There they are loaded on iron bogies and carried off, or rolled along as before to the weighing machines; everything is paid for according to the weight of the finished material.

Punchings and drillings are also treated by the process known as 'puddling.' In this case, the furnaces will have a cavity in the floor, into which the small scrap material is shovelled or tipped. The door is now made fast and the heat applied, which must not be too fierce, however, or the whole mass would soon be burned and spoiled. When the drillings and chippings have cohered, the puddler, by an aperture through the iron door, inserts a steel bar, curved at the end, and prises the lump and turns it over and over. This is called 'balling up.' By and by, when the iron is thoroughly heated and fairly consistent, it is brought to the 'shingler,' who soon gives it shape and solidity. At the first few blows a terrific shower of sparks shoots around, which travel for a great distance, burning everything they meet. To protect themselves against this the shinglers wear heavy iron jackboots, reaching above the knees, with an iron veil over their eyes and faces. As the steam-hammer block upon which the pounding is done is only a few inches above the floor level and the sparks and splinters fly out with the precision of shot from a gun barrel, the danger is confined to a space within two feet of the floor.

When the heats come from the puddling furnaces they look soft and spongy and soon become dull on the outer parts, so that a stranger might think them not sufficiently hot to beat up, but after the first light blow or two he will find himself mistaken. First of all the huge hammer – able to strike a blow equal to a hundred tons pressure – is merely allowed to squeeze the mass, without beating it. Then it rises gently and travels up and down, scarcely touching the metal. Gradually the blows fall harder and harder until the piece is fully consistent; then it is rapidly drawn away to the rolls. Very rarely are the hammers required to expend their full powers upon the melting slabs, unless they happen to be of steel, which is very hard, even when whitehot. Then the blows fall terrific. The steam spouts, roars and hisses; the chains jingle and the ground under your feet shakes as though in an earthquake.

When a better quality of iron is required the punchings, bolts, and rivets are placed in a large drum which is afterwards set in motion and continues to revolve for several hours. By this means all the rust, paint, and dirt are removed from the metal, and when it is taken from the cylinder it shines like silver. Special regard is had for this in the furnaces. Care is taken to save it from over-heating and waste, and when it finally emerges from the rolls it is set apart by itself and labelled for its superior quality.

Various prices, ranging from 15s. to 50s. a ton, are paid for shingling and forging. These depend upon the weight of the piece and the degree of finish required. The shingler is clever and expert, and he is not highly paid at the works, considering his usefulness, for he is a great manufacturer. Thousands of tons of metal must pass through his hands in the course of a year, and the work is very hot and laborious. By the age of fifty the shinglers and forgemen are usually worn out and superseded at the forge. When they can no longer perform their duties at the steam-hammer they are removed from the manufacturing circle and presented with a broom, shovel, and wheel-barrow. Their wages are cut down to that of a common labourer, and thus they spend their few remaining years of service. At an early age they drop off altogether, and their places are filled by others who have gone through the same experience.

The running of the iron from the furnace to the steam-hammer and back again to the rolls is chiefly performed by boys and young men. The majority of these come from the villages round about, for the town lads, as a rule, are much too wideawake for the business; the work is too hard

---

Overleaf: Men and steam-hammer. Young Tom Hamblin (second from right) when sent by Alfred to check the time, got into trouble with a foreman

for them. Living close to the factory they know by report which shops to avoid, and if, by misadventure, they happen to get a start in such a place they are very quickly out of it. Accordingly the more laborious work usually falls upon those who dwell without the town. It is the same with the men. Those who live in the borough nearly always obtain the easier berths; John and George do the heavy lifting and heaving.

Accidents are frequent at the rolling mills. Burns are of common occurrence, and they are sometimes very serious and occasionally fatal.

West End Terrace in Westcott Place, near the works but only five minutes walk from country. Railway workers occupied nearly all this row of houses

Great care is requisite in moving about amid so much fire and heated material, for everything – the floors, principals, rollers, the bogie handles, tools and all – is very hot. Some of the carrying is done with a kind of wheel-barrow that requires a special balance. The least obstruction will upset it, and a little awkwardness on the part of the workman is sufficient to bring the weltering burden down to the ground. Not long ago, as a youth was drawing a large, whitehot pile from the furnace to the steam-hammer, he slipped on the iron floor and fell at full length on his back upon the ground. As he fell the bogie inclined forward and the huge pile slid down and lodged on his stomach, inflicting frightful injuries. He was quickly rescued from his tortuous position, but there was no hope of recovery from such an accident, and he died a day or two afterwards. He, too, was of the neighbouring village.

You can always tell these young men of the steam-hammer or rolling mills, whenever you meet them. They are usually lank and thin and their faces are ghastly white. Their nostrils are distended; black and blue rings

Detail of the picture opposite. Alfred and Mary loved children, but had none of their own. Alfred was more at ease with children than with adults

encircle their eyes. Their gait is careless and shuffling, and their dress, on a holiday, is a curious mixture of the rural and urban styles. On week-days they are as black as sweeps, and the blacker they are the better, in their opinion, for they take pride in parading the badge of their profession and are not ashamed of it as are their workmates who dwell in the town.

I have said that formerly much more iron was manufactured on the premises than is the case at this time. Then the steam-hammer shed, in

Workman, probably from railway factory, with spectators who were encouraged by photographers in 1890's. Wellington Commercial Hotel in background

Looking across Fleet Street Bridge into Milford Street, route from railway station to town centre. 1890's, before the trams came. Workmen and posters

Woman and workman, same date and place as opposite page. Area now virtually obliterated by office blocks and new bus station

which nothing but forging is done, was a flourishing place. All the wheels for the engines and waggons, together with piston rods, driving gear, axles, and cranks, were made there. These are obtained elsewhere now, some in England and Scotland, and other parts from abroad. Steel has superseded iron in a great degree, too, being harder, tougher, stronger and cheaper. The combined skill of the chemist and scientist has simplified the manufacture of it, and it is to be obtained in large quantities. But steel rusts much more quickly than iron, and does not last nearly as long in exposed positions on the vehicles.

Formerly all wheels were made of wrought iron and a great part of the work was done by hand. First of all the sections were made under the steam-hammer, in 'T' pieces and boss ends, and shut in the middle. These were for the spokes. Then the 'T' ends were incurved and joined together all round till the rim of the wheel was finished. After that, there remained to form the centre and make the 'boss' solid and compact. As the boss sections were made to fit together in the middle, they only required to be heated and welded. Accordingly they were placed on an open forge, built round with damp coal-dust to contain and concentrate the heat, the boss being exactly over the centre of the fire. Another forge, close at hand, contained a large round iron washer, similarly placed, to which was attached an iron bar for lifting it from the fire. Both heats were prepared simultaneously. Then the wheel, lifted by a crane, was quickly removed from the forge, turned upside down and placed on the steam-hammer block. The washer was brought out at once and clapped on smartly, and down came the heavy monkey. Half-a-dozen blows were sufficient to make the weld. Then it was removed from the steam-hammer and laid on an iron table and the smiths set about it with their tools to finish it off, three or four men striking alternately on one 'flatter' or 'fuller,' with perfect rhythm and precision, the chief smith directing operations and working with the rest.

Those were the palmy days for the smithy. Wages were high and the prices good, and the work made was solid and strong. Now all wheels are manufactured of cast steel and with little hand labour. The molten metal is simply poured into moulds, allowed to cool and afterwards annealed in special furnaces. One can easily imagine the immense amount of labour saved in the operation, though the wheels are not as elastic and durable.

Situated near the piles of new material are the scrap bunks. These are old waggons that have served their turn on the railway and, instead of being broken up, have been lifted bodily from the sets of wheels and deposited on the ground as receptacles for the large quantities of scrap made in the workshop. What miles these old waggons have gone! What storm and stress they have endured! What burdens they have borne! East and west, north and south, over hills and bridges, through valleys, past miles upon miles of cornfields and meadows, green and gold, red and brown by turn, in rain and snow, winter frost and summer sunshine, by day and night, year after year together.

These waggons, if they could speak, would tell you they have visited every station and town on the system. They have crossed the Thames, the Severn, the Kennet, the Upper and Lower Avon, the Wye, the Dee, the Towy, the Parrot and the Tamar, times out of number. They have gone through dark tunnels, over dizzy viaducts, past cathedral cities and quaint old market-towns, villages, and hamlets, sleeping and waking, at all hours of the day and night, drawn on, and on, and on by the tireless iron steeds, piled up with all sorts of goods and commodities for the use of man – stones to build him houses, iron to strengthen them, corn to feed him and his family, and materials to clothe them. They would tell you of many lovely woods and forests through which they have journeyed, and seaside towns, with the strong blue ocean in view, sometimes running perilously near the beach, at others hidden in deep cuttings, where the banks are blue with violets, and yellow with the pale gold of the cowslip, followed by the endless array of the ox-eyes, toadflax, and sweet wild mignonette. And they would tell you of long, dark, winter nights, when the tempest howled madly through the trees and bridges and sang shrilly in the telegraph wires; when the rain fell in a deluge from the inky sky, or the sleet and snow drove in blinding clouds and was piled upon the weatherproof tarpaulins. Or again they would relate of running smoothly on summer nights under the pale southern moon, or when the stars glittered in the frosty heavens, or dense fog, so troublesome and dangerous to the ever-watchful and valiant old driver, shut everything out of view, signals and all, so that their very whereabouts were only known and identified by paying close attention to the loud, shot-like explosions of the detonators placed along the line by the fogmen.

Now all these things are at an end. They have run their race, and grown old in the service. They have fulfilled their period of usefulness on the line and, like old veterans returned from the war, they have come back to their native town to end their days. Being fairly sound of constitution and having escaped the shocks of collision and accident, they were adjudged too solid to be broken up yet, so, as a last use, they were placed here to receive the punchings and trimmings from the shears and presses, and ingloriously waste away in their old age, exposed to all the inclemencies and caprices of the weather.

The scrap, made daily, soon amounts to hundreds of tons. It is of all shapes and sizes. There is plate from an eighth of an inch to an inch and a half thick from the presses, ends and trimmings of rods and bars from the shears and steam-hammers, burs from the stamping plant and scrag ends from the forgings. In addition to this there are scores of tons of old iron and steel, brought from all over the system to be cut up at the hydraulic shears – sole-bars of waggons, stanchions and 'diagonals,' 'T'-iron plates, and hundreds of old draw-bars and buffers. The iron and steel are carefully observed and kept separate and huge piles soon accumulate, far more than the waggons can hold. The iron refuse is by and by passed on to the rolling mills, while the steel scrap awaits a purchaser. No attempt is made to utilise that on the premises. There are secrets in the manufacture of steel which are never betrayed to outsiders, and it would be a waste of time and money for the local furnacemen and forgers to attempt to do anything with it. However carefully the furnaceman tends it in the fire he cannot get it to cohere well in the piles, and if it is at all over-heated it bursts and scatters in all directions, brittle and glassy, as soon as the steam-hammer touches it with a gentle blow.

There is, at the same time, enormous waste in the matter of scrap iron and steel, which intelligent supervision would certainly lessen. Material that might economically be used in the workshop is indiscriminately passed out with the rubbish and sold away at a cheap rate – at a fraction of its real value. Tons of metal – good solid iron, often of the highest quality – which might be used for forging and stamping, are rejected and scrapped because it would take a trifle longer to handle. Other large scrap material might be slabbed and used without sending it to the mill, and thus large profits would accrue to the shed; for the rolling mills people will only purchase, theoretically, at trade prices, that is, at about two pounds a ton for scrap iron.

CHAPTER III

THE SHUNTERS – WATCHMEN – DETECTING A THIEF – FIRES – CARRIAGE
FINISHERS – PAINTERS – 'WASHERS-DOWN' – CUSHION-BEATERS –
CHANGES AND INNOVATIONS – DEPARTMENTAL RELATIONS

A short way off in the yard, in a small space clear of the confusing
network of lines that cross and recross here and there, running in every
direction and connecting the various workshops together, are two old
railway coaches dispossessed of their wheels and lodged upon baulks of
timber let into the ground. Like the old scrap waggons, they have had
their day in active service, and, coming home in fairly good condition,
though antiquated in style and useless for passenger traffic, have yet been
found convenient as occasional storehouses and shelters. They are now
used as cabins, one for the shunters, who conduct their operations round
about, and the other for watchmen, and they are fitted with stoves for
warming the men's food, and for drying their clothes in wet weather.
The roofs and windows are intact, and some of the original seats still
remain. These are of bare wood and are not padded and upholstered in
the comfortable and luxurious style now required and expected by the
railway traveller.

   These old carriages are at this time very rarely met with and are nearly
extinct. For years after they disappeared from the general traffic –
superseded by more commodious and comfortable vehicles – the best of
them were kept stored up in sheds and yards in out-of-the-way places to
await the time of trippers and excursionists. Then they were regularly
hauled out to accommodate the multitude. The windows were hastily
wiped over and the interiors dusted out; they were ready to receive the
people. Goods engines of the old type were brought up to draw them
along. The trippers squeezed themselves inside, and, with the shrieking
of steam whistles and hooters and the playing of concertinas and
melodions, the trains started off and went jolting and jogging away to

their destinations. At the end of the tripping season the coaches were again stored away in the yards and sidings, until they became too crazy and dangerous to run on the main line, when they were either utilised for storehouses and shelters, or broken up. The refuse wood from the destruction of old worn-out rolling stock is sawn up and used for lighting the fires in the furnaces and boilers, and is distributed throughout the system. A large quantity is also sold to the workmen, who use it both for firing and for the construction of outhouses.

View from one of the signal posts, Swindon Station, 1890: looking towards the GWR works. Only a small part of the works is visible

The shunters of the yard are a hard-working body of men, and they are exposed to many dangers. The hours are long and they must cover many miles during the day by running up and down the lines. It is their duty to transfer the carriages and waggons from road to road and from one workshop to another, to dispose of the old ones brought in for repairs, to lead out the new, and distribute the various stores – iron and steel, coal, coke, and timber – at several points. Whatever the weather may be they must be up and doing, or the traffic in the yard would soon be in utter confusion. Rain or snow, cold or heat, sunshine or cloud, July glow or December fog and gloom are all one to them. The busy swarm of workmen comes and goes, the furnaces spout their dense black clouds of smoke into the heavens; the dazzling steam, shot out from the engines and steam-hammers, leaps up in an ascending pillar, the rapid wheels spin round in the roof or under the wall, and the endless toil goes on, all which must be catered for by the shunters.

Great care must be taken to prevent the sidings from becoming blocked by crossing a wrong point. Where two or more engines are operating over a complex siding this may easily be done, and a delay of several hours will be the result. If an inexperienced shunter, mistaking the number of his points, shifts his waggons onto the wrong track and, not perceiving his error, at once proceeds to carry out several other manœuvres, he may shut in the engines so completely and confusedly that he will want all his wits about him to extricate them again; it will be like a mathematical problem. Happily for the shunter's credit, this is not a common occurrence.

Strong, healthy men are selected for the shunter's trade, to carry the pole and whistle. By working in the open air, exposed to all kinds of weather, they become hardy and seasoned and present a far different appearance from that of those who are shut up within the walls of the workshop, amid the smoke and fumes. Instead of becoming lean with the constant running to and fro, they seem to thrive on the exercise, and many of them assume substantial proportions. Their faces are bronzed with the sun and wind, and they are a picture of health – strong, stalwart, and of good physique. The shunters are not under as many restrictions as are the factory workers proper, *i.e.*, those within the sheds. It is their privilege to smoke while on duty, or, at any rate, in the intervals on the premises, an indulgence which is strictly forbidden to all other employees. They remain always about the yard and never go beyond the bounds prescribed for them, so that they really belong to the factory.

The other cabin is used by the watchmen as an out-shelter – a kind of half-way refuge. Their headquarter is at the main entrance, where there are always one or two on duty to check the coming in and going out of the workmen, to keep out intruders and to prevent any from passing out before the regulation hour. They also act in the quality of police to protect the property of the railway company, patrol the shops and yards, and keep a sharp look-out for loiterers and any who should attempt to smoke or read a newspaper on the sly.

Every workshop and building is provided with certain clock-like instruments called 'tell-tales,' which are fixed in many corners and angles, and at frequent intervals along the high board fence that encloses the factory grounds. The watchman appointed for the round is furnished with a key that fits the instrument. It is his duty to visit each of these every hour, or every two hours, according to the time-table given him by his chief. When he comes to the tell-tale he inserts the key and, after turning it round, withdraws it. This leaves a record of his visit and certifies that he has gone his round regularly. At intervals, unknown to the watchman, the tell-tales are removed and privately examined, in order to see that everything is correct, and if there has been any neglect of duty the offender is sought out and punished. Occasionally it transpires that there has been wholesale tampering with the instruments in order to escape going the rounds. The watchmen, like all others at the works, agreed for the time, finally come to loggerheads and play the tell-tale themselves. Someone or other informs of his mate, this one retaliates and the scheme is laid bare. Forthwith the whole staff of watchmen are summoned to appear before the works' manager, and are punished in various ways. Something new and strange is adopted; the men's time and rounds are altered, and they patrol their beats the laughing-stock of the workmen whom it is their duty to observe and supervise.

The watchmen, as a class, are surly and over-officious. Perhaps they were chosen for some qualities they were thought to possess, fitting them for the duties expected of them; they are not popular with the workmen. The fact of their being placed in a supervisory position and of being exempt from manual work induces them to have a higher opinion of themselves than the actual circumstances warrant. They consider themselves above the average at the works and cultivate the pseudo-genteel.

When a new watchman is made it is noised abroad throughout the department; his size, description, and all else that is known of him are passed around the sheds for the benefit of the masses. Developments are anticipated and the results eagerly awaited. Elated at his promotion and great in his own conceit the newly initiated one, before he is well-known and identified by the workmen, slips to and fro in the sheds, eager for surprise captures. Immediately before the hooter sounds for the men's release at meal times he is to be found suddenly opening doors and popping on the scene. If any of the workmen should happen to have on their coats, or to have gathered near the door ready to rush out, they scatter like wood-pigeons when a hawk has darted in the midst of them.

This forms the subject of a report to the shop foreman or to the manager. Dire threats as to the consequences of loitering are launched at the workmen; a few youths are suspended and forced to take a rest; and so the matter is settled.

The watchman, however, is not forgotten or forgiven by the men. Some nickname or other is coined for him on the spot. Perhaps he is hooted for a sneak and teased in various ways, the boys especially enjoying a joke at his expense. They set traps for him, and after racing about the yard and dodging between the waggons and coaches, suddenly decamp and make for the tunnels or entrances. Once a nickname becomes attached to a watchman it seldom leaves him. One has borne the title of 'Long Bill' for a number of years; another is honoured with the appellation of 'Powerful'; this one is 'Flat-foot,' that is 'Rubber-heel,' and another has earned for himself the ridiculous title of 'Chesty.'

Theft is sometimes practised by the workmen, though it is much more rarely committed now than it was formerly. Some of the schemes adopted for getting the stolen materials outside the works have been quite artistic, and others were ridiculously open and daring. Years ago loads of timber and other valuables were regularly smuggled out in the middle of the night, and especially on Saturday nights. They were piled upon big trucks and bogies and got past the entrances with the watchman's consent and connivance. Probably he received a bribe for his silence – a quart of ale at the club, or a share of the stolen goods. On at least one occasion a brazen-faced fellow wheeled out a new wheel-barrow, unchallenged, amid the crowd at a dinner-time and was never suspected. At other times wheel-barrows and other tools have mysteriously disappeared in the night, as though they had been swallowed up by an earthquake. They were quietly lifted over the fence and received into the neighbouring field and so got safely away.

Sometimes a workman will split on his mate whom he knows to be in the habit of purloining things from the shed. Perhaps it is a little firewood or a few screws or nails that were picked up in the yard. Going privately to the watchman he acquaints him of the fact, and at dinner-time, or night, a stand is made at the entrance, and the culprit seized and searched. This invariably means dismissal, however small the amount of the theft may be. Somehow or other, though, the informer is discovered and for ever afterwards he is branded as a sneak and shunned by his fellows. There is no forgiveness for this kind of thing among the workmen. Honesty or not honesty, he is never tolerated but is looked upon with the utmost disgust and contempt.

Occasionally, if you should stand at the entrance as the workmen are leaving, you might see an abject-looking individual, with drawn features, making his way painfully through the tunnel, limping, or dragging a leg behind him. The casual observer would jump to the conclusion that the man had met with an accident, or that he was naturally lame or a cripple. But very likely, if the truth were known, he has a staff of wood, or a rod of iron, four feet long, concealed in the leg of his trousers and reaching up to the breast, and that is what makes him walk with such great difficulty. Another plan is to bend a rod of iron in the shape of a hoop and so fix it around the waist, or to pack the contraband next to the skin, under the armpits and around the stomach. This very often leads to detection. The watchman on duty at the entrance has his suspicions aroused by the shape of the man. Accordingly he steps out, calls him aside and feels the part, and the culprit is discovered.

It sometimes happens that a watchman gets on the track of an innocent workman and makes himself appear ridiculous, for he is sure to be noticed by the crowd and heartily jeered at for his interference. Not long ago a young workman, on his way out from the shed one morning after night duty, was challenged and stopped and required to disclose the contents of his dinner-basket, which, to the watchman's eye, seemed unusually heavy. The young man, who was an enthusiastic Christian, smilingly complied and, opening his basket, took out a big Bible, and presented it to his challenger. That was more than the watchman had bargained for, and he immediately shuffled off in considerable confusion. A few nights ago a surly watchman stopped me and curtly demanded to know what I was carrying 'in the parcel under my arm.' It was merely my daily newspaper.

It is not the rank and file alone that are guilty of taking things that do not belong to them. Some of the principals of the staff have been notoriously to blame in this respect, as is well-known at the works, though their misdeeds are invariably screened and condoned. If one of the managers has stolen materials worth hundreds of pounds he is reprimanded and allowed to continue at his post, or at most, he is asked to resign and is afterwards awarded a pension; but if the workman has purloined an article of a few pence in value he is dismissed and prosecuted. This is no general statement but a plain matter of fact.

Further over the yard, towards one of the sheds that form the boundary on this side, stands a large water-closet, one of many about the factory, built to meet the requirements of about five hundred workmen. These buildings are of a uniform type and are disagreeable places, lacking in sanitary arrangements. There is not the slightest approach to privacy of any kind, no consideration whatever for those who happen to be imbued with a sense of modesty or refinement of feeling. The convenience consists of a long double row of seats, situate back to back, partly divided by brick walls, the whole constructed above a large pit that contains a foot of water which is changed once or twice a day. The seats themselves are merely an iron rail built upon brickwork, and there is no protection. Several times, I have known men to overbalance and fall into the pit. Everything is bold, daring, and unnatural. On entering, the naked persons of the men sitting may plainly be seen, and the stench is overpowering. The whole concern is gross and objectionable, filthy, disgusting, and degrading. No one that is chaste and modest could bear to expose himself, sitting there with no more decency than obtains among herds of cattle shut up in the winter pen. Consequently, there are many who, though hard pressed by the exigences of nature, never use the place. As a result they contract irregularities and complaints of the stomach that remain with them all their lives, and that might easily prove fatal to them. Perhaps this barbarous relic of insanitation may in time be superseded by some system a little more moral and more compatible with human sensibility and refinement.

Near this spot, in the open air, are stored hundreds of gallons of oil, spirits and other liquids of a highly inflammable nature, used for mixing paints for the carriages and waggons, together with chemicals employed in the rapid cleansing of the exteriors of vehicles that come in for repairs and washing-down. The rules of the factory strictly forbid the storing of any of these liquids within the workshops and outhouses. This precaution is taken in order to prevent damage by fire in case of an outbreak and to render the flames more easy of control by the firemen.

At every short distance there is a connection with the water-main and a length of hose always fit and ready for any emergency. The works has its own fire-engine – a powerful motor and pumps – and if by chance a call is made the men are speedily on the spot. Here and there around the sheds are deep pits, walled up and covered with cast-iron tops, to contain water for the fire-engines, for they cannot well draw clear off the main. To these pits, in the afternoon or evening, the engines and firemen occasionally come for practice. Immediately the wells are filled from the main, the hose is coupled up, and a perfect deluge is rained over everything in the vicinity, as though a fire were really in progress. After half an hour's lusty exertion with the hose and the scaling of walls and roofs, the firemen stow their apparatus and the motor rushes off down the yard quickly out of sight.

Though fires at the works are not of common occurrence, there is now and then an outbreak, and sometimes one of serious dimensions. They are generally the result of great carelessness, or the want of ordinary attention on the part of a workman or official. Perhaps a naked light is left burning somewhere or other, or a portion of cotton-waste is smouldering away unobserved. The roof may become ignited through contact with the hot chimney; and very often the cause of the outbreak is not ascertained at all. In several cases incendiarism has been suggested as the cause of a fire, but, notwithstanding all the efforts of the works' detectives to fix the guilt, proof of the crime has never been brought home to any individual. When fires do happen they nearly always originate in the night. One reason of this is that, with so many workmen on the scene during the day, the first sign of an outbreak would be immediately detected and dealt with before it could become dangerous. But at night it would develop rapidly and obtain a good hold on the premises before being discovered by the watchman.

When it is known in the works that a fire is raging round about – if it should happen to be at night – the few workmen employed, without waiting for instructions from the overseers, throw down their tools and rush off to the scene of the accident. They are impelled to do this, in the first place, by the strong natural desire every man has to be of service in times of danger; secondly, by reason of the intense excitement which the cry of 'Fire!' always produces in the most phlegmatic individual, and, last of all – if either of the two causes before-named are wanting – by a natural and uncontrollable curiosity and fascination for the smoke and flames. It is usually the first of these three causes that impels the workmen to throw down their tools and run to help the men with the fire-engines. At such times as these nothing is held sacred. Doors and windows are forced open or smashed in, bolts and bars are wrenched from their sockets, offices and storehouses are entered; the most private recesses are made public. All thoughts of the midnight meal are set aside and there is no returning to the worksheds until morning brings a fresh supply of hands accompanied by the day officials.

Not many years ago the station buildings took fire, shortly after midnight, and most of the men on night duty in the department nearest the scene flocked out to help the station staff and the firemen. By and by the refreshment rooms were involved and there was a wholesale removal of the viands and liquors. Under such circumstances, drinking was naturally indulged in, and more than one – officials, as well as the rank and file – who came out to help returned the worse for liquor. Such adventures as these live long in the memory of the workmen: it is not often they have the opportunity of taking a drink at the company's expense.

Some time after the station fire a much more serious outbreak occurred in an extensive shed used for the construction and storing of carriages. There were in the place sufficient vehicles to compose twenty trains, and the most of them were brand new, representing altogether a huge sum of money. When the watchman passed through on his rounds at midnight everything appeared safe; the place was dark, silent, and deserted. Half an hour afterwards a workman employed in a shed some distance away saw a dull glow above the roof and thought at first it was the moon rising. A few minutes afterwards flames leapt into sight and discovered a fire of some magnitude.

Quickly the signal was given, and every available man rushed on the scene. The centre of the shed was like a raging furnace. The roof was on fire and the flames leapt from coach to coach with great rapidity. These, from their slightness of construction and from their being thickly coated with paint and varnish, caught fire like matchwood and burned furiously, while large sections of the roof fell in. Every now and then, as a coach became consumed down to the framework, the gas cylinders underneath burst with a terrific report, like that of a piece of heavy artillery. The shattered iron and steel flew in all directions and increased the danger to the firemen. Hundreds of people of the neighbourhood, roused with the repeated shocks, left their beds and ran out of doors to ascertain the cause of the explosions. Some thought it was an earthquake and others feared it was the boilers exploding. Many volunteered to help, but their offers were refused, and a strong cordon of police was drawn around the shed to keep out all intruders. So fierce was the heat within that the steel tyres of the wheels were buckled and bent, the rails were warped and twisted into fantastic shapes and the heavy iron girders of the roof were wrecked. The frames of the burnt coaches were reduced to a pile of debris and were totally unrecognisable. The damage to rolling stock and to the premises amounted to many thousands of pounds, yet the fire was all over in two or three hours. As to its origin, that remained a mystery, and completely baffled the detectives. Examination of the tell-tales proved that the watchman had gone his round all right, and though many experiments were made the cause of the outbreak remained inexplicable.

A great part of the repairs to carriages – such as washing-down, smudging, and especially the cleaning and re-fitting of interiors – is done out of doors in the yard when the weather permits, for it would be impossible to contain all the vehicles in the sheds. The whole of this work, even to the most trivial detail, is now done at the piece rate. Experienced examiners decide the amount of repairs to be executed, and the prices are fixed according to their recommendation. It is generally a matter of luck to the workman whether the repair job pays or not. Very often the carrying out of repairs takes a much longer time than had been anticipated. The renewing of one part often necessitates the remodelling of another, or the fitting up of the new piece may prove to be a very tedious process. In this case the workman may lose money on the job, though, on the other hand, he may have finished altogether earlier than he expected. It would be very nearly impossible to have a perfect equation in the matter of repair prices, and this is recognised by all, masters and men, too, at the factory. The workman is commonly told by his chief that 'what he loses on the swings he must pick up on the roundabouts,' *i.e.*, what he loses on one job he must gain on another, and this axiom is universally accepted, at least by all those who do repairs. On new work the labour is uniform and there is no need and no excuse for inequality of prices.

Great consternation fell upon the carriage finishers, painters, and pattern-makers, several years ago, when it became known that piece rates were to be substituted for the old day-work system, especially as the change was to be introduced at a very slack time. It was looked upon as a catastrophe by the workmen, and such it very nearly proved to be. Many journeymen were discharged, some were transferred to other grades of work – that is, those who were willing to suffer reduction rather than to be thrown quite out of employment – and the whole department was put on short time, working only two or three days a week, while some of the men were shut out for weeks at a stretch. Several who protested against the change were dismissed, and others – workmen of the highest skill and of long connection with the company – had their wages mercilessly cut down for daring to interpose their opinion. The pace was forced and quickened by degrees to the uttermost and then the new prices were fixed, the managers themselves attending and timing operations and supervising the prices. Felling among the workmen ran high, but there was no help for the situation and it had to be accepted. Few of the men belonged to a trade union, or they might have opposed the terms and made a better bargain; as it was they were completely at the mercy of the managers and foremen.

The carriage finishers and upholsterers are a class in themselves, differing, by the very nature of their craft, from all others at the factory. As great care and cleanliness are required for their work, they are expected to be spruce and clean in their dress and appearance. This, together with the fact that the finisher may have served an apprenticeship in a high-class establishment and one far more genteel than a railway department can hope to be, tends to create in him a sense of refinement higher than is usually found in those who follow rougher and more laborious occupations. His cloth suit, linen collar, spotless white apron, clean shaven face, hair carefully combed, and bowler hat are subjects of comment by the grimy toilers of other sheds. His dwelling is situated in the cleanest part of the town and corresponds with his personal appearance. In the evening he prosecutes his craft at home and manufactures furniture and decorations for himself and family, or earns money by doing it for others. Very often the whole contents of his parlour and kitchen – with the exception of iron and other ware – were made by his hands, so, since his wages are above the ordinary, provided he is steady and temperate, he may be reasonably comfortable and well-to-do.

The painters are not quite as fortunate as are their comrades the finishers. Their work, though in some respects of a high order and important, is at the same time less artistic than is that of the cabinet-makers and upholsterers. It is also much more wearisome and unhealthy, and the wages are not as high. Very often, too, work for them is extremely scarce, especially during the summer and autumn months, when every available coach is required in traffic for the busy season, and they are consequently often on short time. Their busiest periods are the interval between autumn and Christmas and the time between the New Year and Easter. The style of colouring and ornamentation for the carriages has changed considerably of recent years and there is now not nearly as much labour and pains expended upon the vehicles as in times past. The brighter colours have been quite eliminated and have given place to chocolates and browns, while the frames and ends of the carriages are painted black. The arms of the company, together with figures, letters, initials, and other designs, so conspicuous to the eye of the traveller, are affixed by means of transfers and therefore are not dependent upon the skill of the painters.

The washing-down of the coaches is done by labourers, some of whom live in the town and others in the villages round about. Little skill is required for this, and the operation is very dull and monotonous. The men are supplied with long-handled brushes, soaps, and sponges, hot and cold water and chemical preparations. Large gangs of them are continually employed in removing the accretions of dust and filth acquired by the coaches in their mad career over the railway line, through tunnels and cuttings, smoky towns and cities. Sometimes the vehicles are completely smothered with grease and mud thrown up by the sleepers in bad weather, and every particle of this must be removed before the painter can apply his brush to renovate the exterior.

The washers-down are generally raw youths and many of them are of the shifty type – the kind that will not settle anywhere for long together. The drabness of their employment forces them to seek some means of breaking the monotony of it, and they often indulge in noise and horseplay, singing and shouting at the top of their voices and slopping the water over each other. This brings them into trouble with the officials, and occasions them to take many a forced holiday, but they do not care about that, and when they arrive back upon the scene they practise their old games as boldly as before. Having no trade, and receiving but a scant amount in wages, they do not feel to be bound down hand and foot to the employment, and even if they should be discharged altogether they will not have lost very much. Their youthfulness, too, renders them buoyant and independent; all the world is open to them if they decide to hand in their notices.

The cushion-beaters, formerly well known about the yard, have quite disappeared now. At whatever time you were outside the shed, in fine weather, you might have heard their rods beating on the cushions in perfect rhythm and order. They were taken from the coaches and laid upon stools in the open air, and the beater held a rod, usually of hazel, in each hand. With them he alternately smote the cushion, keeping up the effort for a long time, until every particle of dust was removed and blown away. His dexterity in the use of the rods and the ability to prolong the operation were a source of great interest to the youths; all the small boys of the shed stole out at intervals to see him at work. Now the dust is removed from the cushions and paddings by means of a vacuum arrangement. This is in the form of a tube, with an aperture several inches in diameter and having strong suctional powers created by the exhaust steam from the engine in the shed. It is passed to and fro over the surface of the cushion, and the dust is thereby extracted and received into the apparatus. So strong is the suction within that it will sometimes draw the buttons from the upholstering if they are loose or frayed. The quantity of dust extracted from one carriage often amounts to a pound in weight.

Old customs and systems die hard at the works and, whatever their own opinion of the matter may be, the officials are not considered by the workmen to be of a very progressive type. Many of the methods employed, both in manufacture and administration, are extremely old-fashioned and antiquated; an idea has to be old and hoary before it stands a chance of being admitted and adopted here. Small private firms are usually a long way ahead of railway companies in the matter of methods and processes, and they pay better wages into the bargain. They have to face competition and to cater for the markets, while railway companies, being both the producers and consumers of their wares, can afford to choose their own way of manufacturing them. In addition to this, the heads of small firms usually have an interest in the concern whereas the managers of railway works are otherwise placed; it makes no difference to them what they spend or waste, and they are always able to cover up their shortcomings. Their prodigality and mismanagement would ruin a hundred small firms in as many months, though the outside world knows little or nothing about it. But if the officials creep they urge the rank and file at a good rate and make a pretence of being smart and business-like. The fact of a workman being engaged prosecuting a worn-out method for the production of an article does not make the task lighter or more congenial for him, rather the opposite. Real improvement in manufacture not only expedites production, but also simplifies the toil to the workman, and the newer methods are the better, generally speaking.

In everything, then, except in smart management and supervision, railway sheds now resemble contract premises. Piecework prices are cut to the lowest possible point; it is all push, drive, and hustle. No attempt is made to regulate the amount of work to be done, and short time is frequent and often of long duration. This is not arranged as it was formerly, when the whole department, or none at all, was closed down. Now even a solitary shed, a portion of it, or a mere gang is closed or suspended if there is a slackness at any point. Consequently, one part of the works is often running at break-neck speed, while another is working but three or four days a week and the men are in a half-starved condition. In one shed fresh hands are being put on, while from others they are being discharged wholesale. Transfers from one shop to another are seldom made, and never from department to department. One would think that the various divisions of the works were owned by separate firms, or people of different nationalities, such formidable barriers appear to exist between them.

The chiefs of the departments are usually more or less rivals and are often at loggerheads, each one trying to outdo the other in some particular direction and to bring himself into the notice of the directors. The same, with a little modification, may be said of the foremen of the several divisions, while the workmen are about indifferent in this respect. For them, all beyond their own sheds, except a few personal friends or relations, are total strangers. Though they may have been employed at the works for half a century, they have never gone beyond the boundary of their own department, and perhaps not as far as that, for trespassing from shed to shed is strictly forbidden and sharply punished where detected. Thus, the workman's sphere is very narrow and limited. There is no freedom; nothing but the same coming and going, the still monotonous journey to and fro and the old hours, month after month, and year after year. It is no wonder that the factory workmen come to lead a dull existence and to lose interest in all life beyond their own smoky walls and dwellings. It would be a matter for surprise if the reverse condition prevailed.

CHAPTER IV

THE OLD CANAL – THE ASH-WHEELERS – THE BRICKLAYERS – RIVAL
FOREMEN – THE ROAD-WAGGON BUILDERS – THE WHEEL SHED –
BOY TURNERS – THE RUBBISH HEAP

West of the workshop the yard is bounded by a canal that formerly
connected the railway town with the ancient borough town of Cricklade, eight miles distant. But things are different now from what they
were at the time the cutting was made, for great changes have taken place
during the last half century in all matters pertaining to transport. Then
the long barges, drawn by horses, mules, and donkeys, and laden with
corn, stone, coal, timber, gravel, and other materials, proceeded regularly by day and night, up and down the canal to their destinations –
north to Gloucester, west to Bristol, east to Abingdon, and thence to
far-off London. At that time, instead of being filled with mud, weeds,
and refuse, and overgrown with masses of rank vegetation – grasses,
flags, water-parsnip, and a score of other aquatic plants – the channel was
broad and free, and full of clear, limpid water. The cattle came to drink
in the meadows; there the clouds were mirrored, floating in fields of
azure. The fish leapt and played in the sunshine, making innumerable
rings on the surface, and the swallows skimmed swiftly along, dipping
now and then to snatch up a sweet mouthful to carry home to their
young in the nest under the eaves of the neighbouring cottage or shed.

Occasionally, too, a steamboat passed through the locks out beyond
the town and proceeded on its way to the Thames or Avon. The dredger
plied up and down to prevent the accumulation of mud and refuse, and
the towpaths and bridges were kept in good repair. The railway had not
everything its own way then. The fever of haste had not taken hold of
every part of the community, and a few, at least, could await the arrival
of the barges and so save a considerable sum in the conveyance of their
goods. But now all that is changed. Goods must be loaded, whirled

---

Overleaf: North Wilts Canal to Cricklade, 1912: dried up bed where children
        stand, below Telford Road Bridge and Lock, now Cheney Manor
        Road

rapidly away and delivered in a few hours, for no one can wait. The pace of the freight trains has been increased almost to express speed. Every possible means that could be thought of have been devised to facilitate transport, and the barges have disappeared from this neighbourhood. Here and there at the wharves may still be seen a few rotten old hulks, falling to pieces and embedded in the mud; the bridges are shattered and dilapidated and the lock gates are broken. The towpaths are overgrown with bushes and become almost impassable, and the channel is blocked up.

Wilts. and Berks. Canal, about 1912: disused. Did Alfred, a botanist, walk along the tow-path from work to South Marston? Slightly further than by road, but botanically richer

The only person who benefits by the change is the botanist. He, from time to time, may be seen busily engaged in grappling for rare specimens of weeds and grasses, or the less learned student of wild flowers comes to gather what treasures he may from the wilderness: the beautiful flowering rush, golden iris, graceful water plantain, arrowhead, water violet, figwort, skull-cap, gipsy wort, and celery-leaved crowfoot. Formerly, too, the works derived a considerable quantity of water through the canal, but that has long ceased to be. There is no water at hand now, and supplies have had to be sought for among the Cotswold Hills, at a great distance from the town. The engines at the old pumping station, near the canal path, once so familiar a feature to travellers that way, are silent now and will be heard there no more. They, too, have become a thing of the past.

The factory premises extend along both banks of the canal and are protected on the far side by a high wall, while that part nearest the

York Road Bridge, about 1912. Wilts. and Berks. Canal went east/west through town. To conserve water for it, Coate Reservoir made, 1822. Hawthorn hedge (right) is still growing today!

workshop is open to the water's edge. On this side, first of all, is a high platform, called the stage, which is used to load the ashes and refuse, slag and clinkers from the furnaces and forges. This refuse is wheeled out twice daily – at six in the morning and again in the evening after the furnaces have been clinkered – by labourers, upon whom the duty devolves. To remove the clinker properly and economically from the grate of the furnace the fire must have been damped for a short while. This allows the whitehot coals to cling together underneath, and they form a kind of arch above the bars. When this has been accomplished the furnaceman inserts a strong steel bar at the bottom, resting it upon the 'bridge,' and, with a heavy sledge, breaks the clinker, working along from side to side. That is in a compact layer or mass, often six or eight inches deep, considerably thicker in the corners, and it is very tough while it is hot. After it has been thoroughly broken up, several of the fire bars are removed together, beginning at one side, and the heavy clinker drops through, spluttering and hissing, into the deep boshes of water disposed underneath. If the fire has not been sufficiently damped it is loose and hollow, and as soon as the bars are removed the white-hot coals rush through into the water, raising clouds of hot, blinding dust and dense volumes of steam.

Immediately the furnaceman, warned of the fall, springs backwards and escapes from the pit, or, if he is tardy in his movements, he is caught in the hot vapour and scalded severely. Sometimes the fall is very sudden and he has not time to escape. Then his face and arms take the full force of the rushing steam and he is certain to receive painful injuries. When the operation of clinkering is over the men bring their wheel-barrows and, with the aid of long-handled shovels, remove the refuse from the pits and run it outside and upon the stage. This is hot work, whenever it is performed; the men are always sure of a wet shirt at the task. Whatever the weather may be, wet or fine, frost or snow, they come to it stripped to the waist and quickly run their wheel-barrows to and fro. If the rain should pelt in torrents it makes little or no difference to them, they still go on with their work, half-naked and bare-headed. Hardy and strong as they may be, this is bound to affect their health, sooner or later. It is not an uncommon thing to find one or other of them breaking down at an early age, a physical wreck, unfit for further service.

The ash-wheelers belong to the same class as the coalies and are sometimes identical with them. They are usually some of the strongest men in the shed, new hands, perhaps, who have not yet earned for themselves an installation into the ranks of the regular machine staff. Sometimes, however, they have proved themselves smart with the shovel and wheel-barrow and have been considered too serviceable to shift to other employment, for, as it is well known that 'the willing horse must draw double,' so the workman who is willing to perform a hard duty without murmuring and complaint is always imposed upon and forced to do extra. The natural fool or the systematic skulker is pitied and respected. Once his general conduct is understood he is taken for what he is worth, and no more is expected of him. In time he is rewarded. He may come to be a checker, a clerk, or an inspector; while the sterling fellow, the hard worker, the 'sticker,' as he is called, may stop and work himself to death like a slave. Thus, deserving men, because they have proved themselves adepts at the work, have been kept on the ash-barrows for ten or twelve years, sweating their lives away for the sum of eighteen shillings a week. Several, however, disgusted with the business, have left the shed and gone back to work on the farms, in the pure surroundings of the fields and villages. This branch of work has recently been overhauled and estimated at the piece rate, and the wages somewhat improved, though the amount of work to each man has been almost doubled. The refuse and clinker from the furnaces are transported to various parts and used for filling up hollows, and for the making of banks and beds of yards and sidings.

Beyond the stage, lodged on the ground, are two old iron vans that were formerly used in the goods traffic. They have no windows or lights of any kind, merely a double door opening outwardly. These are the cabins and stores of the bricklayers, and they contain cement, fireclay, and firebricks for the furnaces and forges. A permanent staff of brick-layers is kept in each department at the works to carry out whatever repairs are necessary from time to time and to see to the construction and renovation of the furnaces. If there is any building on a large scale required, such as a new shed, stores, or offices, extra hands are put on from the town and afterwards discharged when the work is done. This procedure gives the officials an opportunity of selecting the best men, so that it often happens that new hands, temporarily engaged, become fixtures if they have shown exceptional skill at their trade and are otherwise suitable. In that case some of the old hands must go, and it needs not to be said that such an opportunity is welcomed by the foreman, as it provides him with an excuse for removing undesirables without being too much blamed himself.

The bricklayers are a distinct class and do not mingle well with the other men at the works. Their having to do with bricks and mortar, instead of with iron and steel, seems to exclude them from the general hive, and the fact of their being dressed in canvas suits and overalls, and smeared with cement and fireclay, instead of being blackened with soot and oil, tends to emphasise the distinction. As with the rest of the staff, they are recruited from all parts of the country, and some of them have served a rural apprenticeship. In shrewdness and intelligence they do not rank with the machinists; that is to say, they may be smart at their trade, but they do not discover extraordinary faculties beyond that. Perhaps the nature of their toil has something to do with it, for that is at best a dull and uninspiring vocation. There is no magic required in the setting together of bricks and mortar, and little exertion of the intellect is needed in patching up old walls and buildings. They are nevertheless very jealous of their craft, such as it is, and deeply resent any intrusion into their ranks other than by the gates of the usual apprenticeship. Occasionally it happens that a bricklayer's labourer, who has been for many years in attendance on his mate, shows an aptitude for the work, so that the foreman, in a busy period, is induced to equip him with the trowel. In that case he at once becomes the subject of sneering criticism; whatever work he does is condemned, and he is hated and shunned by his old mates and companions. The foreman, too, takes advantage of his position and pays him less than the trade rate of wages, so that, after all, he is really made to feel that he is not a journeyman.

Very often, when there is no building to be done, the bricklayers must turn their hands to other work, such as navvying, whitewashing, painting, and so on, all which falls under their particular department. Armed with pick and shovel, or pot and brush, they must dig foundations and drains, or scale the walls and roof and cleanse or decorate the shed. This is always productive of much grumbling and sarcastic comment, but it is better than being suspended. On the whole the bricklayers have a fairly comfortable billet at the works and they are not subject to frequent loss of time through wet weather and other accidents, as are their fellows of the town, though they do not receive as much in wages.

It is astonishing what a prodigious amount of work the labourers will get through in a short time, and apparently with little exertion, when they are digging out drains and foundations for new furnaces, steam-hammers, or other machinery. These foundations are generally huge pits, twelve or fifteen feet deep and double the size square. Stripped to the waist in the heat of the workshop, and armed with the heavy graft tool, with a stout iron plate fixed underneath their right foot, they will dig for hours without resting and yet seem to be always fresh and vigorous. Occasionally, as they throw up the solid clay, some workman of the shed will steal along to examine the fossil remains, pebbles, and flints, that were embedded in the earth, and slip back to his place at the steam-hammer, preserving some relic or other for future examination. The sturdy labourer, however, keeps digging out the clay and hurling it up to the light. He knows nothing of geological data, theories and opinions, and cares not to inquire. He is there to dig the pit and not to trouble himself about the nature of soils and deposits, and though you should talk to him ever so learnedly of old time submersions, accretions, and formations, he only answers you with a blank stare or an unsympathetic grin. His private opinion is that you are something of a lunatic.

There is one among the bricklayers' labourers that is remarkable. This is the silent man, generally known as Herbert. The story goes that Herbert was once in love and thought to take a wife. But the course of true love did not run smooth in his case, and, in the end, the young lady jilted Herbert. That is according to the story. It may or may not have been true; perhaps Herbert could tell, but he is not at all communicative. Whatever the circumstances were, they made a profound impression upon Herbert's mind and he has never been the same man since. Now he does not speak to any except his near workmate, and only then to answer the most necessary questions. It is useless for an outsider to attempt to make him speak; he ignores all your attentions. To cause him to smile would be akin to working a miracle. The set features never relax. The eyes are vacant and expressionless, the mouth is firm and stern, and the whole countenance rigid.

Yet Herbert is a fine-looking man. His features are regular – almost classic – his face is bronzed with working out of doors, and he is a picture of health. In height he is medium. His shoulders are broad and square, his arms strong and muscular, and he has the endurance of an ox. Would you tire Herbert? That is impossible. Whatever labour you set him to do he performs it without a murmur. He does the work of three ordinary men. Must he dig? He will dig, dig, dig, and throw up the huge spits of heavy clay as high as his head, one might say for ever. Must he wheel away the debris? He will pile up the wheel-barrow till it is ready to break down under the weight, and trundle it off and up to the stage without the slightest exertion and be back again in a breath. He will lift enormous weights and strike tremendous blows with the sledge. He is tireless in his use of the pick and shovel; in fact, whatever you set Herbert to do he accomplishes it all in about a fifth of the time ordinarily required for the purpose. He is the butt of his masters and of his workmates. Whatever uncommonly laborious task there is to be done Herbert is the man to do it, and the more he does the more he must do, though he does not know it, or if he does, he shows no indication of the knowledge. Now and again the foreman stands by and watches him approvingly, and this stimulates him to fresh efforts. He revels in the work and, whatever he thinks about it all, he is still silent and inexplicable.

This sort of thing is all right from the point of view of the foreman, but it is very inconvenient and unfair to the other labourers who are sane in their minds and mortal in their bodies, for everything they do is adjudged according to the standard of this indefatigable Hercules. The overseer, used to seeing him slaving endlessly, thinks light of the others' efforts, and imagines that they are not doing their share of the toil, so uneven is the comparison of their labours. In reality, such a man as Herbert is a danger and an enemy of his kind, though as he is quite unconscious of his conduct and does it all with the best intentions he must be forgiven. Such a one is more to be pitied than blamed.

The foremen of the bricklayers are not bricklayers themselves, and never have been, but were selected apparently without any consideration of their specific abilities. This one was a shunter, another was a carpenter, a third was a waggon-builder, and so on. Perhaps So-and-so and So-and-so went to school together, or worked formerly in the same shed; or consanguinity is the cause, for blood is thicker than water in the factory, as elsewhere. Accordingly, it often comes about that the most fitting person to take the responsible position is thrust aside at the last moment for an utter stranger, one who has no knowledge whatever of the work he is to supervise. With a certain amount of 'pushfulness,' however, and an extraordinary confidence in himself and his abilities, the new man is able to make a pretence of knowledge and, somehow or other, the work proceeds. Very often it would go on for months just as well without the foreman to interfere, and in many cases even better, for it is the chargemen and gangers who have the actual control of operations and who possess the real and intimate knowledge of the work.

Should an aspirant to the post of foreman through his own merits be set aside for a stranger – as is sometimes the case – there is bound to be jealousy existing between the two for ever afterwards, which now and again breaks out into heated scenes and may result in brawls and dismissals. Of the workmen, some will take the one side, and some the other; they are mutually distrustful, and have recourse to whispering and tale-telling. If it has been proved that one workman is guilty of getting another his discharge by any unfair means he is not forgiven by his mates. The dismissed man, in such a case, will frequently wait for his informer outside the gates, and will not be satisfied until he has given him a good thrashing. Perhaps he will walk boldly in through the entrance with the other men and take him unaware at his work and punish him on the spot. It is superfluous to say that this is not tolerated by the officials, and anyone who is so bold as to do it must be prepared to stand the consequences and appear at the Borough Police Court.

Now and again a foreman, who has been guilty of some underhanded action, is taken to task by the exasperated victim and treated to a little surprise combat of fisticuffs. Perhaps the foreman is a sneak or a bully, or both, and has carried his tyrannical behaviour too far for human endurance; or private jealousy may have impelled him to some cowardly turn or other, and the workman, driven to desperation, takes the law into his own hands and gives him a thrashing. This – provided the reprisal was merited – will be a source of huge delight to the other men in the shed, and everyone will rejoice to see the offender 'taken down a notch,' as they say; but if it was merely an exhibition of unwarrantable temper on the workman's part, the overseer will be commiserated with and defended. Whether right or wrong the pugnacious one is dismissed. His services are no longer required at the shed; he must seek occupation elsewhere.

Running along for some distance near the canal is a shed in which the road-waggons are made – trollies, vans, and cars for use in the goods yards and stations about the line – and inside this, and parallel with it, is the wheel shop, where the wheels, tyres, and axles are turned and fitted up for the waggons and carriages. Besides the making of new work in the first-named of these sheds, there is always a considerable amount of repairs to be carried out. A great part of this is done outside, in fine weather, in order to give increased room within doors.

The road-waggon builders are of a sturdy type. Many of them are inclined to be old-fashioned and primitive in their methods, and they are solid in character. This is accounted for by the fact that the greater part of the older hands received their initial training in small yards, in little country towns and villages, where they worked among farmers and rustics. The work they did there was necessarily very solid and strong – such as heavy carts and waggons for the farms – and everything had to be done by hand, slowly and laboriously perhaps, but efficiently and well. This taught them the practical side of their trade, as how to be self-sufficing and independent of machinery, which are the most valuable features of a good apprenticeship and are of great service to the workman in after years. By and by, when the time came for them to leave the scene of their apprentice days – for few masters will pay the journeyman's rate of wages to any who, at the end of their term, have not gone further afield for new experience – they shifted out for themselves. Some went one way and some another. This one went to London, that one to Bristol, and others came to the railway town. Whatever peculiarities of workmanship they acquired in their youth they brought with them and practised in their new sphere, and so the individual style is maintained in spite of totally different methods and processes.

At the present time – in large factories, at any rate – there is machinery for everything, and this is highly destructive of the purely personal faculty in manufacture. But in the case of the road-waggon builder, though a great many, or perhaps all, of the parts have been shaped for him by steam power, there yet remains the fitting up and building of the vehicle, which is reasonably a task requiring considerable care and skill. The iron frame of the locomotive or railway waggon may be clapped together quite easily, for there is no very elaborate fitting or joining to be done. Good strong rivets are the chief things required there. The wooden bodies of the vans and cars, however, must be fitted and built with the nicest precision and finish, or the materials would shrink away and the parts would gape open, or fall to pieces. Thus, the road-waggon builder, as well as the carriage body-maker, must be a craftsman of the first order, and while some journeymen may be at liberty to sacrifice their dearly gained experience and individual characteristics in the face of newer methods and improved mechanical processes, it is well for him to hold fast to what he has found useful and good in the past.

The workmen of every shed have their own particular tone and style collectively as well as individually; different trades and atmospheres apparently producing different characteristics and temperaments. Accordingly, the men of one shed are well-known for one quality, while those of another are noted for something quite different. These are famed for steadiness, civility, and correct behaviour; those for noise, rudeness, horse-play, and even ruffianism. The men of some sheds are remarkable for their extreme docility and their almost childish obedience to the slightest and most insignificant rules of the factory, counting every official as a thing superhuman and nearly to be worshipped. Others are notorious for ideas quite the reverse of this, for riotous conduct within and without the shed, an utter contempt of the laws of the factory, for thieving, fighting, and other propensities. These characteristics are determined as much by the kind of work done in the sheds and the quality of the overseer, as by the men's own nature and temperament. Most foremen are excessively autocratic and severe with their men, denying them the slightest privilege or relaxation of the iron laws of the factory. Others are of a wheedling, pseudo-fatherly type, who, by a combination of professed paternal regard and a cunning manipulation of the reins, contrive to make everything they do appear just and reasonable and so hold their men in complete subjection. Some foremen, again, are of the ceremonious order, who, from pure vanity, will insist upon the complete observance of the most trivial detail and drive their workmen half-way to distraction. A few, on the other hand, are generous and humane. They hold the reins slack, and, without the knowledge of their chiefs, grant a few small privileges and are rewarded with the confidence of the workmen and a willingness to labour on their part amounting to enthusiasm. For, as the horse that is tightly breeched draws none too well, neither do those men work best who are rigidly kept down under the iron rod of the overseer. Discipline there is bound to be, as everyone knows, but there is no excuse for treating a man as though he were a wild beast, or an infant just out of the cradle. Whatever dissatisfaction exists about the works is chiefly owing to the behaviour of the officials, for they force the workmen into rebellion. If the directors of the company are anxious for the welfare of their staff – as they profess to be – let them instruct their managers and foremen to show themselves a little more tolerant and kindly disposed to the men in the sheds. Actions speak louder than words, and kindness shown to workmen is never forgotten.

The wheel shop is a large building, containing many rows of lathes for the wheels, tyres, and axles, which are nearly all tended by boys. The lines of shafting stretch in the roof, up and down from end to end of the place, and the pulleys whirl round almost noiselessly overhead. Everything is spotlessly clean, for there are no furnaces belching out their smoke, dust, and flames. The temperature is low and the shed, even in the hottest part of the summer, is cool in comparison with the other premises round about. In the winter it is heated with steam from the boilers and the exhaust from the shop engines. This prevents the boys from catching cold. The heavy steel axles and tyres are exceedingly chill in the winter, especially in frosty weather.

The boys come from all parts, from town and country alike, immediately after leaving school, and go straight to the lathes. There are labourers to fix the wheels and tyres in the machines, and the boys attend to the tools, working carefully to the gauges provided. Coming to the work at a time when their minds are in a receptive state, they soon master the principal parts of the business and before long become highly skilled and proficient. Their wages are no more than five or six shillings a

Swindon boys, future railway workers. Milford Street, near the station, 1890s.
Niblett sold mineral waters

More boys, potential railway workers, further along Milford Street, 1890s.
A.E. Tunley, picture framer, supplier of paint and artists' materials, still trades
in Swindon, in Fleet Street. Details left and right below

week for a start, with yearly rises of one or two shillings until they reach a pound or twenty-two shillings. Upon arriving at this stage – unless work is plentiful – they are usually removed from the lathe and set labouring, or otherwise transferred or discharged as too expensive for the work. Sometimes, after this, they migrate to other towns and earn double or treble the wages they received before, for good wheel- and axle-turners are in constant demand and a clever workman may be sure of securing a high rate of remuneration.

The boys are an interesting group, and one that is well worthy of consideration. They are of all sorts and sizes, of many grades and walks

Boys and men, probably aiming at a life in GWR works. Cromwell Street, during coal strike. Waiting for supplies at coal merchant's, with wheeled truck. Hoop for fun

in life. There is the country labourer's lad, who formerly worked on the land amid the horses and cattle; the town labourer's lad, who has been errand-boy or who sold newspapers on the street corner; the small shopkeeper's lad, the fitter's lad, tall and pale, in clean blue overalls, and the engine-driver's lad, fresh from school, whose one ambition is to emulate his father and, like him, drive an engine, only one that is two or three times as big and powerful. There are tall and short boys, boys fat and lean, pale and robust-looking, ragged and well-kept, with sad and merry faces. And what pranks they play with one another, and would play, if they were not curbed and checked with the ever watchful eyes of the shop foreman! They are always ready for some game or other – football, hide-and-seek, or 'ierky' – at any time of the day, and whatever

More of the group, with cheeky errand boy. Coal merchants flourished in Cromwell Street area

they do, it does not seem to tire them down; they are still fresh and active, cheerful and vivacious.

Many of them begin the day well with running regularly to work, perhaps for two or three miles. At five minutes past six in the morning they commence at the lathe, and when breakfast-time comes they scamper off, food in hand, and play about the yard, or in the recreation field beyond. From nine till one their labour is continuous; there they stand, bound as with chains to the machines they serve, for ever watchful, so as not to spoil the cut and waste the axle, which would mean an enforced holiday for them. When one o'clock comes, smothered with oil and with faces like those of sweeps – often blackened purposely to give themselves the appearance of having perspired much – they race off as before, and play recklessly until it is time to return to the shed. And after the day's work is finished and they go home in the evening, they wash away the grime and oil and play about the streets and lanes till bed-time, utterly indifferent to the wearisome occupation awaiting them on the morrow. Their sleep is sound and sweet, for their hearts are happy and light. Of the cares of life they know nothing; the future is full of hope for them; all the world is before them. Their chief concern is for the holidays. All these are anticipated and awaited with

Another group, with potential railway boys, 1913. Regent Street, looking into Cromwell Street: now obliterated

great joy and eagerness; it is by this alone that they discover the extreme tedium of the daily drudgery of the workshop.

The boys' foreman is an experienced official, shrewd, keen, and very severe; a good judge of character, cautious, and careful, civil enough, but unbending in a decision, a very good formative agent, one who will exercise a healthy restraint upon the intractables and encourage the timid,

but who exploits them all for the good of the firm. His keen eyes and
sound judgment enable him to at once sum up a lad's capabilities. He
takes the youth and sets him where he will show to the best advantage,
instructs him on many of the crucial points, advises him as to the best
means of getting on, and very often furnishes him with hints of a
personal nature which – whatever the lad may think of them at the time –

Continuation to the right. Briggs Shoes remains, though corner gone. Tomkins
and Bassetts printed postcards, such as this

bear fruit in later life. If the youngster is inclined to be wild and
incorrigible he tries his best to reform him and gives him sound advice.
He has also been known to administer a corrective cuff in the ear and a
vigorous boot in the posterior, but he usually succeeds in bringing out
the good points and suppressing, if not entirely eradicating, the bad.

Whenever he walks up or down the shed the boys fix their attention
more firmly upon their machines, for they feel his keen, penetrating eyes
upon them, and they know that nothing ever escapes his notice. If there
is a slackness at any point the word is passed rapidly on – 'Look out,
here's J—y coming,' and the overseer is sometimes amused with the

various expedients resorted to in order to deceive him and cover up the juvenile shortcomings. As to wages, prices, and systems, they are not altogether his fault. If he could suit himself he might possibly be willing to pay more, but he is always being pressed by the staff to reduce prices and expenses, and, like the other foremen, he is not prepared to offer effective resistance. Being an official of long standing, however, he is secure in his place, and has no occasion to betray his hands to the firm, as is too often the case with young foremen, who wish to secure personal notice and advantage. That is one of the most damning features of all, and is becoming more and more a practice at the works. One young 'under-strapper' I knew is in the habit of standing over the boys at the lathe, watch in hand, for four hours without once moving, and, by his manner and language, compelling them to run at an excessive rate so as to cut their prices. Without doubt he is deserving of the birch rod, though the managers, who allow it, are the more to blame.

A short way from the canal, north of the road-waggon shed, is the rubbish heap, at which most of the old wood refuse and lumber, with hundreds of tons of sawdust, are brought to be burned. At one time all this was consumed in the boiler furnaces, but since the amount of refuse has enormously increased it has been found expedient to transport some part of it there and so do away with it. One small furnace is used for the purpose, and by far the greater part of it, especially the sawdust, is burned in big heaps upon the ground. This is a slovenly, as well as a dangerous method, and the inconvenience resulting to the men in the sheds is considerable. If the wind is in the west the dense clouds of smoke sweep along the ground and are blown straight in through the open doors upon the stampers, and are a source of extreme discomfort and disgust. There is always plenty of smother in the shed, arising from the oil furnaces, without receiving any addition from outside. Once the workshop is filled with the bluish vapour it takes hours to disperse, for, though there are doors all round and hundreds of ventilators on the roof, they do not carry off the nuisance. Very often the smoke will travel from end to end of the shed, like a current of water, but just as it reaches the doorway and you think it is going to pass outside, it suddenly whirls round like a wheel and traverses the whole length of the place, and so on, over and over again.

If the wind is in the north, then the road-waggon builders must suffer the persecuting clouds of smoke and be tormented with smarting and burning eyes at work; and if it should blow from over the town, across the rolling downs from the south, the smother is carried high over the fence and sweeps along the recreation field to the discomfort of small boys and lovers, or of whoever happens to be passing that way. If the nuisance arose from any other quarter complaints might be made and steps taken towards the mitigation of it. As it is, no one, not even a member of the local bodies and the Corporation, summons up the courage to make a protest, for everyone bows down before the company's officials and representatives in the railway town and fears to raise objections to anything that may be done by the people at the works.

CHAPTER V

'THE FIELD' – 'CUTTING-DOWN' – THE FLYING DUTCHMAN –
THE FRAME SHED – PROMOTION – RIVET BOYS – THE OVERSEER

On the north the factory yard is bounded by a high board fence that runs along close behind the shed and divides the premises from the recreation grounds, which are chiefly the haunt of juveniles during the summer months and the resort of football players and athletes in the winter. Here also the small children come after school and wander about the field among the buttercups, or sit down amid the long grass in the sunshine, or swing round the Maypole, under the very shadow of the black walls, with only a thin fence to separate them from the busy factory. The ground beneath their feet shakes with the ponderous blows of the steam-hammers; the white clouds of steam from the exhaust pipes shoot high into the air. Dense volumes of blackest smoke tower out of the chimneys, whirling round and round and over and over, or roll lazily away in a long line out beyond the town and fade into the distance.

The fence stretches away to the east for a quarter of a mile from the shed and then turns again at right angles and continues the boundary on that side as far as to the entrance by the railway. About half-way across are several large shops and premises used for lifting, fitting, and storing the carriages; beyond them is a wide, open space commonly known as 'the field.' As a matter of fact, the whole area of the yard was really a series of fields until quite recently. Fifteen years ago, although the space was enclosed, you might have walked among the hedgerows and have been in the midst of rustic surroundings. Numerous rabbits infested the place and retained their burrows till long after the steel rails were laid along the ground. Hares, too, continued to frequent the yard until the rapid extension of the premises and the clearing away of the grass and bushes deprived them of cover. It was a common thing to see them and the rabbits shooting in and out among the old wheels and tyres that had been removed from the condemned vehicles.

If you should follow the fence along for a short distance you might even now soon forget the factory and imagine yourself to be far away in some remote village corner, surrounded with fresh green foliage and drinking in the sweet breath of the open fields. One would not conceive that in the very factory grounds, within sight of the hot, smoky workshops, and but a stone's throw from some of them, it would be possible to enjoy the charm of rusticity, and to revel unseen in a profusion of flowers that would be sought for in vain in many parts about the countryside. Yet such is the pleasure to be derived from a visit to this little frequented spot. The fence, to the end, runs parallel with the recreation ground alongside a hedgerow that once parted the two fields when the whole was in the occupation of the people at the old farmhouse that has now disappeared. In the hedgerow, with their trunks close against the board partition, still in their prime and in strong contrast to the black smoky walls and roofs of the sheds opposite, stand half-a-dozen stately elms that stretch their huge limbs far over the yard and throw a deep shadow on the ground beneath. At this spot the field gradually declines and, as the inner yard has been made up to a level with the railway beyond, when you approach the angle you find yourself out of sight, with the raised platform of cinders on the one hand and, on the other, the high wooden fence and thick elms.

At the corner the steel tracks have had to make a long curve, and this has left the ground there free to bring forth whatever it will. Here, also, the trees are thickest, and, within the fence, a small portion of the original site still remains. A streamlet – perhaps the last drain of a once considerable brook – enters from the recreation ground underneath the boards and is conducted along, now within its natural banks and now through broken iron pipes, into the corner, where it is finally swallowed up in a gully and lost to view. Stooping over it, as though to protect it from further injury and insult, are several clumps of hawthorn and the remains of an old hedge of wych elm. Standing on the railway track of the bank are some frames of carriages that were burnt out at the recent big fire. Near them are several crazy old waggons and vans, that look as if they had stood in the same place for half a century and add still further to the quiet of the scene.

It is alongside the fence, and especially about the corner, that the wild flowers bloom. Prominent over all is the rosebay. This extends in a belt nearly right along the fence, and climbs up the ash bank and runs for a considerable distance among the metals, growing and thriving high among the iron wheels and frames of the carriages and revelling in the soft ashes and cinders of the track. Side by side with this, and blooming contemporary with it, are the delicate toadflax, bright golden ragwort, wild mignonette, yellow melilot, ox-eye daisies, mayweed, small willow-herb, meadow-sweet, ladies' bedstraw, tansy, yarrow, and cinquefoil. The wild rose blooms to perfection and the bank is richly draped with a vigorous growth of dewberry, laden with blossoms and fruit.

Beside the streamlet in the corner is a patch of cats'-tails, as high as to the knees, and a magnificent mass of butter-bur. The deliciously scented flowers of this are long since gone by, but the leaves have grown to an extraordinary size. They testify to the presence of the stream, for the butter-bur is seldom found but in close proximity to water. Here also are to be found the greater willow-herb with its large sweet pink blossoms and highly-scented leaves, the pale yellow colt's-foot, medick, purple woody night-shade, hedge stachys, spear plume thistles, hogweed and garlick mustard, with many other plants, flowering and otherwise, that have been imported with the ballast and have now taken possession of the space between the lines and the fence.

The shade of the trees and beauty of the flowers and plants are delightful in the summer when the sun looks down from a clear, cloudless sky upon the steel rails and dry ashes of the yard, which attract and contain the heat in a remarkable degree, making it painful even to walk there in the hottest part of the day. Then the cool shade of the trees is thrice welcome, especially after the stifling heat of the workshop, the overpowering fumes of the oil furnaces and the blazing metal just left behind; for it is impossible for any but workmen to enjoy the pleasant retreat. No outsider ever gains admittance here, and though you should often pace underneath the trees in the recreation ground you would never dream of what the interior is like. Nor do even workmen – at least, not more than one or two, and this at rare intervals in the meal-hours – often come here, for if they did they would be noticed by the watchmen and ordered away. Their presence here, even during meal-hours, would be construed as prejudicial to the interests of the company. They would be suspected of theft, or of some other evil intention, or would at least be looked upon as trespassers and reported to the managers. In times gone by men and youths have been known to escape from the factory during working hours and while they were booked at their machines, by climbing over the fence, and this has made the officials cautious and severe in dealing with trespassers. It would not be a difficult matter, even now – and especially in the winter afternoons and evenings – to climb over the top of the fence and decamp.

This part of the factory yard is by far the most wholesome of the works' premises. There is plenty of room and light, and happy were they who, in the years ago, were told off for service in the field, breaking up the old waggons, sorting out the timber, and running the wheels from one place to another. At the time the old broad-gauge system of vehicles

Mixed gauges, broad and standard. The mixture caused great complexity of points and crossings. Broad gauge was finally dispensed with in 1892

was converted to the four-foot scale, large gangs in the yard were regularly employed in cutting-down; that is, reducing the waggons to the new shape. First of all the wood-work was removed; then both sides of the iron frame – a foot each side – were cut completely away. Two new 'sole-bars' were affixed, and the whole frame was riveted up again. The wheels, also, were taken out and the axles shortened and re-fitted. The carpenters now replaced the floors and sides and all was fit for traffic again. The locomotives, on the other hand, were condemned. The boilers and machinery were built on too great a scale to be fitted to the narrow-gauge frames. They were accordingly lifted out and the boilers distributed all over the system, while the frames were cut up for scrap and new ones built in place of them.

The old type of broad-gauge engine has never been beaten for speed on the line. By reason of its occupying a greater space over the wheels and axles the running was more even, and there was not so much rocking of the coaches. The broad-gauge Flying Dutchman express was

The Flying Dutchman, built and photographed 1892, took eighty-seven minutes (average speed 53¼mph) from Paddington to Swindon, then waited ten minutes to encourage refreshment-buying

noted for its magnificent speed and stately carriage, and for many years after the abolition of the system stories of almost incredible runs were current at the works. One old driver, very proud of his machine, was said to have sworn to the officials that he would bring his engine and train from London to the railway town, a distance of seventy-seven miles, in an hour, dead time, with perfect safety, and he was only prevented from accomplishing the feat by the strong stand made by the officials, who threatened him with instant dismissal if he should exceed the limit of speed prescribed in the time-tables.

At the same time, it is well known that the official time-table was often ignored, and stirring tales might be told of flying journeys performed in defiance of all written injunctions and authority. The signalmen knew of these feats and were often astounded by them, but they are only human, and they often did that they ought not to have done in order to shield the driver. The passengers, too, are always delighted to find themselves being whirled along at a high rate. There is an intoxication in it not to be resisted, and when they leave the train at the journey's end, after an extraordinary run, they invariably go and inspect the engine and admire the brave fellow who has rushed them over the country at such an exciting speed.

When the broad-gauge was converted great numbers of men from all quarters were put on at the works. Every village and hamlet for miles around sent in its unemployed, and many of the farms were quite deserted. These were engaged in 'cutting-down' or in breaking up the waggons and engines – little skill being necessary for that operation – and when, after several years, the system was quite reduced and slackness followed the busy period, the greater part of them were discharged and were again distributed over the countryside round about. It is impossible to go into any village within a radius of eight or ten miles of the railway town without finding at least one or two men who were employed on 'the old broad-gauge,' as they still call it. After their discharge the majority, by degrees, settled down to farm life. Many, however, continued out of work for a long time, and some are numbered among the 'casuals' to this day.

The only tools, besides hammers, required by the cutters-down, were cold sets to cut off the heads of the rivets and bolts, and punches to force the stems and stays out of the holes. They were held by hazel rods, that were supplied in bundles from the stores for the purpose. To bind them round the steel tools they were first of all heated in the middle over the fire. Then the cutter-out took hold of one end, and his mate held the other, and the two together gave the wand several twists round. After that the rod was wound twice about the set or punch and the two ends were tied together with strong twine. This gave a good grip on the tool, which would not be obtained with the use of an iron rod. The repeated blows on the set from the sledge would soon jar the iron rod loose and cause it to snap off, while the hazel rod grips it firmly and springs with it under the blow.

Formerly all the repair riveting was done by hand. When the hot rivet was inserted in the hole the 'holder-up' kept it in position, either with the 'dolly' or with a heavy square-headed sledge. Then the riveters knocked down the head of the rivet with long-nosed hammers, striking alternately in rapid succession and making the neighbourhood resound with the blows. Afterwards the chief mate held the 'snap' upon it and his mate plied the sledge until the new head was perfectly round and smooth. The 'snap' is a portion of steel bar, about ten inches long and toughly tempered, with a die, the shape of the rivet head required, infixed at one end. Now, however, pneumatic riveting machines are used out of doors. These, being small and compact, can be employed anywhere and with much fewer hands than were required by the old method. The air is supplied from accumulators into which it is forced by the engine in the shed, and it is conducted in pipes all round the factory yards.

The repair gangs are an off-shoot of the frame shed that is situated at a distance of nearly half a mile from the field. There the steel frames for the waggons and carriages and all iron-topped vehicles, such as ballast trucks, brake and bullion vans, refrigerators and others are constructed. That is essentially the shop of hard work, heavy lifting and noise terrific. The din is quite inconceivable. First of all is the machinery. On this side are rows of drills, saws, slotting and planing machines; on that are the punches and shears, screeching and grinding, snapping and groaning with the terrible labour imposed upon them. The long lines of shafting and wheels whirl incessantly overhead, the cogs clatter, the belts flap on the rapidly spinning pulleys, and the blast from the fan roars loudly underground. All this, however, is nearly drowned with the noise of the hammering. Hundreds of blows are being struck on 'tops' and 'bottoms', steel rails and iron rails, sole-bars and headstocks, middles, diagonals, stanchions, knees, straps and girders. Every part of the frame is being subjected to the same treatment – riveted, straightened, levelled, or squared, most unmercifully used. Every tone and degree of sound is emitted, according to the various qualities and thicknesses of the metal – sharps and flats, alto, treble and bass. There is the sharp clear tone of the highly-tempered steel in the tools used; the solid and defiant ring of the sole-bar or headstock, strong and firm under the hammer of the 'puller-up,' the dull, flat sound of the floor plates, the loud hollow noise of the 'covered goods' sides and ends, and the deep heavy boom of the roofs of the vans. Everyone seems to be striking as hard and as quickly as he is able. All the blows fall at once, and yet everything is in a jumble and tangle, loud, vicious, violent, confused and chaotic – a veritable pandemonium. And then, to crown the whole, there are the pneumatic tools, the chipping and riveting machines. It is dreadful; it is overpowering; it is unearthly; but it has to be borne, day after day and year after year.

Yet even the frame shed must yield to the boiler shop in the matter of concentrated noise. The din produced by the pneumatic machines in cutting out the many hundreds of rivets and stays inside a boiler is quite appalling. There is nothing to be compared with it. The heaviest artillery is feeble considered with it; thunder is a mere echo. What is more, the noise of neither of these is continuous, while the operation within the boiler lasts for a week or more. The boiler, in a great degree, contains the sound, so that even if you were a short distance away, though the noise there would be very great, you could have no idea of the intensity of the sound within. Words could not express it; language fails to give an adequate idea of the terrible detonation and the staggering effect produced upon whosoever will venture to thrust his head within the aperture of the boiler fire-box. Do you hear anything? You hear nothing. Sound is swallowed up in sound. You are a hundred times deaf. You are transfixed; your every sense is paralysed. In a moment you seem to be encompassed with an unspeakable silence – a deathlike vacuity of sound altogether. Though you shout at the top of your voice you hear nothing – nothing at all. You are deaf and dumb, and stupefied. You look at the operator; there he sits, stands or stoops. You see his movements and the apparatus in his hands, but everything is absolutely noiseless to you. It is like a dumb show, a dream, a phantasm. So, for a little while after you withdraw your head from the boiler, you can hear nothing. You do not know whether you are upon your head or your heels, which is the floor and which is the roof. The ground rises rapidly underneath you and you seem to be going up, up, up, you know not where. Then, after a little while, when you have removed from the immediate vicinity of the boiler, you feel to come to earth again. Your senses rush upon you and you are sudddenly made aware of the terrific noise you have encountered. Even now, it will be some time before the faculty of hearing is properly restored; the fearful noise rings in your ears for hours and days afterwards.

And what of the men who have to perform the work? It is said that they are used to it. That is plainly begging the question. They have to do it, whether they are used to it or not. It is useless for them to complain; into the boiler they must go, and face the music, for good or ill. All the men very soon become more or less deaf, and it is inconceivable but that other ailments must necessarily follow. The complete nervous system must in time be shattered, or seriously impaired, and the individual become something of a wreck. This is one of the many ills resulting from progress in machinery and modern manufacturing appliances.

The personnel of the frame shed is individual and distinct in a very marked degree. Most of the men seem to have been chosen for their great strength and fine physique, or to have developed these qualities after their admission to the work. The very nature of the toil tends to produce strong limbs and brawny muscles. It is certain that continual exercise of the upper parts of the body by such means as the lifting of heavy substances tends to improve the chest and shoulders, and many of those who are engaged in lifting and carrying the plates and sole-bars are very stout and square in this respect. There is a number of 'heavy weights,' and a few positive giants among them, though the majority of the men are conspicuous, not so much by their bulk, as by their squareness of limb and muscularity. A proof of the strength of the frame shed men may be seen in the success of their tug-of-war teams. Wherever they have competed – and they have gone throughout the entire south of England – they have invariably beaten their opponents and carried off the trophies.

There was formerly a workman, an ex-Hussar, named Bryan, in the shed, who could perform extraordinary feats of strength. He was nearly seven feet in height and he was very erect. His arms and limbs were solid and strong; he was a veritable Hercules, and his shoulders must have been as broad as those of Atlas, who is fabled to have borne the world on his back. It was striking to see him lift the heavy headstocks, that weighed two hundredweights and a quarter, with perfect ease and carry them about on his shoulder – a task that usually required the powers of two of the strongest men. This he continued to do for many years, not out of bravado, but because he knew it was within his natural powers to perform. Notwithstanding his tremendous normal strength, however, he was subject to attacks of ague, and you might have seen him sometimes stretched out upon the ground quite helpless, groaning and foaming at the mouth. If he had been working in the shed recently, since the passing of the new Factory Acts, he would have been promptly discharged, for no one is kept at the works now who is subject to any infirmity that might incapacitate him in the shed among the machinery. Later on, when work got slack, Bryan was turned adrift from the factory, a broken and a ruined man. All his past services to the firm were forgotten; he was cast off like an old shoe. However valuable and extraordinary a man may have proved himself to be at his work, it counts for little or nothing with the foreman and managers; the least thing puts him out of favour and he must go.

The men of the frame shed are of a cosmopolitan order, though to a less extent than is the case in some departments. The work being for the most part rough and requiring no very great skill, there has consequently been no need of apprenticeships, though there are a few who have served their time as waggon-builders or boiler-smiths. They are not recognised as journeymen here, however, and so must take their chance with the rank and file. Promotion is supposed to be made according to merit, but there are favourites everywhere who will somehow or other prevail. The normal order of promotion is from labourer to 'puller-up,' from puller-up to riveter, and thence to the position of chargeman. Here he must be content to stop, for foremen are only made about once or twice in a generation, and when the odds on any man for the post are high, surprise and disappointment always follow. The first is usually relegated to the rear, and the least expected of all is brought forward to fill the coveted position. It may be design, or it may be judgment, and perhaps it is neither. It very often looks as though the matter had been decided by the toss of a coin, or the drawing of lots, and that the lot had fallen upon the least qualified, but there is no questioning the decision. The old and tried chargeman, who knows the scale and dimensions of everything that has been built or that is likely to be built in the shed in his lifetime, must stand aside for the raw youth who has not left school many months, but who, by some mysterious means or other, has managed to secure the favour and indulgence of his foreman, or other superior. Perhaps he is reckoned good at arithmetic, or can scratch out a rough drawing, though more than likely his father was gardener to someone, or cleaned the foreman's boots and did odd jobs in the scullery after factory hours.

Another reason for the selection of young and comparatively unknown men for the post of foreman is that they have a smaller circle of personal mates in the shed, and, consequently, a less amount of human kindness and sympathy in them. That is to say, they will be able to cut and slash the piecework prices with less compunction, and so the better serve the interests of the company. The young aspirant, moreover, will be at the very foot of the ladder, hot and impetuous, while the elder one will have passed the season of senseless and unscrupulous ambition.

A feature of the frame shed is the rivet boy. It is his duty to hot the rivets in the forge for his mates and to perform sundry other small offices, such as fetching water from the tap in the shed, or holding a nail bag in front of the rivet head which is being cut away, in order to keep it from flying and causing injury to any of the workmen. The forges for hotting the rivets are fixtures and are supplied with air through pipes laid beneath the ground from the fan under the wall. Several boys usually work from one fire, and there is often a scramble for the most advantageous position in the coals. An iron plate is used to facilitate the heating. This has been perforated with holes at the punch to allow its receiving as many rivets as are required. It is then placed over the whitehot coke in the forge and the rivets inserted. Each boy has a certain number of holes allotted to him and he must not trespass on his mates' territory.

Young apprentices pre-1914, on strike because their wages were not raised, although men's were. Lads like these were Alfred's mates when he was a rivet-hotter

It sometimes happens that one of the boys proves to be a bully and a terror and plays ducks and drakes with the rights and privileges of the others. This is always a matter of great concern to the juveniles, and they will not be satisfied till the tyrant has been humbled and punished. They have many minor differences and quarrels among themselves, and challenges to fight are frequent. Honour looms big in the eyes of the rivet boys, and they are quick to resent a taunt or affront and to wipe off all aspersions. Perhaps a sneer has been levelled at one by reason of his name, his father's occupation, or the name of the street or locality in which he lives. With true pluck the matter is taken up. An hour and a place for the meeting are fixed: it is generally – 'Meet me in the Rec at dinner-time.' There they accordingly assemble with their mates and supporters and fight the matter out. It is usually a rough-and-tumble proceeding, but they do not desist till one or the other has been worsted and honour satisfied. More than once it has happened that they have been so intent on the match they have lost count of the time and have all – a dozen or more – got locked out for the afternoon. This requires some explanation, and the next day the whole circumstance has to be related. Here the boys' fathers might interfere and administer a sound corrective lesson to each one of them.

Getting locked out is also very often the result of over-staying at football, which is regularly practised by the youngsters in the recreation field all the year round. The boys club together and buy a ball and race out to play every dinner-time. There, for three-quarters of an hour, they exert themselves to the utmost and are forced to run back to the shed at the top of their speed, often returning in an exhausted condition. A spell of five minutes puts them right, however, and they go on with their work as though they had enjoyed an infinite period of refreshment. In the evening they race home to tea and afterwards go out again while it is daylight, never seeming too tired for sport and play.

Many queer nicknames, such as 'Bodger,' 'Snowball,' 'Granny,' 'Chucky,' and 'Nanty Pecker,' are in vogue among the boys. These become fixtures and remain with them for many years. It must not be thought that all the rivet boys submit to become permanent hands in the shed. A good many of them, as soon as they are sufficiently old and big, go to the recruiting sergeant and try to enlist. Some enter the Army and others the Navy; some go this way and some that. Very often boys who spent their early days at rivet-hotting in the shed and enter the Service, return in after years to obtain another start in the old quarters, and grow old amid the scenes of their boyhood. Some never return at all, but die, either in battle, of sickness, or other accident. More than one, too, has gone the wrong way in life and ended in suicide.

The boys are much given to reading cheap literature of the 'dreadful' type, and they revel in the deeds of Buffalo Bill, Deadwood Dick, and other well-known heroes of fiction. Sometimes a boy, unknown to his parents, actually possesses a firearm – a pistol or revolver – and, with a group of companions, scours the countryside round about in search of 'game.' Once, at least, mischief was done in the shape of bursting open a letter-box with bullets, and at another time a poor calf received a bullet-shot through the hedgerow. This last-named deed, however, was purely accidental. Great fear fell upon the juveniles after this untoward experience and the pistol was forthwith cast into the canal. At another time a careless lad shot himself through the hand with a pistol and inflicted a dangerous wound.

A great change has come over the frame shed during the last twelve years. The old foreman has gone; a great many of the old hands have disappeared also, and the methods of work have been revolutionised. The prices have been cut again and again; a different spirit prevails everywhere; it is no longer as it used to be. Considerable liberty and many small privileges were allowed to the men by the governing staff in those days, and the foreman, if he felt disposed, could do much to make them comfortable and satisfied. Then the overseer was practically master of his shed and could make his own terms with the workmen, though it is only fair to remember that under those conditions he was sometimes inclined to be summary and despotic.

The old foreman of the frame shed was an excellent example of this kind of overseer. As an engineer he was clever, intelligent, sharp-sighted, and energetic. In addition to this he was a good judge of character, a natural leader of men, and one strongly sympathetic. If he was in want of new hands he needed not to ask a dozen ridiculous questions, or to stand upon any kind of ceremony; he came, saw, and decided at once. One glance was sufficient for him; he had summed the man up in an instant. In the shed he was free, easy and spontaneous, praising and blaming in the same breath. At one moment he was livid with passion; the next he was kind, conciliative, and condescending. His temper was hot and fiery. When he frowned at you his expression was as black as a thunder-cloud, but you knew that everything would soon be well again. His behaviour was at least open and genuine, and whatever his attitude to his superiors might have been, he was free from dissimulation with the workmen. Nothing escaped his attention in the shed. As he walked his eagle eye comprehended all. If a stanchion or girder was in the least out of square he perceived it, and it had to be put right immediately.

He never made himself too cheap and common with the workmen, but held himself in such a relation to them that he could always command respect. He often came to the shed late and left early, but there was then no rigid law compelling the foreman to be for ever at his post, and the work usually proceeded the same. He was an inventor himself, and he was always ready to encourage independent thought and action among his workmen. He recognised merit and rewarded it. He was not jealous of his workmen's brains, and he was at all times willing to consider an opinion and to act upon it if it seemed preferable to his own. He was a mixture of the fatherly ruler and the despot, but he was very proud of his men and he lauded them up to the skies to outsiders, whenever an opportunity presented itself. There was nothing they could not make, and make well, according to him. If he blamed them to themselves he stoutly defended them against others, and he would not have dreamed of selling and betraying them to the management, as is commonly done at this time.

Of the boys he was extremely fond, and especially of such as were well-behaved and attentive, however ragged and rough their dress might be, and he often stood and talked to them with his hand on their shoulder, or gave them pennies or marbles. But if he saw one of the 'terribles' bullying a younger lad he ran up to him and gave him a sound cuff, or a vigorous kick. Under his foremanship work was plentiful and wages were high. The shed was nearly always on overtime, and money flowed like water. The men bore the strain of the overtime complacently. They worked without fear and turned out a hundred, or a hundred and twenty waggon frames a week. Those were prosperous days for the frame shed and many a one saved a little pile from his earnings.

Together with all this, however, the foreman discovered some remarkable characteristics and he was possessed of the most amazing effrontery. If strangers connected with other firms came in to inspect the plant and process and to know the price of things, he hood-winked them in every possible manner and told them astounding fables. He would take up an article in his hand, describe it with pride, and tell them it was made for a fifth of what it actually cost to produce. If the manager came through and any awkward questions were asked, he skilfully turned the point aside and motioned secretly to the men to support him if they should be consulted. He hated all interference and would not stand patronage even from his superiors, and where argument failed clever manœuvring saved the situation.

Whatever he saw in the shape of machinery he coveted for his own shed. More than once he was known actually to purloin a machine from the neighbour foreman's shop in the night and transfer it to his own premises. Once a very large drilling machine, new from the maker and labelled to another department at the works, came into the yard by mistake but it never reached its proper destination. Calling a gang of men, he removed the drill from the truck, caused a foundation to be made for it, fixed it up in a corner half out of sight, and had it working the next morning. A hue and cry was raised up and down and around the yard for the missing machine, but it was not discovered till a long time afterwards. It still stands in the shed, a proof of one of the most brazen and impudent thefts possible.

At another time three large drop-hammers were shunted near the shed, and on seeing them he quickly had them unloaded, but he was not successful in retaining them. On being discovered he made profuse apologies for his 'mistake' and there the matter ended. At last he fell into the disfavour of someone and defiantly handed in his resignation. Now everything proceeds upon formally approved lines, though many a one wishes the old foreman were still in his place, grumbling and scolding, and pushing things forward as in the days ago.

CHAPTER VI

THE SMITHY – THE SMITH – BUILDING THE FIRE – GALLERY MEN –
APPRENTICES – THE OLDEST HAND – DEATH OF A SMITH –
THE SMITH'S ATTITUDE TO HIS MATES – HIS GREAT GOOD-NATURE –
THE SMITHS' FOREMAN

Adjoining the frame-building shed is the waggon smithy, where the thousand and one details for brake systems for the carriages and waggons, and other articles and uses are manufactured. Here, also, all kinds of repairs are executed, and a great number of tools of every description made for the permanent way men and for other workshops round about. It is said that the forge is the longest in England, and this is probably correct. It is slightly under two hundred yards in length, and it contains one hundred fires. These are built at equal distances, on each side of the shed, with crowns like large bee-hives, and the chimneys are joined in with the walls. Every fire is supplied with a boshful of water in which to cool the various tools, and there is also a tap and a rubber pipe for damping the coals.

Behind the forge is a recess for the coke, which is crushed by machines outside and wheeled in ready for use. Above this is a rack for the tongs and tools, of which the smith possesses a considerable number. They are of all sorts and sizes, capable of holding and shaping every conceivable article. Of tongs there are flat-bits, hollow-bits, and claws large and small, with sets and 'set-tools,' 'fullers,' flatters, punches, 'jogglers,' and many others with no specific title but conveniently named by the brawny fellow who uses them. Standing in one corner, or soaking in the water of the bosh, are large and small sledges and one or two wooden mallets. Every fire has its sieve or 'riddle,' as it is called, for sifting the coke before it is put in the forge, for every particle of dust must be removed from the fuel so as to obtain a clear, bright heat. If there is welding to be done the coke will have to be broken up small – about the size of a walnut – with the mallet, in order to concentrate the heat, and to allow of the iron being easily moved in the fire and well-covered with the fuel.

The task of making up the fire falls upon the smith's mate or striker. Perhaps, if the piece of work is of big dimensions, two fires are needed; if it is small or moderate-sized, one will be sufficient. It is the mate's duty to get everything ready for the smith. First of all the clinker is removed and the dust taken out from the centre of the fire with an iron shovel. The live coals are now raked to the middle and the blast applied. When this is performed the fresh coke is 'riddled' up, and carefully distributed in the forge. Every smith is very particular as to the *shape* of his fire. In general disposition it will be high at the back with the corners – right and left – well filled, rather full in front and even in the centre. If the weather is hot and the coke dry it may receive a good watering – once before the smith begins his heat, and several times during the operation. A good smith will be sparing of water, however, for too much of it makes the fire burn too fiercely in the centre, contracts the area of heat and causes the iron to be dirty and slimy. The harder the coke, the better it is, and the more brilliant the heat will be. Soft coke is soon consumed and completely reduced to dust, while good, hard coke will last a considerable time in the fire.

It must not be assumed that the smith is idle while his mates are employed in renovating the forge. He is busy preparing his tools and taking dimensions of the job to be made, and pondering on the best means of doing it. For this he usually has a large board whitened with chalk, upon which he sketches out the article and by means of which he determines the best method of forming his bends and angles. He may not be much of an artist, but in his rude way he will make a very commendable drawing of his job and will thus be enabled to determine beforehand exactly what to do to effect it, just the time to begin his tapers and angles, the direction of the bend, and the tools for doing it. He never leaves the method undetermined till he has his iron on the anvil, but takes pains to have everything settled and every phase of the operation well in view before he begins it. It is the inferior or the unintelligent workman alone that heats his iron and trusts to a chance idea to complete the job.

Meanwhile the cloth cap has been removed from the head, and the waistcoat and braces hung up behind the forge. The long leathern apron is produced from the wooden tool-chest and tied around the waist, or fastened with the belt, about three inches of the top of the trousers being often turned down outside. The smith's trousers are usually of blue serge, and they are made very loose and baggy, so as to allow of much stooping. The strikers more frequently use aprons made of canvas or of old thin refuse leather that has been stripped from the worn-out carriages and horse-boxes and consigned to the scrap-heap. While the finishing touches are being put to the forge the burly smith takes his can and goes to the tap for a drink of water. Arrived there he fills the vessel, removes the quid of tobacco from his cheek – a great many smiths chew tobacco – raises the can to his lips, rinses out his mouth once or twice and spouts the water out again to a great distance. Then he takes a long drink, fills the can again and carries it back to the forge, where he hands it to his mates, or sets it down for future refreshment.

By this time the iron will have been placed in the forge and the blast applied by the strikers. The sets also will have been ground, the shafts of the hammers examined and the wedges tightened. The floor, too, will be cleanly swept round about, for the smith is most particular in the matter of neatness and will not have loose ashes and cinders, or other rubbish, lying under his feet. A light, square table, sometimes of wood and sometimes of iron plate, is set by the anvil, and of a height with it, to contain the tools. A handful of birch, bound together after the manner of a little besom, is placed conveniently upon the table. This is used for brushing the heat when it comes from the coals, and for removing the dust and scale from the anvil. As the blast rushes through the pipe from underground and into the forge it roars loudly, sounding in the coke like a strong wind among trees. Long, yellow flames rise and leap high up the chimney, and the air around is filled with clouds of dust and sulphur fumes from the burning coke. As the heat of the fire increases this diminishes; in a short time the gaseous properties are entirely consumed and there is no smell of any kind.

Our smith is a perfect giant in stature. In height he is well over six feet, solid and erect, with tremendous shoulders and limbs. His head is massive and square, with broad deep forehead and bushy brows. His grey eyes, frank and fearless, are rather deeply inset. The nose is Roman and slightly crooked; the mouth, with thick lips a little relaxed, is pleasant and kind. He has a heavy, bronze moustache, a clean shaven chin and plump, ruddy cheeks. The whole countenance is square, and exhibits the marks of good-nature and honest character. His ponderous arms are hard and brown, full of rigid bone and muscle, and his hands are large and horny with continual holding of the tongs and hammer. His breast is remarkably broad and hairy – his woollen shirt is always thrown open at work; he has hips and belly like an ox, legs like those of an elephant, and large flat feet, and he weighs more than eighteen stone. When he walks his motion is rather slow and deliberate. He goes heavy on his soles, and his shoulders rise and fall alternately at every step he takes.

He is at all times steady and cool, and he seems never to be in a hurry. At the anvil he gives one the same impression, so that a stranger might even think him to be sluggish and dilatory, but he is in everything sure and unerring, never too soon or too late. Every action is well-timed; nothing is either over- or under-done. He performs all his heats with a minimum amount of labour. Where a nervous or spasmodical person would require forty or fifty blows to shape a piece of metal he will accomplish it with about twenty-five. His masterly eye and calculating brain are ever watchful and alert. He understands the effect of every blow given, and while the less experienced smith is still engaged with his piece nearly black-hot, his is finished, complete, with the metal still yellow or bright red. He moves always at the same pace, and his work is of a uniformly superlative character. When strangers are about, watching him at his weld, he makes no difference whatever in his usual methods of procedure, but behaves just as coolly and deliberately and takes no notice of any man.

Some smiths and forgemen, on the other hand, hate to be watched at work by strangers – 'foreigners,' as they call them – and very quickly give evidence of their dislike and irritation. They will every now and then dart an angry look at the visitors, and, after using the tools, throw them down roughly, muttering under their breath and telling the strangers to 'clear off,' though not sufficiently loud to be heard. By and by the unoffending strikers will come in for a castigation; whatever kind of blow they strike it will be wrong for their mate. At last he shuts off the blast from the forge, and, laying down his hammer, turns his back towards the 'interlopers,' and waits till they have passed on up the shed. After their departure he resumes his labour and quickly makes up for lost time.

Some smiths, again, though extremely nervous under the eye of a stranger, do not object to being watched, while others positively like the attention. Such as these are always anxious, under the circumstances, to impress the stranger with their great skill and dexterity in the use of tools and in twisting and turning the iron about on the anvil. They are the 'gallery men.' As soon as visitors appear afar off they begin to prepare for an exhibition. The blast is steadied down, or shut off, and the fire is cooled round. The tools are all most conveniently disposed upon the anvil or table, and everything is made ready for a 'lightning' weld. The strikers are as well agreed as the smith, and brace themselves up for an extra special effort. They wait till the visitors are nearly opposite them and certain of viewing the operation. Then on goes the blast, roaring loudly in the firebox, while the smith, with the perspiration streaming down his brow and cheeks, turns his heat over and over in the forge and glances quickly across to take care that he is ready at the right moment. The visitors notice the unusual activity of the men at the fire and stand still, waiting to see the heat. This is the signal for the iron to leave the coals. With exaggerated celerity the sections of metal are withdrawn from the forge and brought to the anvil. The fused parts are clapped smartly together, the striker throws down his tongs viciously, grips his hammer and, following the directions of his mate, rains a shower of blows on the spluttering iron. The sparks whizz out, and reach the visitors, singeing the dresses of the ladies – if there happen to be any among them – and causing them to cry out and step backwards a few paces, while the anvil rings merrily under the blows. Now the smith lays down his own hammer quickly and takes up the steel tool for finishing and squaring the heat. His mate follows, striking rapidly, at all angles, heavy and light, light and heavy, according to what is required, though the smith utters not a word during the process, for the whole routine is known by heart. Over and over the piece is jerked on the anvil – a fine flourish being given to each movement – until it is finished. Upon its completion the smith hands it to the striker, who receives it dexterously and places it on the ground, or in the pile, the pair of them looking several times at the visitors as much as to ask them if they do not think the job well and quickly done, and begging a compliment. The visitors usually accord them an admiring glance in recognition of their prowess and pass on up the forge.

The gallery men are smart and quick by nature, and are fairly sure of being successful in 'exhibition' work. The slightest blunder would spoil the whole act and make them appear ridiculous, consequently none but those who are really skilful ever attempt the business. The average smith, however, and especially the one we have in view, never breaks his rule or goes out of his way to oblige visitors, but continues at a steady, uniform rate. The workman who is showy and energetic before visitors is often remiss when they have gone by; it is the continual plodder that gets through the most work in the long run. The visitor, moreover, if he is gifted with an ordinary amount of insight and commonsense, may easily recognise the superior workman and discriminate between the genuine and the superficial effort. Occasionally, when strangers pass through, after such a performance as I have described, the striker, more in jest than in earnest throws his cap at the feet of the visitors, suggesting that a tip would be welcomed. It is but fair to say that the hint is seldom or never taken.

Though the striker, or inside mate, must perform the task of preparing the fire for the smith, he is no longer responsible for it. Henceforth the smith takes it under his care, and only hands it over to his mate when the heat is finished and a stop has to be made to renew the forge. If the job upon which he is engaged is of any dimensions and two fires are needed, that will make it increasingly hard for the strikers. The heaviest work is naturally more usually assigned to the strongest men, though the rule of adaptability also holds here and the various jobs are given to those who have proved themselves to be the most efficient at them. Of the smiths, some are famed for their skill in one direction, and some for their ability in another. This job requires strength, that speed and cleverness, and another needs a combination of all those qualities and is difficult to do at any time. Occasionally it transpires that an inferior smith has been kept at one class of work for such a long time that he gets out of touch with the other jobs in the shed, and would shape awkwardly if he were suddenly called upon to undertake something new and unusual to him. This is a mistake not often committed by the foreman, however. He periodically changes and interchanges the work and so gets the smiths accustomed to many and miscellaneous toils.

The skilled and clever smith will be at home anywhere and every-where. He will do anything, anyhow, and by any method you please, for he is a complete master of the trade. He will make all kinds of tools with the utmost ease and simplicity. He will also forge chains, wheels, joints, and levers, work in iron or steel, in 'T' stuff, or angle iron; every conceivable shape and form of work is subject to his operation. If you put him at the steam-hammer he is still at home; he will forge out an ingot or bloom with the best man on the ground.

All the lightest work falls upon the young apprentices and the very old men, who are too feeble to undertake heavy and trying tasks, but are yet far too valuable to be dispensed with altogether. The apprentices perform such work as simple setting and bending, the making of bolts and eyes, rings and links for chains and so on. They usually come to the work at the age of sixteen, and stay for five or six years, when they voluntarily hand in their notices and migrate to other towns. There they are received as improvers, or as journeymen, and are forthwith paid the trade rate of wages. This varies considerably in many localities, and it is to be noted that railway sheds almost always provide the very lowest wages. Since the work is constant and sure, however, and is not subject to the many fluctuations of the contract shop, the stability of employment is counted a certain compensation for lower wages, and the majority of smiths accept the conditions philosophically.

The young apprentices are strong and sturdy, and invariably of a sound constitution; one never sees a sickly-looking youth taking up the occupation of smithing. This accounts for the fine physique and often big proportions of the senior smith; the reason being that the youths chosen were hardy and suitable, and showed signs of physical development. The sons of smiths usually choose the trade of their fathers and follow in their footsteps. There is consequently often a hereditary quality in the workman; they have been a family of smiths for generations.

The smiths, provided they are strong and healthy, are usually retained at the forge till they have reached the age of seventy when, under the present rule, they are required to leave. Even this is a kind of concession to them, for, generally speaking, the other workmen are turned off long before they reach such an advanced age. The smith's usefulness, even in his age, is the cause of this; though feeble, he is still able to do good work and to help with his knowledge and experience. He is usually employed at tool-making, or at other light occupations. His poor old hand, almost as hard as iron, shakes with the weight of the hammer; his head trembles visibly, and his legs totter beneath him. He comes in early in the morning, in order to avoid the crush. He brings his meals with him and eats them in the forge, and he is the last going out at night. In his decline he is forced to live near the works – only a street or so from the entrance – and even then it takes him a long time to hobble to and fro. In the evening and at week-ends he usually stays at home to rest, or he may possibly look in to see a friend, or to take a mug of ale at the neighbouring inn.

It is a sad day for him when he receives intelligence of his discharge. Feeble as he is become, he has a real affection for the smithy, and is never so happy as when he is at his forge and anvil. As long as he can drag himself backwards and forwards, see the old faces, and snuff the breath of the fires, he is content. His health, too, which has been maintained by the constant exercise of his trade, is passable while he can do a little work. When he is forced to lie idle, and to forego his regular habit of early rising and the exertion of his muscles with the hammer, that suffers as a matter of course. His joints forthwith become stiff and set; his little store of strength, instead of increasing with the change, wastes and declines. In a very short while he is dead, and his old bones are haled away to the cemetery on top of the hill. A number of his mates and fellow-smiths follow him to the grave and witness the last rites, not for the sake of formality, but out of pure friendship and respect. His name is certain to live long in the annals of the smithy.

The oldest hand in the forge at the present time is aged sixty-eight, though there were recently several above this age who have now been placed on the retired list or superannuated by their societies. He has led a hard life, and affords a very good example of the average type of smith. He was apprenticed at Cheltenham and made a journeyman at Gloucester. From that city he passed on to Worcester, and went thence to Birmingham, working for about a year at each place. Afterwards he migrated to Sheffield – the home of furnaces and forges – and shifted thence in turn to Liverpool, Lancaster, Rotherham, Durham, and several other manufacturing centres, settling finally in the railway town. He has brought up a big family and seen them all established in life. Of his sons several are smiths; one is in America, one in Africa, and one at home in England. He has saved enough money to buy his house, and he has a few pounds besides, so that he has no fear of being reduced to want. He has worked hard and lived well, and he has always drunk his glass of ale. He is associated with several bodies and committees, and he has presented a bed to the local hospital out of his earnings, with the natural condition that smiths have the first claim upon it. Though his hand is a little unsteady with continual use of the tools, he can still manage a fair day's work. He is very proud of his trade and takes great delight in telling you of his travels and adventures. Every summer he passes the examination of old smiths made by the works' manager to see that they are fit for duty, and he still looks forward to years of activity at the forge.

Nearly all the smiths live in the town and within easy reach of their work. A few only of their number have had a rustic apprenticeship. The great majority of those in the shed have learnt the rudiments of their trade in factories, and have migrated from place to place. By living in the midst of large towns and cities, they have become almost indifferent to surroundings and are able to make themselves happy and comfortable in the most crowded and uncongenial situations. For the beauties of external nature they care but little; they appear to be wholly wrapt up in and concerned with their own vocation. They nearly all belong to unions and organisations, and are the most independent of men, though they do not make a great parade of the fact. Their independence is born of self-confidence – the knowledge of their own usefulness and worth, and the strength of their position. If they should choose to leave one place they are certain of getting employment elsewhere, for a good smith is never out of work for long together. Other trades suffer considerably through slackness of employment, but there is a constant demand for smiths and hammermen. The fact is that fewer smiths and forgemen are made, in proportion to their numbers, than is the case with some other trades. The work is hard and laborious, and the life must be one of toil and sacrifice.

Although some smiths drink an enormous quantity of cold water at the forge there are others who seldom taste a drop of the liquid. If you ask them the reason why, they will tell you that it is not a wise plan to drink much cold water at work. They say that it causes cramp in the stomach, colds, rash, and itching of the skin, and add that it makes them sweat very much more than they would otherwise do. The more you drink, they say, the more you want to drink, and it is but a habit acquired. If you care to use yourself to it you may work in the greatest heat and feel very few ill effects from it if you are abstemious in the taking of liquids. At the same time, the majority of smiths do drink water, and that copiously, and seem to thrive well upon it. Such as do this, and are fat and well, when spoken to upon the matter, always smile broadly and tell you it is the result of having a contented mind and of drinking plenty of cold water.

It is certain that those who drink most perspire most, but that does not appear to hurt them in the least, and you often hear it said by a workman who is not addicted to perspiring freely that he feels very 'stuffy' and congested and that he should be better if he could sweat more. A delightful feeling is experienced after a good sweating at work. Every nerve and tissue seems to be aglow with intensest life; the blood courses through the body and limbs freely and vigorously, and produces a sense of unspeakable physical pleasure. Sweating as the result of physical exercise has a powerful effect upon the mind, as well as upon the body; it clears the vision and invigorates the brain, and is a perfect medicine for many ailments, both mental and physical. If many of the languid and indolent, who never do any work or indulge in sturdy exercise, were suddenly to rouse themselves up and do sufficient physical labour, either for themselves or for someone else, to procure a good sweating at least twice a week, they would feel immeasurably better for it. Life would have a new meaning for them. They would eat better, rest better, and sleep better. They would feel fresher and stronger, altogether more active and vigorous, more sympathetic and satisfied. Though he is, as a rule, quite unaware of it, the workman derives considerably more physical pleasure from life than do those persons, mistakenly envied, who do nothing, for everything has a relish to him, while to the others all is flat and insipid. Truly work is the salt of life, and physical work at that, though there is a most passionate desire in many quarters to be well rid of it.

The majority of the smiths, even though they do not drink much cold water in the forge, are fond of a glass of ale; there are very few teetotalers among them. No one would wish to imply by this that they are 'wettish customers.' The very nature of their work makes them thirsty, and though they constrain their appetites while they are at the fires, nevertheless when they come to the town they feel bound to go in somewhere or other and 'wet the whistle,' as they term it. After a hot turn in the shed the foaming ale goes down with a delicious relish and the smith feels that he is entitled to enjoy that pleasure, considering how hard he has toiled all day in the heat and dust. There is also the evening paper to be read, after which follows a chat with his mate, and all the hard toil is for the moment forgotten. Rested and refreshed, the man of the forge goes home to his wife and children and partakes of a good tea, feeling very fit and on excellent terms with himself and others.

It is rather remarkable that smiths do not smoke very much tobacco. In the use of the weed they are very moderate, though the strikers and mates easily make up for the deficiency. Every day, after having their meals in the smithy, they walk out into the town or stand under the bridge to 'have a draw' and read the morning newspaper, returning leisurely about ten minutes before it is time to start work again.

To his mates and strikers, while at the forge, the smith is rather quiet and reserved, often speaking very little and seldom discussing with them matters apart from the work. This is not out of any undue feeling of pride in himself or unsociableness, but because he is full of his work, and disinclined to talk much. Neither is he given to the discussing of political and social problems and continually seeking an opportunity for holding an argument with this or that one. It is characteristic of him to view everything calmly and soberly; he is imbued with the genuine philosophical temperament. It is a certain and invariable rule that the one who has the most ready tongue and is always ripe for an argument is not the most energetic and proficient at his employment. If such a one as this should desire to entangle the sturdy smith in a cobweb of discussion he is bluntly and unceremoniously told to 'clear out,' for he has no time to listen to such 'stuff.' Off the premises, however, he is friendly and indulgent to his mates and strikers. When he meets them in the town he stops and speaks to them and invites them to have a glass of ale at his expense.

The religious beliefs of the smiths are not as well-known as are those of some classes of workmen, for they are not in the habit of discovering themselves to outsiders. Though he who has his forge in the village, under the old elm or spreading chestnut, may go regularly to church, there is no evidence to prove that those who dwell in the town imitate him in that respect. Their Sundays appear to be spent chiefly at home in rest and quietness, in company with their wives and families. A few, plainly and simply dressed – for the smith heartily hates all foppishness and superficial ornament – may be seen in the evening walking out towards the fields. The majority, however, stay indoors and recuperate for the coming week's work, or merely go to see their friends who live a few streets away. But if they do not go to church or chapel they are far from being deficient in charitableness and true piety. They merely aim to live the best life they can and to do good wherever possible. Their religion is one of kindness to all; they are at once large-hearted and broad-minded, honest, just, and liberal. Their sympathy for their fellows arises largely from the fact that they are well acquainted with hard toil; they know what it is to work and sweat, to be hot and thirsty, beaten and tired. Theirs is no gentlemanly occupation, such as is that of some other journeymen; not merely the theoretical exercise of a craft, but one that requires good, solid exertion, such as brings out all that is best in a man.

A proof of their utter good-nature and kindness to their fellows may be seen in the fact of their having, for the last twenty years, made a voluntary weekly offering of a halfpenny per man to the local Cottage Hospital. This is taken once a fortnight, the condition being that it must be unsolicited and a straight gift. In twenty years the sum collected has amounted to over two hundred pounds. This is quite independent of the annual collections made for charities, in which the smiths again always head the list by a large margin. There is no other example at the works of such spontaneous good-nature, and this will show, more than any words, the true characteristics of the brawny men at the forges.

The smiths' foreman is the very personification of his class, and is a highly interesting study. He is of great stature – he is over six feet in height – with broad, square shoulders and large limbs; fleshy, but not corpulent. His forehead is wide and steep; he has bushy brows, iron grey hair and beard, and red cheeks. His eyes are frank and honest; his voice deep and gruff, but not unkind; and when he speaks to you he looks you full in the face. His whole figure is striking; he towers above the majority

---

Overleaf: Steam-hammer forge, 1907. Maximum blow of a 5-cwt hammer produced a crushing effect, on the piece of hot iron, equivalent to about 30-ton load

of his workmen. His weight, as he tells you himself, with a mixture of pride and modesty and the suspicion of a smile, is nineteen stone six. After this he hastens to inform you that he is not the heaviest at his house, for his good wife turns the scale at twenty-two stone. He has been once married and is the father of a large family – nineteen in all – twelve of whom are yet living. His age is well over sixty, and he will soon have to retire from the forge, though he is still hale and hearty, fond of a glass of good beer, and, as he frequently and forcibly tells you, he is 'a great eater of beef.'

As for scholarship and culture, he makes no claim to either, for he never had the opportunity of much education, though he is a famous smith, and is gifted with the rare faculty of getting his men into a good humour and keeping them there. He is on good terms with all his staff; is jealous of their interests, open and honest in his dealings with them, and he has the satisfaction of being respected in return. He is one of the old school, of a type that is nearly extinct now; a bold defender of the rights of smiths, a hard and fast believer in the hand-made article. Naturally, for him, he is suspicious of all modern machinery that tends to do away with the trade of the smithy, and he swears by the most unbreakable oaths that whatever is done by the newer systems of forging and stamping he is able to equal it on the anvil, both as regards strength and cheapness. When the managers recently attempted to bring about sweeping reductions in the prices throughout the smithy he opposed them at every point, swore that he was master in his own shed, and that no one but he should be allowed to fix prices. 'When I am gone you can do just whatever you like, but I'm going to have a say in things as long as I'm about here,' said he. On the managers insisting to cut the prices, he unceremoniously took off his coat, and, turning up his shirt-sleeves, presented the representative with a pair of tongs and a hammer and challenged him to have a trial at the game himself. 'Here's my fire, guvnor, and there's yourn. Come on with you and let's see what you can do, and if you can make it at your price I'll give in to you, but you'll never do it in the world.' Only one or two prices fell in the whole shed. The managers abstained from further interference and since that time the smiths have been but very little molested.

No one could walk through the forge and observe the splendid physique and bearing of the smiths, their skill and dexterity with the tools at the fires and anvil, without a feeling of pride and genuine admiration for them. They are a fine body of men, and their frankness and good-nature, their freedom from ostentation, and general straightforwardness impress one even more than do their physical qualities, and help to fix them more deeply and truly in his regard and esteem. They are not little and petty; they are not spiteful and malicious. They are not jealous of each other's skill and position; they are no tale-bearers. They seldom quarrel about politics or religion, or hold any other controversy in the shed or out of it. Their attitude to each other is fair and unquestionable; they are natural and spontaneous, very free and gener-ous. If proof is needed of this you have but to come into the smithy and see for yourselves. You will find it written in their faces in unmistakable characters. You will discover it in a greater degree if you converse with them. You will be completely satisfied as to their genuineness and quite convinced of the justice of these observations.

CHAPTER VII

FITTERS – THE STEAM-HAMMER SHOP – FORGEMEN – THEIR
CHARACTERISTICS – BOILERMAKERS – THE FOUNDRY –
THE BLAST FURNACE – MOULDERS

There are two large fitting sheds at the works – for engine- and carriage-
fitting. They differ in several respects but are on the whole consimilar,
both in the nature of the work done and in the composition and
individuality of the staffs employed. The duties of the fitters are very
well indicated by their denominative: they prepare and fit together all the
machinery parts for the locomotives and carriages as well as the steam-
brake details and other apparatus of a complicated nature. The sheds also
serve as centres for supplying the other shops with their small staffs of
fitters who superintend repairs to the local machinery, attend to the
steam-hammers, fix new shafting, and so on.

The fitting sheds are large buildings and are packed with machinery of
every conceivable shape and kind. Within them are lathes large and
small, machines for slotting, shaping and drilling, drills for boring round
and square holes, punches and shears, hydraulic tackle, and various other
curious appliances almost incapable of description. There are hundreds of
yards of steel shafting, pulleys and wheels innumerable, and miles of
beltage. The space between the roof and the floor seems to be entirely
occupied with swiftly-revolving wheels and belts. To view the interior is
like peering into a dense forest where all is tangled and confused and
everything is in a state of perpetual motion. At the same time there is a
minimum of noise. Here are no steam-hammers beating on the stubborn
masses of iron and steel and making the foundations of the earth tremble
beneath you, no riveters' hammers battering on the hollow plates of the
frames and boilers, and no pneumatic tools ringing out sharply and
driving one to distraction with the unspeakable din. The wheels revolve
almost without sound; the shafting turns and spins silently. The lathes

are nearly noiseless in operation, and the drills only creak a little now and then as a small portion of the detached metal becomes blocked underneath the tool and runs round with it. The greatest noise is made by those who are busily chipping at the benches; otherwise there is comparative quiet when we remember the tremendous din of the neighbouring workshops.

As there are no furnaces or forges in the fitting shed, and abundant ventilation, the air is cool and free from smoke and fume. The work is less laborious than is that of the smithy or frame shed, and the men are not required to perspire much. Both the fitters and the machinemen wear cloth suits, with a thin blue jacket or 'slop' and overalls, and you rarely see them stripped or with their shirt-sleeves turned up. This is so much the rule that if they should be seen to take off their coats at a job in either of the outlying sheds the circumstance will be noted as of unusual occurrence by the rank and file. They will immediately raise a good-natured laugh and jokingly tell them to 'put their jackets on if they don't want to catch a cold.' One local fitter, by reason of his great fondness for carrying a drawing with him wherever he goes and the readiness and ease with which he has resort to it in order to explain away the most trivial detail, has earned for himself the title of 'The Drawing King.' A second, as the result of his artificial activity with the callipers, is styled 'Calliper King,' while a third, by his volubility, has secured the expressive nickname of 'Fish-mouth.'

An amusing and true story is told of a chargeman of the fitting shed. He was lying seriously ill and believed himself to be at the point of death. While in that condition he was conscience-striken at the thought that he had had one or two very good prices for work in the shed. He accordingly sent for his foreman to come and visit him. When he arrived the sick man unburdened his soul and begged him to cut the prices forthwith; he said he 'could not die with it on his mind.' In due time the prices were cut. The old fellow's period had not yet come, however. He got better and had the satisfaction of returning to the shed and working at the reduced rates, the laughing-stock of his companions.

The fitters are usually looked upon as the men *par excellence* of the shed. Like the smiths, they have usually travelled far. Some have visited every part of the kingdom, while others may have served abroad – in America, at the Cape of Good Hope, in China, or Egypt. A few have been artificers in the Navy or in the Mercantile Marine; here is one, for instance, who, by reason of his nautical experiences, has gained the nick-name of 'Deep Sea Joe.' It will commonly be found that those who have gone furthest from home are not only the best workmen – as having had a more varied and extensive experience – but they are also more broad-minded and sympathetic towards their mates and labourers.

The majority of the fitters are members of Trades Unions, and of all other classes at the works, perhaps, they take the greatest pains to protect themselves and their interests. By contributing to the funds of their organisations they are insured against accidents, strikes, or dismissal, and are thus placed in a position of considerable independence. They are required to serve an apprenticeship of five or seven years' duration before they are recognised as journeymen and they are, by a common rule, compelled to go further afield in order to obtain the standard rate of wages. Nearly all the foremen of the different sheds are appointed from among the fitters; whatever qualities an outsider may discover he stands but little chance of being preferred for the post.

Before a fitter has been promoted to the position of foreman he is a bold champion of the rights of Labour, one loud in the expression of his sympathy with his fellowmen, a staunch believer in the liberty of the individual and a hearty condemner of the factory system. If he has been appointed overseer, however, there is a considerable change in his manner and attitude towards all these and kindred subjects. A great modification of his personal views and opinions soon follows; he begins to look at things from the official standpoint. He is now fond of telling you that 'things are not as they used to be.' Possibly they are not, as far as he himself is concerned, but there is another view of the situation. At the same time, he will be fairly loyal to his old mates, the journeyman fitters, and treat them with superior respect. To the labourers, however, he will not be so well-disposed. He will ignore their interests and rule them with a rod of iron.

I have said that steam-hammer forging is on the decline in the railway town. The chief cause of this is the recent development of the process of manufacturing malleable cast steel, which has largely taken the place of wrought iron forging both in the locomotive and elsewhere. Formerly all wheels were forged in sections and were afterwards welded up, and the work provided constant employment for the steam-hammer men. Now they are obtained elsewhere, more cheaply, it may be, though they are of a inferior quality. Engine-cranks also, which at one time were made exclusively on the premises, are nearly all bought away from the town, and this was a second great loss to the shed. All that remains is the manufacture of the less important details, such as connection rods and levers, with a few special or repair cranks now and then.

The steam-hammer shed has thus been deprived of much of its importance. The big machines, capable of striking a blow equivalent to a hundred or two hundred tons' pressure have been removed and put on the scrap-heap, and their places have been filled by other and less powerful plant. The old forgemen, too, with their mates who worked the furnaces, are missing. Of these, some are dead, some have been discharged, while others have been reduced and are scattered about the yard. He who formerly shouted out his orders at the steam-hammer and controlled the mighty mass of iron or steel with the porter, turning it round and round to receive the tremendous blow, is now hobbling about with a shovel and wheel-barrow, cleaning up the refuse of the yard, in receipt of a miserable pittance. Perhaps he is lame as the result of a blow, or he has a withered arm through its having been 'jumped up' with the driving back of the porter, or he may have lost an eye. A portion of steel has fled from the hammer rod, or from the 'ram,' and struck him in the eye and he is blind as a consequence.

Several years ago there was at the factory a splendid forger, a cool and highly-skilled workman, and one possessed of fine physique. He was tall, square and broad built, full of bone and muscle, solid and strong, and, though of seventeen or eighteen stone in weight, he was very nimble and of unerring judgment. One day he received the offer of a job in the Midlands, at nearly double the wages he was getting in the railway town, and he decided to accept the post. Accordingly he left the shed and took over his new duties. He had not been away long, however, before he met with a serious accident that quite incapacitated him from following his occupation as a forgeman. A careless or unskilful hammer-driver had struck a terrific blow out of time, and the porter-bar, driven out suddenly, forced the forger's hand and arm violently to the shoulder, completely crippling him. A ruined man, he came back to the town and gained a wretched livelihood by helping to serve the bricklayers and masons with his one arm.

The steam-hammer forger is one of the most skilful and useful, as well as the most interesting of men. He may possibly have learned his trade in the town, or he may hail from Sheffield, Middlesborough, Scotland or Wales. All these places are noted for extensive manufactures in iron and steel and for the efficiency of their workmen, and especially for their forgers and furnacemen. If any forger in the shed is reputed to have come from the Midlands, the North, or the iron region of Wales, he is sure to be considered something of a prodigy. He comes bearing with him a part of the laurels of his township and all eyes will be upon him to see how he acquits himself of the responsibility. Very often, however, he quite fails to fulfil the expectations entertained of him and is easily beaten by the local men. After all, it was but the name; he is no better than many who have learned their trade in the shed. Perhaps he is not even as efficient as they, though he did come from 'Ironopolis' and forged very many tons of steel ingots in an incredibly short space of time, though this happened 'years ago,' if you chance to press him at all concerning the matter.

The former is not always a man of big physical proportions. On the contrary, he is more usually of a medium, or even of a diminutive type; you seldom or never find one as stout and heavy as is the average smith. The nature of the toil forbids this. The smith, at his work, is more or less stationary. His forging, moreover, is not so heavy, nor is he exposed to such great heat. The forgeman's ingot may weigh four or five tons, all blazing hot, with a porter-bar of thirty hundredweight or more attached, and though this will be suspended from the crane and he will have several mates to help him, it will yet require the whole of their powers to remove it from the furnace to the hammer and to turn it over or push it backwards and forwards to receive the ponderous blow. But if the forgeman is inferior to the smith in the matter of stature and bulk, he easily beats him in strength. He is a very lion in this respect. Underneath his thin, shrunken cheeks and skinny arms are sinews almost as tough as steel itself. In the most blinding and deadly heat of the furnace, with three or four tons of dazzling metal exactly in front of him and the sweat pouring out of the hollows of his grimy cheeks and running down his nose and chin to drop in a continual stream on the ground beneath, he still pushes, heaves, and shouts loudly to his mates, and works and slaves quite unconcernedly. He is almost as fresh at the end of the operation as he was at the beginning. Nothing seems to tire him down; he is for ever active and vigorous.

The forgeman often proves to be a rather irritable individual, one sharp and sour to his mates and hasty in his temper. His companions at the hammer – with the exception of the furnaceman – are so many children to him; he orders them here and there with the slightest ceremony and shouts out his orders at the top of his voice. At every command he utters they hasten to obey, fearing his testiness, and when he roars out at them they shake in their boots. Perhaps they are slow in handing him a tool, or they have applied the wrong gauge, or the hammer-drive has struck too hard a blow. Whatever it is, the forgeman's wrath is aroused and they must suffer for it. In his anger he calls them many names that could not be styled complimentary and withers them with looks. Then, whatever kind of blow the hammerman strikes, it will be wrong. If it is light, he wanted it heavy; if heavy, he required it light – the mere suggestion of a blow. He will often, in the same breath, roar out at the top of his voice – 'Hit 'im! Hit 'im! Light! LIGHT! LIGHT!' and will immediately explode with passion because his order was not acted upon to the letter. By and by the exasperated hammer-driver will venture to reply to his autocratic mate, and a smart battle of words ensues, in which the forgeman, however, usually comes off best. The old furnaceman, greyheaded, or totally bald with the heat, will fire away with his coals and wink at the gaugeman now and then, but never a word will he utter. He knows his mate thoroughly, and understands his temper perfectly. Accordingly, he hears all and says nothing; it makes but little difference to him which way the forging goes as long as he has performed his heat properly. Perhaps, after this, things may run a little more smoothly for a time, or matters may even become worse. I have known mates to work at the same hammer and not speak to each other for a year, not even to give the necessary instructions as to carrying out the forging.

Though there could be no excuse for this foolish exhibition of ill-nature, many apologies may yet be made for the nervous and irritable forgeman. In the first place, his work is enormously hard and exacting; and in the second, there is a great responsibility resting upon him which is not shared by his workmates. The value of the forging in his hands is often considerable, and the least error on the part of his furnaceman or hammer-driver might completely spoil it. If the metal should be in the slightest degree overheated it would burst all to pieces at the first blow of the hammer, and if the hammer-driver should happen to strike a heavy blow at a critical moment, he might spoil the piece in that way, or otherwise necessitate a considerable amount of labour to get it into shape again. All this is a matter of serious care to the forgeman, and as his mates are very often raw hands or careless, dull-headed fellows, it is not to be wondered at that he should now and then discover some perverseness of temper.

It is interesting to note the style of working adopted by different forgers. This, of course, will vary with the man's capability for the job, his gift, his skill acquired, and his natural temper. All forgers are not possessed of a uniformity of skill and capacity, any more than are all musicians and painters equal in their arts; wherever you go you will find good, bad and indifferent workmen. It may at once be said, however, that bad forgemen are not tolerated for any length of time. If they cannot handle the porter and bring their ingot or bloom to a successful finish they are quickly removed and better men put in place of them, for iron and steel ingots are too valuable to be wasted with impunity. As a rule, the quiet workman is the best; that is, he who talks least to his mates, and who does not bawl out every order at the top of his voice. Such a one will often remove his bloom from the furnace, bring it to the hammer and complete it without speaking a word. A nod of the head or a few motions of the hand will be sufficient; his mates understand him perfectly and everything proceeds without a hitch. The hammer-driver, encouraged to use his discretion, knows exactly what kind of blow to strike – heavy or light, light or heavy – when to stop and when to begin. The grimy mate, usually styled the donkeyman, stands by with the gauges; at each pause he fits them to the white-hot mass of iron or steel and again the hammer descends, regularly and evenly. The tremendous 'monkey' goes high up, almost out of sight overhead, and glides noiselessly downwards till it beats the metal, making the pulley chains rattle and jingle and the whole shed to totter and tremble. I have often sat on a gate, or under the trees in the fields on a still evening, towards midnight, and counted the blows struck on an obstinate forging in the shed five miles distant.

It is a pleasure to watch the skilful forgeman perform his heat and shape the ponderous bloom under the steam-hammer. If you observe him closely you will see that he scarcely moves his body. He stands in one position, easily and naturally, all the time, in a slightly stooping attitude, yet he has full power over the heavy weight in his hands. When he shifts the porter, or turns the forging round, his arms are the instruments; it is all performed deftly and simply, with a minimum of exertion. There is a style in it the most casual observer must readily perceive. He cannot help being struck with the extreme simplicity and attractiveness of the whole operation, and he will at once recognise the skilful forger from the unskilful, the gifted craftsman from the mere amateur or improver.

The inferior forgeman will be full of excitement, noise and bustle. He will peer into the furnace half-a-dozen times before he is satisfied as to the heat of the bloom, and grumble and scold the furnaceman all the while. Then, after darting to and fro, backwards and forwards, kicking things out of his way and seeing to this and to that, he bawls out to his mates to 'pull up, and get on the pulley chain.' After a considerable amount of pulling and shoving, grunting, sweating, twisting and turning the ingot, he at last succeeds in bringing it to the hammer, having lost a great part of the heat in the transit. Even now he is undecided as to how to begin the shaping of the piece and has to consider a moment or two before giving the word to start. At last he shouts out to the driver, and the preliminary blows fall. A dozen times, where there is no need of it, he stops the hammer and makes his mate try the gauges. Then he goes on again, thump, thump, thump, now shouting out 'Light!' at the top of his voice, following up with a very loud 'Whoa!' If his mate happens to be in the way he gives him a rough push and tells him to 'get out,' takes up the gauges and fits them himself and afterwards throws them down with violence, and repeats the performance till the bloom is in some manner completed. When the porter-bar has been lopped off and the forging placed on the ground he examines it several times, going to the furnace and coming back to view his half-finished labour and making as much fuss as though he had just forged a battleship, till even the door-boy is disgusted and passes sarcastic remarks upon his ceremonious chief. Considerably more slotting and shaping will always be required on his piece than on that of the other forgeman, and his work will be left till last in the machine shop. The skilful forger will shape his bloom perfectly, so that there will be but a very small amount of facing to do to it; his work will be sure to receive praise, while the other's will as certainly be execrated.

The men of the steam-hammer shed differ from the rest of the factory hands in having to work a twelve-hour day. Very often the heats are ready to draw out at meal-times, and it would be ruinous to leave them to waste in the furnace while the men went home to breakfast and dinner. Accordingly, the forger and his mates boil water in a can on the neck of the furnace, or over a piece of hot metal, and make their own tea to drink. Occasionally the mid-day meal is brought to the factory entrance by the forgeman's little son or daughter, or he may bring in a large basin full of cooked meat and vegetables and warm it up himself. Perhaps the fare is a rasher of bacon. This the workman brings in raw and either roasts it over the furnace door, or on a lump of hot iron. Perhaps he uses a roughly-made frying-pan; or he may place it in the furnaceman's shovel in order to cook it. If the furnaceman sees him, however, he will certainly forbid this, for heating the shovel will spoil the temper of the steel and cause it to warp. He will say, moreover, that coal charged into the furnace with a shovel that has had 'that mess' in it will never heat the iron, and I have more than once seen the half-cooked food unceremoniously turned out into the coal-dust. A common name for the roughly-made frying-pan is a 'rasher-waggon.'

At night, when the day's work is over and everything has been left neat and tidy for the succeeding shift, the forger stows his leathern apron, cap and jackboots, rinses his hands in the bosh, and leaves the shed, walking a little in advance of his mates and preserving the same temper he has displayed at the toil. His mates, however, together with the ingenuous and mischievous door-boy, are not so conventional in their behaviour. Since they are free to go home and roam the streets or trudge off into the country once more, they indulge in games and fun before they leave, and sing and whistle to their heart's content. Meanwhile the old furnaceman has damped his fire and made everything ready for the mate who succeeds

F. Sparkes, Family Butcher, 47 Regent Street, 1910. All classes of railway workmen ate 'great quantities' of meat. (Jefferies, 1875)

him. Now he, too, swills his hands in the bosh and gives his sweaty old face an extra special rub with the wiper, puts the muffler around his neck, slips on his jacket, and, taking his dinner-can under his arm, proceeds through the tunnel and out into the town.

Very few of the forgemen were born in the town; they have nearly all come in from the villages round about and become urbanised. After their toils in the hot shed they do not want to have to journey far to their homes. Their dwellings are consequently usually within easy distance of the forge, though here and there is to be found one who has the courage to continue in his native village. As their wages are above the average paid at the works – though the rate is not nearly as high as it is at most steam-hammer sheds – the forgers are enabled to indulge themselves in the matter of living. Their food will accordingly be of the very best quality, and when that has been paid for there is yet a fair supply of pocket money remaining. Most forgemen are fond of a glass of ale; it is a rare thing to find a teetotaler in their ranks. They are much given to talking of their achievements at all times and in all places, and they occupy long hours in telling of the famous jobs they have done on many occasions – a special crank for this or that engine, a big piston-rod or monkey for an outside firm, or a mighty anchor for an ocean-going vessel.

In point of real usefulness and importance the boiler-makers stand second to none at the works. Though they may not be as highly skilled as are the fitters individually, collectively they form a much more imposing and vigorous body, and one that is far more essential to the absolute needs of the firm. To whatever extent the forger or fitter may be done without, or unskilled men put in place of them, that is not possible in the case of the boilersmith. His labour, as well as being very important, is distinct from that of all others at the factory; his is an exclusive profession. In the making of locomotives for the line the boiler is by far the greatest item, and it is very difficult and expensive to construct. The work must be performed with exquisite care and everything must be conscientiously well done. There must be no shoddy work in a boiler; no 'nobbling over,' concealment of flaws, or deception of any kind, or disastrous consequences would be inevitable. The plates must all be admirably shaped and fitted, the bolts and stays very strong and sound, and the whole most carefully adjusted and riveted. The time required for the construction of a first-class boiler for a locomotive is about six months, and the cost is near about a thousand pounds. All the inner plates are of copper, which is used in order to allow of regular expansion and contraction. The tubes are of iron or steel, and number several hundreds. Tubing is a branch of work distinct from boilermaking properly so-called, and is undertaken by those less skilful than are required for the other processes.

Boilermakers are divided into two classes – the platers and the riveters. Those of the first grade prepare the plates, perform the marking-off and cutting-out, see to the drilling of the holes and afterwards bolt the parts together. The riveters follow and make everything solid and compact.

Nearly all the riveting is done by hand; very little is left to the chance work of the machine, which is often faulty and unreliable. Rivets put in by hand are far more trustworthy than are those done by the machine. The hammered heads will be tougher and more durable than those that have been squeezed up by the hydraulic apparatus.

The two grades of boilermakers are kept separate and distinct. Every man is provided with a card certifying to which class he belongs, whether to the platers or riveters, and he can – as a general rule – only obtain a job upon that kind of work specified by his ticket. Similarly, if he has been employed on repair work for any length of time he will have great difficulty in getting re-admittance into the ranks of those engaged on the new boilers. The trade throughout is jealously guarded and protected. The rules are well-defined and published far and wide; there is no setting aside the regulations. Notwithstanding the division of work on a boiler the efficient boilersmith is qualified to construct one throughout, from the marking of the plates to the insertion of the tubes. The valves and other fixings are usually attached by the fitters.

The din of the frame shed and the unearthly noise of the pneumatic apparatus on the headstocks and plates is not to be compared with the tremendous uproar of the boiler shop. Here are no less than two hundred huge boilers, either new ones being made, or old ones undergoing repairs and engaging the attentions of four or five hundred boilersmiths, to say nothing of tubers and labourers hammering and battering away on the shells and interiors. There are boilers in every stage of construction and in every conceivable position on the stocks. Some are upright, some are upside down, some are standing on end, some lying on their sides, and others are scattered broadcast. The workmen swarm like ants everywhere, crawling over the tops, inside and out, in the smoke-box and fire-box, and lying on their backs underneath. Hundreds of tools are in operation at once. Hundreds of hammers are falling, banging and clanging perpetually, with an indescribable noise and confusion. If you would be heard you must shout at the top of your voice and make yourself hoarse in the attempt. The boilersmiths, who are used to the conditions, do not try to address each other at their work; they have discovered an expedient. Instead of straining their throats and lungs in the vain effort to make themselves heard they simply motion with the head or hands; their mates come to know what is required and obey the telegraphic intimation, and so the work proceeds.

The boilermakers are a bold and hardy class, sturdy in their views and outlook, and very independent. As in the case of the fitters, smiths, and

other journeymen, they have travelled far and wide and become acquainted with many workshops and sets of conditions. Very often they will
have tramped the whole country, from end to end, in search of
employment, for though as a class they are indispensable their ranks are
often over-crowded, and when trade is slack the services of many of
them are dispensed with. As with the majority of other journeymen, if
they are thrown out of employment, though they may be idle for a long
time and reduced to dire straights, they seldom deign to do other work,
but shift from place to place and beg food along the highways and
through the villages. Though verging on starvation they cannot, even
for a short period, be prevailed upon to abandon the idea of their trade,
but still crowd around the factory doors and hope for a revival of the
industry.

A short time ago a party of boilermen, who had been discharged from
the town, made weekly visits to the villages round about pretending that
they had walked from Sunderland and Newcastle – where a big strike
had been declared – and calling themselves a deputation empowered to
collect money for their mates at home in the North. The spokesman, a
voluble and impudent scoundrel, told impressive stories of hardships and
suffering and drew a great many coins from the credulous and sympathetic rustics. By and by, however, a second party, with exactly the same
story, came on the scene and professed to be highly indignant on being
told that they had been anticipated in their office as collectors. The
second batch of visitors did not solicit money; they demanded it, and any
who refused were subjected to abuse and threatening language. At last
the suspicions of the villagers were aroused. They doubted the genuineness of the tales of distress and of the long march from far-off
Sunderland, and closed their doors to the importunate strangers. Very
soon trade in the railway town revived; the majority of the men were
reinstated and the countryside knew them no more.

The iron foundry is but a few yards from the boiler shed; you may
very quickly be introduced to it, with the noise of the hammers and the
clatter of the pneumatic apparatus still ringing loudly in your ears. After
the din of the boiler shop the quietude of the foundry will be the more
remarkable. Here are no plates to be beaten, no rapidly revolving pulleys
and shafting, and no uproar. All that can be heard is the dull roar of the
blast furnace half-way up the shed, and the subdued noise of the
traversing table in the roof above you. The floor is of soft, yielding sand,
similar to that of which the moulds for the castings are made, and it is
noiseless under the feet. The men sit or kneel on the ground, with their

---

Overleaf: Iron foundry, 1907, with finished casting of combined cylinder and
saddle for 'Star' class locomotive. Total annual output of finished
casting: 20,000 to 25,000 tons

patterns beside them, and construct the duplicates to receive the molten metal. As soon as the moulds are finished the dark, grimy labourers bring the molten liquid, either carrying it in a thick iron vessel lined with firebricks and having a spout on one side – as you would carry a stretcher – or wheeling it along in a big cauldron that swings like a pot, and pour it in through a small space left for that purpose.

The chief interest to the visitor centres in the furnace that contains the molten fluid. This is a large, cylindrical structure, enclosed in a steel frame, towering high into the roof and emitting a terrific heat all around. Near the top is a large platform, reached by an iron stairway, up which you are invited to mount by the grimy furnaceman, more often in jest than in earnest, for the heat there is overpowering. The handrail of the stairway seems nearly red-hot, and the air, puffed out from the furnace, strikes you full in the face, so that you are almost suffocated with it. On the platform is the feeding-place where the fuel and metal are charged – coke to produce the heat and material for the molten fluid, either old broken up castings, or bars of new pig iron. Both iron and coke are thrown in and fused up together. The fluid metal collects and flows out in front, while the debris of the coke – what little remains after combustion – is ejected through a small aperture at the rear. The iron, by its weight, sinks to the floor of the furnace, while the filth and ashes of the coke remain floating on the top – there is no fear of the two intermixing. An iron conduit, working on a hinge, conveys the liquid metal into the pots for the moulds. When the vessels are filled the shoot is raised, and this stops back the metal that goes on accumulating till the next pot is in position.

There is a great attractiveness in the operation of filling the vessels with the molten fluid that, yellowish-white in colour, flows like water from the interior, sparkling and spluttering as it drops into the receptacle beneath. The heat is very intense at all times, and the toil continuous; hundreds of moulds are waiting to be filled from the furnace. Having occasion to visit the shed recently I pushed a way through the crowd of labourers waiting to have their pots filled and stood beside the furnace-man as he was running out the metal. He took no notice of my presence, but kept his eyes fixed upon the conduit.

'Very hot today!' I shouted.

'Yes, 'tis,' he replied, without turning round.

'How much metal does the furnace hold?'

'Don' know.'

'What's your heat?'

'Don' know.'

'How many tons of metal do you run out in a day?'

'Don' know.'

'You must have an idea.'

'Don' know. Got no time. We're busy.'

'Are you always on at this rate?'

'We kips on till us stops, same as the rest on 'em, an' has a sleep in between.' Then, turning round to one of the new arrivals he shouted – 'What! bist thee got back 'ere agyen, Charlie? Thee't eff to wait a bit. I got none for thee yet awhile.' Charlie nodded and grinned, with the sweat streaming down his nose and chin; the whole company smiled appreciatively. Perhaps Charlie was carrying metal for one of the less important moulds, and was used to being put aside and made to wait a few moments, or he may have been one of the day men, of whom there are but a small number in the shed. Nearly everything is done at the piece rate; a few special jobs alone are done according to the day work rule. Under these circumstances Charlie might have no objection to waiting five or ten minutes.

Most of the moulders dwell in the town, though many of the labourers prefer to inhabit the region round about the borough, in those villages of easy access to the railway centre. Some of the journeymen have served their apprenticeship at small country towns and villages – perhaps in the same county and district – at which agricultural machinery is manufactured. Such as these will be sure to import local methods and characteristics and they will always retain some part of their individual style acquired during their term of apprenticeship. Though the difference of method may not be very great, it will be productive of good results; it is by a combination of several practices and systems that perfection is ultimately attained. Very often, in the midst of a teasing operation, a mate or passer-by may suddenly call to mind a similar difficulty he had in some far-off village yard and thus he will be able to supply the key to the situation. According to the theory of the works' officials, no difficulties should ever be encountered – they should not even exist. In practice, however, difficulties will often be met with, and when the workman is compelled, by the lowness of his prices, to push ahead at a great speed he is sometimes apt to become confused with a difficulty and to overlook a point that, to the leisured overseer, will be quite obvious and simple.

CHAPTER VIII

GETTING TO WORK – THE AWAKENING IN THE COUNTRY –
STEALING A RIDE – THE TOWN STIR – THE ARMY OF WORKMEN –
'CHECKING' – EARLY COMERS – CLERKS AND DRAUGHTSMEN –
FEATURES OF THE STAFF

At an early hour the whole neighbourhood within a radius of five or six
miles of the factory is astir; there is a general preparation for the coming
day's work. The activity will first begin in the villages furthest from the
town. Soon after four o'clock, in the quiet hamlets amidst the woods and
lanes, the workmen will leave their beds and get ready for the long tramp
to the shed, or to the nearest station touched by the trains proceeding to
the railway town. Many of the younger men have bicycles and will pedal
their way to work. They will not be forced to rise quite as early as the
rest, unless they live at a very great distance. A few workmen I know
have, for the past twenty years, resided at not less than twelve miles from
the town and have made the journey all through the year, wet and dry
together. The only time at which they cannot get backwards and
forwards is when there are deep floods, or after a heavy snowstorm.
Then, if the fall has been severe and the water or snow lies to any depth
on the roads, they will be compelled to walk or to lodge in the town.
Sometimes the fall of snow has taken place in the night and the
workman, under these circumstances, will be forced to take a holiday
until it melts and he is able to journey along the road again.

I have heard many accounts, from workmen who had long distances to
walk to the factory, of the great and terrible blizzard of 1881, when the
drifts in many places along the highways were from sixteen to twenty feet
deep. One sturdy fellow took great pride in relating how he made the
journeys daily – of six miles each way – during the whole time the snow
lay on the ground, though many were frozen to death in the locality.
Another workman whom I knew walked regularly to and from the village

for fifty years, and at the end of that time bethought himself to get a tricycle. It was amusing to see him, with snow-white hair and the perspiration pouring down his weather-beaten old face, pedalling home from
work after a very hot and scorching day at the rolling mills. What with the
fatigue of the day's work and the extraordinary exertions required to
propel the machine, he was very nearly exhausted by the time he reached
home. Everyone along the highway turned to have a second view of the
old man as he trundled his machine along, puffing and blowing with the

Drove Road, seventeen years after the blizzard: freak snowstorm near the end of
April. All the photographers went out and photographed it

effort, his face red and fiery; but he was not to be deterred from the innovation. It is probable that walking would have been the easier way of
getting backwards and forwards, for the machine was nearly as heavy as a
farm cart. There was a slight saving of time, however, and it is a common
saying among work-people of all sorts that 'Third-class riding is better
than first-class walking.' After the old man's death the tricycle became the
property of a band of farm boys who used it as a training machine; it was
for a long time a source of fun and amusement to the villagers.

Very often, in the remote villages, where there is no access to the
stations at which the factory trains call, a party of workmen club

together and hire a conveyance to bring them daily to the town; or they may subscribe the money and buy a horse and cart and contribute equally towards the expense of keeping them. An arrangement is made with the proprietor of a public-house in the town. The horse is stabled and the vehicle stored for a small sum, and the men ride backwards and forwards, comfortable and independent. It was the custom, years ago, during haymaking and harvest-time, for farmers to come in with conveyances from the out-lying villages and meet the men and drive them home. They went straight from the factory to the farmyard or hayfield, and, after a hearty tea in the open air, or a square meal of bread, cheese and ale, turned in and helped the farmer, both enjoying the change of work and earning a couple of shillings a night as additional wages. This practice was very popular with the factory men, who never ceased to talk about it to their town mates in the shed and rouse them to envy with the frequent narration. Of late years, however, the custom has died out. Labour is too cheap and machinery too plentiful for the farmer to have any difficulty in getting his crops together nowadays.

The majority of the villagers, though compelled to leave home for the town at such an early hour, will yet rise in time to partake of a light breakfast before starting for the shed. The country mothers are far more painstaking in the matter of providing meals than are many of those in the town; they think nothing of rising at four a.m. in order to boil the kettle and cook food for their husbands and sons. Though the goodman may protest against it and declare that he would rather go without the food than give his wife so much trouble, it makes no difference. Every morning, at the usual hour, the smoke goes curling up from the chimney; a cup of hot, refreshing tea is invariably awaiting him on the table when he arrives downstairs. After the repast he starts off in abundant time and takes his leisure on the road; one rarely sees a countryman hurrying to work in the morning.

The boys, on the other hand, will not be as punctual in starting off to work; they will usually be late in setting out, very often delaying till the last moment. They will, moreover, often loiter on the way bird's-nesting or reading, or perhaps they may start into the farmer's orchard and carry off the rosy-cheeked apples to eat in the shed or to divide out among their mates and companions. At one time there were three brothers of one house in the village, all working in the factory, though they never under any circumstances went to the town together. The eldest of the three always led the way, the second following five minutes later, and the youngest brought up the rear at a similar interval. The return home at night was made in the same manner: it is unusual to see the members of a family or household going to work together.

Very often the village resident will work for an hour in his garden or attend to his pigs and domestic animals before leaving for the rail-way shed. If the neighbouring farmer is busy, or happens to be a man short, he may help him milk his cows or do a little mowing with the scythe and still be fresh for his work in the factory. I have known those who, during the summer months, went regularly to fishing in the big brook, or practised a little amateur poaching with the ferrets, and never missed going to gather mushrooms in the early mornings during autumn.

Several boys of the village, especially on the dark winter mornings, used to watch for the freight-trains that sometimes stopped at the signal station and steal a ride down to the works, hanging on to the rails of the brake van, or clinging to the buffers. The practice was attended with considerable risk, and the punishment, had they been detected, would have been sharp and severe. It was difficult to see them sitting in the shadow of the tail lamps, however, though once or twice we were reported by the signalmen and chased by the goods guards. At one time the train ran through the station without stopping, with three youngsters clinging to the rails of the guard's van; and it was only checked by accident twelve miles higher up the line. A great chase across fields in a drenching downpour of rain followed, but the goods guard had to own himself beaten and returned to the van. One of the boys was fond of lying down between the metals, and of allowing the trains to thunder along above him – certainly a dangerous proceeding, though he did not think so at that time. All these practices are well-nigh impossible now. Greater care is taken to keep trespassers off the line and the modern system of transverse sleepers for the track hardly permits of lying down between the metals.

One morning, nearly dark, as a village lad was going to work down the line, he was much frightened at seeing a man behaving in a mysterious and suspicious manner underneath one of the bridges. He appeared to be selecting a spot in which to lie across the rails, and as there was a fast train approaching close at hand, the youngster soon became considerably alarmed. To his relief, however, as the engine drew near, the unknown one got off the track, ran up the bank and disappeared. At the same spot, soon afterwards, a young man, suspected of a criminal offence, threw himself in front of an express and was cut to pieces. After that occurrence we boys shunned the line, for that winter at least, and passed to work along the highway. We had many narrow escapes from being knocked down by engines, trains and waggons in the station yard at different times. One morning, being very late, I ran between some waggons that were being shunted, when only a very narrow space remained before the vehicles closed up. In spite of warning shouts, I skipped through quickly, but as I cleared the rails an old shunter, who was waiting on the other side, swung his arm round and struck me a terrific blow behind the ear with his open hand, and loudly scolded me

Men pushing hand-cart and barrow over the level-crossing.
(Detail of illustration on page 34)

for taking such risks. Half stunned with the blow, I ran off, and freely forgave the old man for his well-meant chastisement. I often meet him now in the town, many years after the escapade, and always remember the incident, though he has doubtless forgotten it long ago.

By five o'clock the people of the inner circle of the radius without the town are well awake, and twenty minutes later the dreaded hooter bellows out, like the knell of doom to a great many. The sound travels to a great distance, echoing and re-echoing along the hills and up the valley seventeen or twenty miles away, if the wind is setting in that direction. This is the first warning signal to the workman to bestir himself, if he has not already done so; to awake from dreams to realities, to shake off the warm, comfortable bedclothes and don his working attire. It is now the turn of the town dweller to stir. Very soon, here and there, a thin spire of smoke arises from the chimney, telling of the early cup of tea in preparation. The oldest hands, a good many of them grey and feeble, are to be seen making their way towards the entrances to the works. It will

Broad gauge tender and standard engine side by side.
(Detail of illustration on page 34)

take some of them quite half an hour to reach the shed, though that is no more than three-quarters of a mile away. By and by others will come from their houses and join those who are just arriving from the country. These are the town's early risers. Some time will elapse yet before the regular stream comes forth to fill the street and make the pavements ring with their countless footsteps. Although a few may prefer to come leisurely to work and perhaps wait in the shed some ten minutes before it is time to start at the machines, the great majority loiter till the very last minute and spend not a second of time, more than they are absolutely bound, upon the company's premises.

At ten minutes to six the hooter sounds a second time, then again at five minutes, and finally at six o'clock. This time it makes a double report, in order that the men may be sure that it is the last hooter. Five minutes' grace – from six till six-five – is allowed in the morning; after that everyone except clerks must lose time. As soon as the ten-minutes hooter sounds the men come teeming out of the various parts of the town in great numbers, and by five minutes to six the streets leading to the entrances are packed with a dense crowd of men and boys, old and young, bearded and beardless, some firm and upright, others bent and stooping, pale and haggard-looking, all off to the same daily toil and fully intent on the labour before them. It is a mystery where they all come from. Ten thousand workmen! They are like an army pressing forward to battle. Tramp! tramp! tramp! Still they pour down the streets, with the regularity of trained soldiers, quickening in pace as the time advances, until they come very nearly to the double and finally disappear through the entrances. Some of the young men's faces are ghastly white, very thin and emaciated, telling a story of ill-health – consumption, very likely – while others are fresh and healthy-looking – there are fat and lean among them. Some there are still bearing traces of yesterday's toil – large black rings around the eyes, or sharp lines underneath the chin and continued round the back of the neck. A little more soap and water would have removed them, but in all probability the youngster was extra tired, or in a great hurry to get off to play, or go a-fishing, and so could not endure a tedious toilet. Others, again, come blundering along with eyes only half open – having obviously missed the morning swill – with their shirt unbuttoned at the neck, their boots not laced up, untidy and unkempt, and in a desperate hurry. This one is bare-headed, that one carries his hat in his hand, and another wears his hind before. Many have had no time even to look for their working clothes, but have clapped on the first that met their eyes on arising from bed; you often see one enter the shed dressed in odd garments, and sometimes wearing a shoe of a sort.

The boys and youths are usually the last. They always experience greater difficulty in leaving the comfortable bed, and the *pater familias* will often have had trouble in inducing them finally to wake up and think about work. They do not realise the seriousness of the business as he does, and are very careless on first awaking. By and by, however, the truth dawns upon them; up they scramble, dress, and run out of doors and up the street, and very often do not stop till they come to the shed. I have many a time, as a boy, run from the village to the factory, four miles distant, in thirty-five minutes, as the result of oversleeping. When the youngsters reach the shed, after a long run, they will require a spell of a few minutes before they can start work, and the forgers and hammer-men will often have to shout at them several times before they are sufficiently rested to begin.

A great many of the crowd bring their breakfast and dinner with them, either to eat it in the shed, or in the mess-rooms provided for the purpose. Some of the men carry it in a canteen, held under the arm or slung with a string over the shoulder and back. Others bring it tied up in red handkerchiefs, and very many, especially of the town dwellers, wrap it up in old newspapers. The country workmen are more particular over their food than are their mates of the town. Though their fare will be plainer and simpler – seldom amounting to anything more tasty than bread and butter, cheese or cold boiled bacon – they will be at great pains to see that it is very fresh and clean.

That which strikes one most forcibly about the morning crowd is the extraordinary quiet and soberness, both of the men and the juveniles. They seldom speak to each other as they hurry along through the streets and tunnels towards their several destinations – not even those who toil side by side at the same forge or machine, however much they may talk later on in the day. They do not – except in somewhat rare instances – even wish each other 'Good morning.' If they happen to speak at all it will usually be no more than to utter a curt 'Mornin',' which is often responded to with a very impolite and often positively churlish ''Ow do!' And as for a smile! A morning smile on the way to work is indeed a rarity. Now and then the careless-hearted lads may indulge in a little playful banter, though even this is not common, but the men never smile in the early morning. There is the day's work to be faced, the smoke and heat, the long stand at the machine, the tedious confinement, the hard word and bitter speech, the daily anxiety, the unnatural combat for the necessaries of life, and it all looms big on the horizon. By and by, as the day advances and the hands of the clock slowly but surely record the death and burial of the hours, the set features will relax, and the tongue will regain its office. The fire of human sympathy will be rekindled and man and boy will be themselves again. But this will be not yet. For the present everyone is concerned with his own necessity. He is marching to battle, the issue of which is doubtful and uncertain. When the first victory has been won, which is at dinner-time for him, he will dissolve and be natural and genial, but not now. It is noteworthy that the country workmen will prove to be more sympathetic than those of the town. Many of them will bid 'Good morning' to everyone they meet, whether they know them or not. They do not stand upon any kind of formality; answered or not they persist in the salutation, and always add the christian name of the individual where it is known to them.

In the street, near the entrances, are coffee stalls, where, for the modest sum of a halfpenny, the workmen may obtain a cup of the steaming beverage, which is usually of a weak quality and not at all likely to derange the stomach of the individual who swallows it. Another halfpenny will purchase a bun or scone, a slice of 'lardy' or currant cake, if anyone shall desire it, so that there is no need for any who can afford a copper each morning to go hungry to work. Some workmen bring food from home in their hand and eat it standing by the stall, where they have stopped to partake of a cup of tea or coffee.

It is pathetic, especially on cold, wintry mornings, to note the rivet boys and others of the poorest class as they approach the entrance by the coffee stalls. Their eyes are fixed longingly on the steaming urns and piled-up plates of buns; they would like to gulp down a good big cup of the liquid and munch several of the cakes. But such luxuries are not for them. They have not a halfpenny in the world, so they content themselves with a covetous look and pass on to the labour. Now and then a father, with his little son, will stop to share a cup of coffee, or they may have one apiece, but this is not a common occurrence. All the money is needed elsewhere – for clothes, boots, and household requirements. The better class of work-people – journeymen and such like – never drink tea or coffee at the stalls. That is beneath their dignity. They do not like to be seen breaking their fast in public, and they speak of beverages as 'messes' and 'slops.' A few of the workmen will loiter about the street till six o'clock, by which time some of the public-houses will be opened. They will require a mug of ale or a little spirit to put them in order; perhaps they were drunk overnight and want a 'livener' before starting in the morning.

At about three minutes past six a smart rush for the entrance is made, and those bringing up the rear will be forced to put on a good spurt in order to gain the shed in time. They have either dawdled about at home, or were late in rising; whatever the reason may be, every morning finds them in the same predicament. The same workmen are always first or last; year in and year out there is little variation in the individual time-table. What a man is this morning he will be tomorrow morning; there is no change week after week or month after month. Moreover, he that is late at the first beginning of the day's work will most certainly be in the same position at breakfast-time and dinner-time, too. He will come to be noted for that characteristic; he is bound to be late in any case. Such men always parcel out their time with exquisite nicety, so that when the hooter begins to sound they have about twenty yards to run in order to reach the check-box. Immediately after the rear part of the crowd has disappeared within the entrance the ponderous doors are closed with a loud bang, and the town without looks to be deserted. The men inside the yard scatter, some this way and some that, and are soon out of sight in the different sheds. All that can be seen now are a few clerks sauntering along, usually wearing a flower in their button-hole, and glancing at the morning newspaper.

Every workman is provided with a brass check or 'ticket,' round in shape like a penny, or oblong, with a number stamped upon it, corresponding to his name in the register. This has to be placed in the check-box each time the man enters the shed, and it is the only accepted proof of his attendance at work or absence from it. If he loses or mislays the ticket he will be fined a sum equal to half an hour's wages, whether he likes it or not, and he will consequently often be forced to pay fourpence or fivepence for a portion of metal that is worth no more than a farthing. This will be the price of having his name registered, or, if he is dissatisfied with the arrangement, he can return home and wait till after the next meal-time. Similarly, in the morning, after the five minutes' grace, whoever is late is charged quarter of an hour for the first five minutes, and half an hour for the next, *i.e.*, till six-fifteen, though there is no reason whatever why a workman should be fined so heavily. A fairer thing to do would be to fine all late-comers a quarter of an hour's wages and allow them to check till quarter-past six. This is the latest time for checking the first thing in the morning. No workman is admitted later than that hour, but must wait till the re-start after breakfast.

The country workmen will be among the first arrivals at the shed, though they are not usually the earliest comers of all. Some of the townsmen are early risers, and come regularly to the premises half an hour before it is time to begin work. It is remarkable that those who are addicted to very early rising, that is, earlier than is really necessary, will most certainly be found to be deficient in brains and intellect. You will invariably find such ones to be dull-witted, and lower in the mental scale than are many who hurry and come late to business. The old adage –

'Early to bed and early to rise,
    Makes a man healthy, wealthy, and wise,'

may be true enough in all the three particulars, but it does not necessarily follow that a strict observance of the rule will also endue him with a plentiful supply of brains and intellectual keenness. Healthy it will certainly make him. The application of a little common-sense will easily demonstrate that one reason of his retiring early is the fact that he has no mental pursuits, nothing in which to interest himself outside his daily occupation, so that he is already deficient, and must perforce betake himself to bed. Being free from mental worry and not troubling about intellectual hobbies, he will sleep soundly, enjoy the maximum amount of rest, and wake up fully refreshed and vigorous in the morning. All that such men as these think of is their day's work, their food and sleep; they have no other object or ambition in life.

As to the entire wisdom of the rule, that is another matter. It was counted sufficiently wise formerly, but we of this day are made of sterner material. Horses and oxen work hard, rest well, enjoy very good health, and appear to be satisfied, if not actually happy, but one man is of more value than many horses or oxen. Work and sacrifice are the only things that will raise a man in the estimation of the world and set him up as a worthy example to his fellows. To those who are content merely to live, and not to shine, may be addressed the words of the Ant spoken to the Fly in the Fable: *Nihil laboras; ideo nil habes* – 'You do nothing, and consequently you have nothing.' At the same time it must be admitted that those who retire early and rise early nearly always prove to be the strongest workmen; they will be capable of great physical exertions and staying powers. But when all has been said, such men are rather to be pitied than envied. They are little more than mere tools and the slaves of their employers – the prodigal squanderers of their powers and lives.

It is a privilege of the shop clerks to arrive a little later than the workmen, and to leave a little in advance of them at meal-times and in the evening. The members of the principal office staff enjoy a still greater dispensation, for they do not begin work at all before nine o'clock in the morning and finish at five-thirty in the afternoon. The clerks are the most numerous of all the trained classes at the factory. With the draughtsmen they form an imposing body, yet though they rank next the foremen and heads of departments, they are not taken very seriously by the rank and file, except when they appear in the shed with the cashbox to pay the weekly wages.

For the sake of distinction the shop clerks are called the 'weekly staff,' and the managers' and other clerks, with the draughtsmen, are denominated the 'monthly staff.' The first-named of these are paid weekly with the workmen; the others receive their salary once a month. The shop clerks are chiefly recruited from the personnel of the sheds, while those of the monthly staff are chosen from over a wider area. In the case of them considerably more training and experience will be required. They must be possessed of specific abilities, and have gone through classes and taken examinations in order to qualify for the positions. It is usual for the more intelligent lads at the higher elementary schools of the town to be recommended to the chiefs of the factory offices. If their qualifications are considered satisfactory, they are started in one or other of the clerical departments and instructed in the several duties. By entering the offices young, and passing from point to point, they have every opportunity of becoming proficient, and are in course of time promoted according to their abilities.

The clerks of the sheds naturally enjoy the confidence of the overseers. They know everything pertaining to piecework prices and output, and are consequently able to furnish the chief with whatever information he desires upon any point. In addition to the clerk there is a checker, who books every article made and supervises the piecework outside the office, and, as if that were not sufficient, a piecework 'inspector,' who is commissioned with the power to report upon any price on the spot and to make any reduction he thinks fit. All these co-operate and together supply particulars of the workman and his job, how much he makes on a shift, the precise time it takes him to finish an article; and if it is necessary one or the other stays behind after working hours and computes the number of forgings, or other uses made, and is a perfect spy upon his less fortunate mates of the shed.

An unscrupulous clerk may thus work incalculable mischief among the men. He often influences the foreman in a very high degree, or he even dictates to him, so that you sometimes hear the clerk spoken of as the 'boss' and the foreman himself styled the 'bummer.' Under such circumstances it will not be wondered at that the clerk is sometimes an unpopular figure in the shed and is looked upon with disfavour, though very often unjustly so. A great deal depends upon the temper and honesty, or dishonesty, of the overseer, for the clerk, in most cases, will take the cue from him. If he is honourable and 'above board,' he will not tolerate any covert dealings and tale-bearing. If, on the other hand, he is shifty and cunning, he will encourage all kinds of slimness and questionable proceedings on the part of his clerks.

The members of the monthly staff and draughtsmen occupy quarters grouped around the managers' offices, and do not often appear in the workshops. When they do so it will be on account of some extraordinary business, or they may come in with the foreman to take a look round and view the machinery. They usually bring a book or drawing in their hand, or under the arm, so as to have some kind of excuse in case they should be challenged by a superior, for even they are not allowed to go wherever they will. I have known draughtsmen to come regularly to the

G.W.R. Institute, Swindon

GWR Mechanics' Institution, about 1910. Alfred took a four-year correspondence course in English Literature with Ruskin Hall, Oxford. Now a society in Swindon, 'Friends of Alfred Williams', honours him

shed provided with a tape-measure, books, and plans, and take the dimensions of a machine again and again. No doubt they were in need of a little exercise and anxious to see the stampers and forgers at work.

Very few clerks, in spite of their leisure and opportunities, are bookish or endowed with a taste for literature; out of over a thousand at the factory less than twenty are connected with the Literary Society at the Works' Institute. The students and premiums have their debating classes on matters connected with engineering. They meet and read papers on technical subjects, but have little interest in anything natural or *spirituel*.

CHAPTER IX

FIRST OPERATIONS IN THE SHED – THE EARLY DIN – ITS EFFECT ON
THE WORKMEN – CHARGING THE HEATS – THE OIL FURNACE –
THE 'AJAX' – HARRY AND SAMMY – THE 'STRAPPIE' –
HYDRAULIC POWER – WHEEL-BURSTING

Arrived in the shed the workmen remove their coats and hang them up
under the wall, or behind the forges. If any shall be seen wearing them by
the foreman when he enters they will be noticed and marked: it is a
common rule, winter and summer, to take them off on coming into the
workshop, except in places where there are no fires. A terrible din, that
could be heard in the yard long before you came to the doors of the shed,
is already awaiting. Here ten gigantic boilers, which for several hours
have been steadily accumulating steam for the hammers and engines,
packed with terrific high pressure, are roaring off their surplus energy
with indescribable noise and fury, making the earth and roof tremble and
quiver around you, as though they were in the grip of an iron-handed
monster. The white steam fills the shed with a dense, humid cloud like a
thick fog, and the heat is already overpowering. The blast roars loudly
underground and in the boxes of the forges, and the wheels and shafting
whirl round in the roof and under the wall. The huge engines, that
supply the hydraulic machines with pressure, are chu-chu-ing above the
roof outside; everything is in a state of the utmost animation. If you were
not fully awake before and sensible of what the day had in store for you,
you are no longer in any doubt about the matter. All sluggishness, both
of the mind and body, is quickly dispelled by the great activity
everywhere displayed around you. The very air, hot and heavy, and
thickly charged with dust as it is, seems to have an electrical effect upon
you. You immediately feel excited to begin work; the noise of the
steam, the engines, the roar of the blast, and the whirling wheels compel
you to it.

At the same time the morning freshness, the bloom, vigour, the hopeful spirit, the whole natural man will be entirely quelled and subdued after the first few moments in this living pandemonium. Wife and children, friends and home, town and village, green fields and blue skies, the whole outside world will have been left far behind. There is no opportunity to think of anything but iron and steel, furnaces and hammers, the coming race and battle for existence. Moreover, as everything is done at the piece rate, the men will be anxious to make an early start, before the day gets hot. It is especially true of the stampers and hammermen that 'A bird in the hand's worth two in the bush,' and a good heat performed before breakfast is far better than depending upon exertions to be made at a later part of the day.

So, before you can well look around you, before the foreman can reach the shed, in fact, the workmen are up and at it. Those who are earliest on the place usually make the first start. They, and especially the furnacemen and forgemen, often begin before the regulation hour, and make haste to get their fires in a fit condition to receive the metal. First of all, the coal furnaces have to be clinkered. A large steel bar and a heavy sledge break the clinker; the fire-bars are withdrawn, and down plunges the white-hot mass into the 'bosh' of water beneath. When this is performed new fuel is laid on, light at first, and sloping gently to the rear wall. The corners are well filled; the floor of the furnace, recently levelled with fresh sand, is firmly beaten down with the heavy paddle, and all is ready to receive the ingots or blooms.

Immediately the forger and his mates swarm round with the metal, either using the crane and pulley, or charging it in upon the peel. The chargeman grunts and scolds and the furnace door is raised, lighting up the dark corners behind the forges. Now the hammer-driver winds the wheel that opens the valve, and fills his cylinder with the raucous vapour; the heavy monkey travels noiselessly up and down, preparing to beat the iron into the shape required. Little by little, as the steam is absorbed by the engines and hammers, the din of the boilers subsides. The tremendous amount of power required to drive the various machines soon reduces the pent-up energy, and by and by the priming ceases altogether. The steam will continue gradually to diminish until the first meal-hour, when it will have reached a low figure, as indicated by the pressure gauge. During the interval, however, it will have risen again, and long before it is time to recommence work the boilers will be roaring off their superfluous energy with the same indescribable din and fury.

To obviate the noise of the simultaneous priming of the boilers an escape valve was recently constructed, and a pipe affixed to carry it through the roof. Owing to the incapacity of the tube, however, the noise, instead of being diminished, was considerably intensified. People heard it in every quarter of the town and thought it was an explosion. No one in the vicinity of the shed could sleep at night, so at last complaints were made to the manager, and the use of the valve was discontinued.

Now the oil furnaces will have been lit up and the smiths' forges kindled. The two foremen will have arrived and made their first perambulation of the shed, and everything will be in a state of bustle and confusion. Certainly the sparks will not be flying, nor the anvils ringing yet. It will take fully twenty minutes to get everything into order and to produce the first heat. But there is a deadly earnestness evident all round. It will not be long before the busy Titans are stripped to the waist, turning the ponderous ingots and blooms over and over, and raining the blows upon the yielding metal.

The oil forge hails from the other side of the Atlantic, and is an innovation at the shed. It is attached to machinery of the American type, and is well suited for the game of hustle. It is not very large, and occupies but a small space anywhere, but it has this advantage, that it may be moved to any position; it is not a fixture, as are the other furnaces. It is oblong in shape, with an arched roof; and the heating space is not more than several cubic feet. The front is of brick, with as many apertures as are required for the bars of metal, and the back and ends are enclosed in a stout iron frame. The oil – derived from water-gas and tar – is contained in a tank as high as the roof, fixed outside the shed, and is conducted through pipes to the furnace. A current of air from the fan blows past the oil-cock and drives the fluid into the furnace. The heat generated from combustion of the oil is regular and intense; the whole contrivance is speedy and simple.

This is so, however, only when the oil is good and clear. Then there will be scarcely any smoke or fume. The slight flame emitted from the vent-hole on top will be of a copperish colour, and the interior will glitter like a star. The furnace will go right merrily; there will be no need for the workman to wait a moment. But when the oil is cheap and inferior, or absolutely worthless – as it often is at the shed – the system is a most foul and abominable nuisance. As soon as the forger attempts to light up in the morning, tremendous clouds of black, filthy smoke pour out of every little crack and hole and mount into the roof. After striking against the boards and rafters this beats down to the ground again and rolls away up the shed, filling the place from end to end, half suffocating the workmen with the sickening, disgusting stench, and making their eyes smart and burn. Several times during the operation of lighting up, by reason of the irregular flow through the feeder, the oil in the furnace will explode with a loud bang, shooting out the flames and smoke to a great distance, and frequently blowing the whole front of the forge to pieces, to the great danger of the stampers and the amusement of the other workmen and smiths – for the oil system of heating is not at all popular with the men of the shed.

The stampers' furnaces, to the number of five or six, are behaving in the same manner, and as there are no chimneys to carry off the smoke the whole smother is poured out into the shed. This will very soon be more than the average man can stand. With loud shouts and curses, down go hammers and tools; the blast is shut off from the fires and a rush is made for the open air until the nuisance is somewhat abated. The overseer walks round and round, viewing the scene with great ill-temper, defending the oil and the furnaces, and blaming the lighters-up for everything, at the same time darting angry looks at those who, half suffocated, have sought refuge outside. So, no matter what the time of year may be, whether summer or the dead of winter, when the chilling winds drive through upon the stampers shivering at their fires, he has every door and window thrown open, and often does it himself and stands like a sentinel in the doorway, that no one shall close them up till he is quite satisfied. If he moves away and the half-frozen workmen steal along and adjust the doors, he returns, closes them entirely, and forces the stampers to endure the whole smother, because they dared to meddle with the doors when he had opened them.

By and by, as the heat in the furnaces increases, the smoke will diminish somewhat, though as long as the oil is inferior they will continue to emit a dirty cloud accompanied with deadly fumes and intense volumes of heat, which are forced out by the blast to a distance of several yards, making it impossible for the youth to get near enough to attend to his bars without having his arms and face scorched and burnt. The roof and walls, for a great distance around, are blackened with the soot. There is no mistaking the cause of it, though it is a favourite recommendation of the oil furnaces that they consume every particle of their vapour. When the oil is of a sufficiently good quality this actually happens; it is only when the fuel is cheap and bad that considerable unpleasantness arises.

Our entry to the shed was made through the large door in the north-west corner, near which the first oil furnace is situated. This furnace is attached to a new kind of forging machine conveniently named the 'Ajax,' by reason of its great strength. Ajax was the name of two of the mighty ones who fought before Troy, but the manufacturer does not inform us whether the machine is named after Ajax, the son of Telamon, or he that was the son of Oileus, though perhaps the latter is intended. Standing alongside the oil furnace is the first of the drop-stamper's forges, and next to that, in a line, are the three drop-stamps themselves. Opposite the Ajax is the foreman's office – a two-storied building – and a little to one side, straight from the door, is a coal furnace, upon which is superimposed a large 'loco' boiler. This reflects a tremendous heat all round, and, together with the furnaces and forges, makes that part of the shed, though near to the door, almost unbearably hot, so that it has come to be called 'Hell Corner' by the workmen.

The line of hammers and furnaces is continued up the workshop to the far end under the wall. There also, fixed to the masonry, are the main shafting and pulleys, whirled round at a tremendous rate by the engine in the 'lean-to' outside. At the end of the line stand the heavy steam-hammers and, under the wall outside, the blower house, containing machinery for forcing the air for the smiths' fires. A huge stack of coal and coke is visible through the door at the other end. A small single fan is attached to the oil furnace with the Ajax in order to supply it with air. This travels at a high rate of speed and makes a loud roar, thereby adding to the confused din of the hammers and other machinery. Standing further out in the shed is a second row of smaller steam-hammers and forges with drills, saws, shears, pneumatic apparatus, other oil furnaces, and the American stamping-hammers with their trimmers and appliances. Beyond them is an open space reserved for future arrivals in the shape of manufacturing plant, and towards the south wall are two lines of powerful hydraulic machines and presses with furnaces and boilers attached for heating the plates of metal for punching and welding.

The Ajax machine operates by up-setting. It is worked by youths, one of whom heats the rods of metal, while the other sets them in the dies and presses the treadle that brings the machine head forward. As soon as the furnace is sufficiently hot fifteen or twenty bars are thrust through the brickwork in front of the forge, the lubricators are filled, the belt pulled over, and the work begins. The belts flap up and down on the pulleys with a loud noise, the cog-wheels rattle and clank, the 'ram' travels backwards and forwards incessantly, clicking against the self-act, the furnace roars and the smoke and flames shoot out. When the bars are white-hot the assistant hands them along; his mate grips them and inserts them in the dies, then presses the treadle with his foot. Immediately the steel tools close up and the ram shoots forward; in about two seconds the operation is complete. Very often the water, running continually over the tools to keep them cool, becomes confined in the dies as they close. The heat of the iron converts it into steam, and, as the ram collects and forces the material, it explodes with a loud report, almost like that of a cannon. Showers of sparks and hot scale are blown in all directions, and if the operator is not careful to stand somewhat aside, his face and arms will be riddled with the tiny particles of shot-like metal ejected by the explosion. It is not uncommon to see his flesh covered with drops of blood from the accident. The bits of metal will adhere tightly underneath the skin, and must be removed with a needle, or otherwise remain till they work out of their own accord.

Both youths of the Ajax dwell in the town, and are known about the corner by the names of Harry and Sammy. Harry's father was an infantryman, and Sammy's parent served in the Navy. There is a little of the roving spirit about both of them – each possesses a share of the paternal characteristic. Harry's father, however, is an invalid, and he is forced to stay at home and help keep him and his mother, otherwise he would long ago have bidden farewell to the shed, Ajax and all. Sammy, on the other hand, is free and unfettered, but though he has made many attempts to enter the Navy, they were all in vain. First, he was not sufficiently tall or broad in the chest, and later, when, after a course of exercises with dumb-bells, he was able to pass the examinations, he was refused on account of his teeth, which were badly decayed. This was a great disappointment to Samuel. He sulked about for several days afterwards, quarrelled and fought with his mate, and was generally inconsolable. The boys' chargeman had to intervene as peacemaker and he comforted Sammy, who shed a few tears and finally became reconciled to the forge again, though he often defiantly affirmed that he would not be beaten, not he! He would go to Bristol and get a job aboard ship; he would not stop there in that hole all his life!

Both Sammy and Harry dress much alike, and they resemble each other in their habits. They are both nimble and strong, active, energetic, and high spirited. Both have commendable appetites, and they are especially fond of drinking tea. They have a passionate regard for sports, including boxing and football, but, over and above all this, they are hard workers; every day they are sure of a good sweating at the furnace and

Ajax. Both wear football shirts – Sammy a green one and Harry a red and white – in the forge, and they have football boots on their feet. If you should turn out Sammy's pockets you would be sure to find, among other things, half a packet of cigarettes, a pack of cards, a mouth organ, a knife, a comb, and a small portion of looking-glass. A great many of the town boys and young men carry a small mirror in their pockets, by the aid of which they comb and part their hair and study their physiognomies. At meal-times, as soon as the hooter sounds, they hasten to the

Policeman and crowd in New Market Hall, Commercial Road, about 1904–05:
now a car park

nearest water-tap, give their faces a rough swill and, with the aid of a portion of looking-glass, examine them to make sure that they are free from the dust and soil of the smoky furnace.

Though the companions of Ajax work hard and perspire much they do not become very tired, apparently, for after the most severe exertions they are still ready to indulge in some sport or other, and run and play or wrestle and struggle with each other on their way down the yard. Arrived home they have their tea, wash and change, and come back to the crowded parts of the town to see and be seen and be moved on by the policeman, returning late home to bed. In the morning they will often be sullen and short-tempered. This invariably wears off as the day advances, however, and they will soon be up to the usual games, singing popular songs and imitating the comic actors at the theatre, where they delight to go once or twice a week.

Close behind the oil furnace, in a recess of the wall, is the fan that drives the blast for this part of the shed, supplying four forges altogether. The fan itself is of iron, enclosed in a stout cast-iron shell or case, and is driven from a countershaft half-way up to the main shafting. Multiplication takes place through this from the top pulley, and whereas the main

Empire Theatre, 1913–14, seating about 1,000. Opened 1898 as Queen's
Theatre with *Dick Whittington* panto. First class touring plays and operas:
some pre-London. Demolished 1959

shaft will make but one hundred and twenty revolutions a minute, the fan below will, in that space, spin round two thousand times. As the engine is running day and night, for more than twenty hours out of the twenty-four, the number of revolutions made by the fan will be over two millions daily. Although, viewed on paper, these figures appear high, yet, if you should stand near and watch the fan itself, it would seem incredible to you that it would require such a long time in which to complete them. The speed is terrific, and this you may know by the sound, without troubling to look at the gear. The rate of the belts, from the pulleys on to the contershaft, is a further proof of the tremendous velocity of the machine. Although strained very tight on the wheels they make a loud noise, flapping sharply all the while; one may easily gauge the speed of an engine by the sound of the belts alone. The fan itself, at normal times, emits a loud humming noise, like that of a threshing-machine, but when the speed of the engine increases through the relaxation of some other machinery, or the sudden rise of steam pressure in the boilers, it seems to swell with a dreadful fury, and assails the ear with a vicious and continuous *hoo-hoo-hoo-hoo-hoo*, *HOO-HOO-HOO-HOO-HOO*, like some savage beast ravenous for its prey. The oscillation of the fan is imparted to everything around. The very ground under your feet trembles, and if you should place your hand upon the outer shell, or on the wooden guard around it, you would experience something like an electric shock, strangely pleasant at first, but very soon necessitating the removal of your hand from the vicinity.

It is dangerous to meddle with the fan while it is in motion. A stout wooden guard is erected around it to prevent any object from coming into contact with the wheels or the interior. If a nut or rivet head should happen to fly and be caught in it, the shell would immediately burst. Very often excessive speed alone will cause a fan to explode. The effect is similar to that of a steam or gas explosion; the heavy cast-iron frame will be shattered to bits, and hurled to a great distance. I remember one in the smithy that exploded and blew up through the roof, making a huge rent. For safety's sake the fans are often constructed underground in order to lessen the danger of explosion, if one should happen.

It is remarkable that while the pulley on the countershaft is travelling at a tremendous speed, so that the spokes are generally invisible, and there appears to be nothing but the rim and centre whirling round, if you look up quickly you will see one spoke quite plainly as it flies over, then it will be entirely lost to view with the rest. The space of time during which it is visible is exceedingly short – it could be no more than a fraction of a second – yet in that brief period the eye perceives it clearly and distinctly: it is something similar to taking a snapshot with a camera.

Formerly, when all the belts were of leather and thickly studded with large broad-headed copper rivets, the boys used to draw near to them and take small lessons in electricity. This could only be done in the case of belts that travelled at a very high rate of speed, such as the one on the fan or the circular saw. Standing dangerously near the wheels they held a finger, or a knuckle, very close to the belt in motion, and were rewarded with seeing a small stream of electric sparks, about as large in volume as the stem of a needle, issuing from the finger-tip or knuckle, accompanied with a slight pain like that produced by the prick of a pin. The velocity of the belt, with the copper, attracted the electricity within the body and drew it out in a tiny visible stream from the flesh. All the belts for high speed work at this time, however, are made of another material, *i.e.*, a preparation of compressed canvas, without rivets. Instead of being laced together they are fitted with a steel-wire arrangement for connection. The ends are inserted, as you would bend the fingers of both hands and thrust them one between the other, and a piece of whalebone is pushed through. Slight as this may seem to be, it is yet capable of withstanding a great strain, and the whole runs much more smoothly than did the old-fashioned leather belts.

A man is specially kept to attend to everything pertaining to the belts. He is known to all and sundry as the 'strappie.' Directly anything goes wrong with the connections he appears on the scene smothered in oil from head to foot, and looking very cloudy and serious. He is usually in a great hurry and is not over-polite to anyone. First of all he gives the signal to have the engine stopped. As soon as the shafting is still, armed with a very sharp knife, he climbs up the wall, in and out among the wheels, and unceremoniously cuts away the defective belt. Arrived on the ground again, he draws out the belt, motions 'right away' to the engineman, then rolls it up and disappears. In a short while he comes back with it strongly repaired, or brings a new one in place of it. The shafting is stopped again, and up he mounts as before. When he has placed it over the shaft and connected the ends, he pulls it half-way on the wheels and ties it loosely in that position with a piece of cord. As the engine starts the belt assumes its position on the wheel automatically; the piece of cord breaks, or becomes untied, and falls to the ground, and everything goes spinning and whirling away as before. If a belt is merely loose the strappie brings a potful of a substance he calls 'jam,' very resinous and gluey, some of which he pours on the wheel and belt while in motion. This makes the belt 'bite,' or grip well, and brings the machine up to its maximum speed with the shafting.

Sometimes, if the shafting has not been oiled punctually, it will run hot, or perhaps a small particle of dust will obstruct the oil in the lubricator and produce friction. News of this is soon published abroad by a loud creaking noise that everyone can hear. The workmen take up the cry and shout 'Oil, oil,' at the top of their voice; then the engine-driver comes forth with his can and stops the screeching. Occasionally the spindle of the fan will run hot, and especially so if the belt happens to be well tight. This, by reason of its great speed, will soon generate a fierce heat; I recently ran to attend to it and found the spindle of the fan a bright red-hot. Thanks to the warning of the belt, which was slipping owing to the greater exertion required through tightening of the bearings by expansion, I was just in time to prevent an accident. In another moment the fan might have been a total wreck.

Through a doorway in the wall, in an extension of the shed, stand several boilers used as auxiliaries, and, near to them, are two powerful pumping engines and their accumulators, which obtain the pressure for the whole hydraulic plant of the department. The engines are of a hundred and twenty horse-power each, and are fitted with heavy fly-wheels that make forty revolutions a minute at top speed. These draw the water from a neighbouring tank and force it into the accumulators, from which the pressure is finally derived. The accumulators are constructed in deep pits that are bricked round and guarded with iron fencing. They are large weights of fifty tons each – there was originally one of a hundred tons – and are built about a central column of iron or steel standing fifteen or twenty feet above the floor level. Contained in the lower part of the weight is a cylinder; into this the water is forced by the engines and the pressure obtained. The power of the water, when a sufficient volume has accumulated, raises the weights high into the roof and keeps them there, with a little rising and falling, corresponding to the action of the presses in the shed. When the weights have risen to a certain point they operate a self-act, and the engines stop. Similarly, when they sink below the point they displace a second small lever that communicates with the engine valves and re-starts the pumps. The pressure put on the water is enormous; it often amounts to two thousand pounds per square inch. Since the operation of water is much slower than that of steam, however, the power is not nearly as effective. It would be impossible by its agency to drive machinery at a high rate without the use of gear, though for punching, pressing, and welding some kinds of work the system is admirable and unsurpassed.

The engine that drives the lesser machinery of the shop stands in a 'lean-to' and is not nearly as powerful as are those that operate the pumps. A little higher up, in another small lean-to, is a donkey engine that drives the 'blower,' which produces blast for the forges and fires. This machine is vastly superior to the old-fashioned fan, and the speed of it is quite low; there is no danger of explosion or other rupture. It is a pleasure, since so much manufacturing plant is introduced to us from foreign countries – America, France and Germany – to reflect that the idea of the blower is English. There is a considerable amount of American-made machinery at the works, and the percentage of it increases every year, though it is often far from being successful. At the same time, it must be conceded that our kinsmen over the sea are very clever in the designing and manufacture of tools and plant, and many of their ideas are particularly brilliant. The English maker of manufacturing tools follows at some little distance with his wares. These, though not actually as smart as the others, are yet good, honest value, the very expression of the Englishman's character. The chief features of American machinery are – smartness of detail, the maximum usefulness of parts, capacity for high speed and flimsiness, styled 'economy,' of structure: everything of theirs is made to 'go the pace.' English machinery, on the other hand, is at the same time more primitive and cumbersome, more conservative in design and slower in operation, though it is trustworthy and durable; it usually proves to be the cheaper investment in the long run. One often sees American tackle broken all to pieces after several years' use, while the British-made machine runs almost *ad infinitum*. At a manufactory in Birmingham is an old beam engine that has been in use for more than a century and a half, and it is almost as good now as when it was new. The same may be said with regard to English-made agricultural machinery. A modern American mower will seldom last longer than four or five years, but I know of English machines that have been in use for nearly thirty years and are as good as ever, generally speaking.

One man attends to the engines that drive the shop machinery and the 'blower.' It is his duty to see that the shafting is kept clean and the bearings well oiled, to watch over the belts and to notify the strappie when one becomes loose or slips off the wheel. Dressed in a suit of blue overalls, and equipped with ladder and oil-can, he remains in constant attendance upon his engines and shafts. He will also be required to keep a watchful eye upon the valves, to regulate the steam to the cylinders, and to maintain a uniform rate of speed for the lathes and drills. Occasionally, if the pressure of steam in the boilers should rise very suddenly – which sometimes happens, as the result of a variable quality of coal and the diversity of heats required by the furnacemen – the engine, in spite of the regulators, will rapidly gain speed and 'run away,' as it is called. This may also result from the disconnecting a particular machine engaged on heavy, dragging work, such as the saw, or fan, both of which require great power to drive them at their high rate of speed.

Considerable danger attaches to the running away of an engine, especially where it is provided with a heavy fly-wheel. This, if it is whirled round at an excessive speed, is liable to burst, and the consequences, in a crowded quarter, would be disastrous. The danger of bursting lies in the tremendous throwing-off power generated from the hub of the wheel, about the shaft; as the sections forming the circle of the wheel are brought rapidly over there is a strong tendency for them to be cast off in the same manner as a stone is thrown from a sling. If the wheel is exactly balanced, however, and every part of precisely the same weight, so as to ensure perfectly even running on the shaft, the danger of bursting will be small. Grindstones burst much more commonly than do metal wheels. There is not the same consistency in stone as in iron; moreover, there may be a flaw somewhere that has escaped the eye of the fitter or overseer. Consequently, if the speed of the engine driving the stone should be immoderately increased, it will not be able to withstand the throw-off, and will fly to pieces, inflicting death, or very severe injuries upon all those in the vicinity.

CHAPTER X

STAMPING – THE DROP-HAMMER STAFF – ALGY AND CECIL –
PAUL AND 'PUMP' – 'SMAMER' – BOILERS – A NEAR SHAVE

The drop-stamps stand in the corner, close under the wall. They are
supplied by three coke forges, and by the coal furnace before mentioned.
A drop-stamp, or drop-hammer, is a machine used for stamping out all
kinds of details and uses in wrought iron or steel, from an ounce to
several hundredweights. It differs from a steam-hammer properly so
called in that while it is raised by steam power it falls by gravity, striking
the metal in the dies by its own impetus, whereas the steam-hammer
head is driven down by a piston. Three hands are employed at each
machine. They are – the stamper, his hotter, and the small boy who
drives the hammer. A similar number compose the night shift; the
machines are in constant use by night and day. All the work is done at the
piece rate, and the prices are low; the men have to be very nimble to earn
sufficient money to pay them for the turn.

The hands employed on the drop-hammers are of a fairly uniform
type, though there are several distinguished above the others by reason
of their individual features and characteristics. Chief among them are the
two young hammer boys, Algy and Cecil, Paul the furnaceman, and a
youth who rejoices in the preposterous nickname of 'Pump.' Algy drives
the end drop-stamp for the chargeman and Cecil the next one to it, larger
and heavier. Algy has several nicknames, one of which, from his
diminutive stature, being 'Teddy Bear,' and the other, carrying with it a
certain amount of sarcasm, is plain 'Jim.' Sometimes, also, he is called
'Dolly' or 'Midget.' Cecil boasts of a string of christian names, the
correct list being Cecil Oswald Clarence. Questioned concerning the
other members of the family he informs you that his brother is named
Reginald Cuthbert, his schoolgirl sister May Alberta, and his baby sister
Ena Merle. From some cause or other he himself has not obtained a

regular nickname; he is rather summarily addressed by his surname. No one in the shed ever deigns to call him by his christian name, it is too unusual and high-sounding, too aristocratic and superb. Bob or Jack would have been preferable; scarcely anyone at the works goes beyond a monosyllable in the matter of names.

The boys are of the same age – fifteen or thereabout – but they are dissimilar in stature and in almost every other respect. Algy is short and small, plump and sturdy, while Cecil is inclined to run. He is tall for his age, and very thin. His body is as flat as a man's hand; he has no more substance than a herring. Algy's features are round, regular, and pleasant; he is quite a handsome boy. His forehead slopes a little, his nose is perfect in shape. He has frank, grey eyes sparkling with fun and good-nature, a girlish mouth, and small, pretty teeth. Cecil, on the other hand, is not what one would style handsome. He has thin, hollow cheeks and small, hard features. His forehead is narrow, and his eyes are rather large and searching – expressing strength and keenness. His mouth is stern, and his lips pout a little: they are best represented by the French *s'allonger – les lèvres s'allongent*, as Monsieur Jourdain's did in Molière, when he pronounced the vowel sound of u. He has a particularly fine set of teeth, and he has a way of grizzing them together and showing them when in the act of making a special exertion that gives him a savage expression.

Both boys are pale. Algy's face, when it is clean, shines like a glass bottle; Cecil's skin is inclined to be yellow. Both have dark rings around the eyes, especially Cecil, who is the more delicate of the two – they are neither very robust-looking. Their hair is very long, and it stands out well from underneath their cloth caps and stretches down the cheeks before the ears. They are consequently often assailed with the cry – 'Get yer 'air cut,' or – 'You be robbin' the barber of tuppence,' or – 'Tell yer mother to use the basin,' suggesting that the boys' hair is cut at home. It is a common charge to lay to small boys in the shed that their mothers used to put a basin over their heads and cut the hair around the outside of it. Both boys wax indignant at being taunted about the basin, and reply to the other remark with, 'You gi' me the tuppence, then, an' I'll have it cut.' Occasionally, more by way of being sarcastic than out of any desire to show good-nature, the stampers will make a collection towards defraying the barber's expenses, and the next morning the boys will turn up at the shed nearly bald: they have had their hair cut this time with a vengeance.

Several times Algy has come to the shed wearing a pair of wooden clogs, but, as everyone teased him and called him 'Cloggy,' he cast them aside and would not wear them any more. Clogs belong rather to the

Midlands and the North of England, and are very rarely seen in the railway town. The least respectable of all the boys' clothing are their shirts. They are usually full of big rents, being split from top to bottom, or torn quite across the back, the lower part falling down and exposing the naked flesh for a space of a foot, and they are of an inscrutable colour. One day an entire sleeve of Algy's shirt dropped clean away, and Cecil's was rent completely up one side so that his entire flank and shoulder were visible. Though the stampers laugh at Cecil and sometimes grip hold of whole handfuls of his flesh, where the shirt is torn, he is not very much disconcerted. Algernon blushed considerably, however, when his mate quietly told him one day that he could see his naked posterior through a rent in his trousers.

Although the boys' clothing is untidy and dilapidated they are not kept short of food, and their appetites are truly enormous. They bring large parcels of provisions to the shed – thick chunks of bread and butter, rashers of raw bacon, an egg to boil or fry, and sometimes a couple of polonies or succulent sausages. The whole is tied up in a red dinner-handkerchief or wrapped in a newspaper; you would often have a difficulty in getting it into an ordinary-sized bucket. The youngsters have to stand a great deal of chaff over their parcels or provisions. The men often take them in their hands and weigh them up and down, showing them about the shed, and asking each other if they do not want to buy a pair of old boots. At breakfast- or dinner-time the lads obtain a roughly-made frying-pan, or take the coke shovel, and, after rubbing it out with a piece of paper, cook their food, usually frying it together and dipping their bread in the fat alternately. Then, if it is fine, still stripped of their waistcoats, they go out in the yard and sit down, or crouch by the furnace door and clear up the food to the last morsel; they will often not have finished when the hooter sounds the first time to warn the men to come back to the shed. When the meal is over, if there is yet time, Algy will produce from his pocket some literature of the Buffalo Bill type, or a school story, of which he is fond, and read it. Cecil will not deign to look at 'such stuff,' as he calls it, but will borrow a newspaper, or some part of one, from his mates, and greedily devour the contents of that.

Though neither of them has left school for more than a year, or, at the outside, fifteen months, they have forgotten almost everything they learned, even to the very rudiments in many cases. Their knowledge of grammar, arithmetic, poetry, geography, and history has entirely lapsed, or, if they remember anything at all, it will be but a smattering of each. To test their memory and knowledge of these matters the boys' chargeman occasionally offers them prizes, and enters them into competition with other lads of the shed, some of whom have not been away from school for more than five or six months, but one and all show a deplorable lack of the faculty of retention. Whether it is the result of too much cramming by the teacher, or whether it is that the rising generation is really deficient in mental capacity, they are quite incapable of answering the most simple and elementary questions. The chargeman's plan is to offer them pennies for the names of half-a-dozen capitals of foreign countries, half-a-dozen foreign rivers, six names of British kings or British rivers, the capitals of six English counties, or the names of the counties themselves, six fish of English rivers, six wild birds, half-a-dozen names of wild flowers, the capitals of British colonies, the names of six English poets, or a few elementary points of grammar, and so on.

The answers, when any are vouchsafed, are often ludicrous and amazing: the intellectual capacity of the boys is certainly not very brilliant. During these tests the chargeman was astonished to learn that Salisbury is a county, Ceylon is the capital of China, and that Paris stands on the banks of the river Liffey. As for the preterite tense, not one had ever heard of it. Only one out of six could give the names of the six counties and kings complete, though another of the lads had strong impressions concerning a monarch he called the 'ginger-headed' one, but he could not think of his name. Not one could furnish the requisite list of fish, fowl, and natural wild flowers, but little Jim, struck with a sudden inspiration, shouted out 'jack and perch,' for he had recently been fishing in the clay-pits with his brother. The others frankly confessed they did not know anything about the matter; if they had ever learned it at school they had forgotten it now. Anyway, it was not of much use to one, they said, though it was all right to know about it. Not one of the half-dozen, though all were born in the town, could give the name of a single Wiltshire river.

Paul is not permanently attached to the furnace in the corner, but came to fill the place of one who had met with an accident. As a matter of fact, Paul is everybody's man; he is here, there, and everywhere. He can turn his hand to almost anything in the second degree, and is a very useful stop-gap. Forge he cannot, stamp he cannot, though he is a capital heater of iron, and makes a good furnaceman; he is a fair all-round, inside man. But somehow or other, everyone persists in making fun of Paul, and contrives to play pranks and practical jokes upon him. Whatever job he is engaged upon his mates address ridiculous remarks to him; they will never take him seriously. Some one or other, in passing by, will knock off his hat; this one gravely takes him by the wrist and feels his pulse, and that one will give him a rough push. Another puts water over him from the pipe, pretending it was by accident; whatever reply he makes his mates only laugh at him. As a rule, Paul takes it all in good part, though sometimes he will lose his temper and retaliate with a lump of coal, or any other missile upon which he can lay his hands.

Paul would be the tallest man in the shed if it were not that he stoops slightly as the result of having had rheumatics. As it is, he is quite six feet in height, bony, but not fleshy, with broad shoulders and large limbs. As he walks his head is thrown forward; he goes heavily upon his feet. His features are regular and pleasant; he has grey eyes and bushy brows. His skin is dark with the heat and grime of the furnace; his expression is one of marked good-nature. In appearance he is a perfect rustic; there is no need to look at him the second time to know that he dwells without the municipal border. It is this air of rusticity, combined with his simplicity of character and behaviour, that makes Paul the butt of the other workmen. They would not think of practising their clownish tricks upon others, for there are many upon whom it would be very inadvisable to attempt a jest without being prepared for a sudden and violent reprisal.

Paul's home is in the village, about three miles from the town. There he passes his leisure in comparative quiet, and, in his spare time from the shed, cultivates a large plot of land and keeps pigs. This finds him employment all the year round, so that he has no time to go to the public-house or the football match, though he sometimes plays in the local cricket eleven. He takes great interest in his roots and crops, and almost worships his forty perch of garden. During the summer and autumn he brings the choicest specimens of his produce in his pocket and shows them to his mates in the shed; he usually manages to beat all comers with his potatoes and onions.

In spite of Paul's simplicity of behaviour, one cannot help being attracted to him by reason of his frankness and open-heartedness; he would not think of doing anything that is not strictly above board. Though rough and rude, blunt and unpolished, he is yet very honest and conscientious. Certainly he is not as sharp and intelligent as are many of the town workmen, but he is a better mate than most of them, and when it comes to work he will stand by you to the last; he is not one to back out at the slightest difficulty.

How Pump came to be Pump is a mystery; no one knows the origin of the nickname. 'They called I Pump a long time ago,' says he. Very likely it was given to him extemporaneously, with no particular relation to anything; someone or other said 'Pump,' and the name stuck there at once. Pump is just under eighteen years of age. He drives the heavy drop-stamp on the day-shift, and, owing to certain characteristics of which he is possessed, he always attracts attention. He is very loud and noisy, full of strong words and forcible language, though he is extraordinarily cheerful and good-natured. He is short in stature, very strong and much given to sweating; in the least heat his face will be very red and covered with great drops of perspiration. His forehead is broad and sloping, he has immense blue eyes, tapered nose, bronze complexion, a solid, square countenance, and a tremendous shock of hair. In driving the hammer he has acquired the unusual habit of following the heavy monkey up and down with his eyes, and the expression on his face, as he peers up into the roof, induces many to stop and take a peep at him as they pass by. To all such Pump addresses certain phrases much more forcible than polite, and warns them to 'clear out' without delay if they do not 'want something.' They usually respond with an extra-special grimace, or work their arms up and down as though they were manipulating the engine from which he derives his nickname.

As a mate Pump is variable. With the men of one shift he can agree very well, but with the others he is nearly always at loggerheads. The fact is that Pump's stamper on one shift does not like him, and will not try to like him, either. He quite misunderstands his driver's characteristics, and will not see his good qualities underneath a certain rugged exterior. Accordingly, they quarrel and call each other evil names all day. Very often the stamper will throw down his tongs and walk off. Thereupon Pump lowers the hammer defiantly, folds his arms, and tosses his head with disgust, while the furnaceman, waiting with his heat, calls to them to 'come on.' Now the stamper picks up his tongs quickly, shouts loudly to Pump, 'Hammer up, there!' and on they go again, the stamper snorting and muttering to himself, and glaring fiercely from side to side, while Pump bursts into song, with a broad grin on his countenance. Sometimes the stamper, in a towering fury, will not come to the chargeman and swear that he will not hit another stroke with 'that thing there,' and demand another mate forthwith, but with a little tact and the happy application of a spice of good-humour, the situation will be saved, and everything will go on right merrily, though the old trouble will certainly recur. Pump confides all his troubles to the chargeman and sheds a few tears now and then. He is full of good intentions and tries to do his level best to please, but he cannot avoid friction with his fiery and short-tempered mates of the fortnightly shift.

He has one very special and ardent desire, which is to go on night duty; he is for ever counting up the days and weeks that must pass before his birthday will arrive, and so raise him to the age necessary for undertaking the shift. In common with most other youths, he looks upon the night turn as something 'devoutly to be wished,' but I very much fear that a few weeks of the change will modify his opinion of the matter, if it does not entirely disillusion him. Notwithstanding a certain amount of novelty attaching to the working on the night-shift, it is attended with many hardships and inconveniences. The greater part of those who have to perform it would willingly exchange it for the day duty.

There was at one time another highly distinctive 'character' attached to the drop-stamps. He revelled in the nickname of 'Smamer.' Where he obtained the pseudonym is unknown, though it is notable that the word has an intelligible derivative. Smamer is undoubtedly derived from the Greek verb $\sigma\mu\hat{\alpha}\nu$=sman, meaning *to smear*, and, afterwards, from $\sigma\mu\hat{\alpha}\mu\alpha$[1]=soap, so that the nickname is meant to designate a smearer. As there are many who are in the habit of smearing their faces with soap, the nickname would seem to have a very wide and universal application. Be that as it may, our Smamer was a smearer of the first order; he usually stopped at that and did not care to prosecute the matter further. His face daily bore traces of the initial process of washing, and that only; it was a genuine smear and little besides. Whoever first honoured him with the appellation was a person of discernment, though he might not have been aware of the origin of the word. You often hear a workman say that So-and-so is 'all smamed up' with oil or some other greasy substance.

Smamer was one of the forge hands and heated iron for the middle drop-stamp. His home was in the country, several miles from the town; winter and summer he tramped to and from the shed. For several years after his father and mother died he lived in the cottage by himself, tilled his own garden, prepared his food, performed his housework, made his bed, and did his own washing, though he was no more than nineteen years of age. He was noted for his eccentric mode of living. Whatever the weather might be he scarcely ever wore an overcoat. He often came to work wet through to the skin, and reached home at night in the same condition, where he received no welcome of any sort, but had to light his own fire before he could dry his clothing or prepare his meal. To every inquiry as to whether he was wet or not he made one reply; he was 'just a little bit damp about the knees,' that was all.

[1] Classical, $\sigma\mu\hat{\eta}\nu$, $\sigma\mu\hat{\eta}\mu\alpha$.

In manner he was quiet and rather sullen; he was never very sweet-tempered, though he was a quick and clever heater of iron and a very good mate. About his native village he was rough and noisy, fond of fighting and disturbance. He was frequently in conflict with the police, and often on the point of being summoned before the Bench for some offence or other, but he usually scraped out of the difficulty at the last moment, either by means of apologies, or by making some kind of restitution to the injured party. At week-ends, with a band of associates, he paid visits to the neighbouring villages and fought with the young men, until the whole of them became so well-known to the police that wherever they went they were recognised and promptly hustled off in the direction of their native place.

During the autumn months Smamer visited all the orchards along the road on the way to work, and came to the shed with his pockets crammed full of apples. These he used to divide out among his mates, who ate them with little or no compunction; there is small searching of conscience among the boys of the factory, especially when the contraband happens to be sweet, juicy apples plucked from the farmer's trees. Very soon, however, the habit of the life began to tell upon him. His continually getting wet, and the having no one to provide him with any kind of comfort, ruined his constitution; in a few months he wasted away and died. A small party of mates from the shed attended the funeral at the little village churchyard: that was the end of Smamer. His place at the forge was soon filled; he was not missed very much. Everyone said he had but himself to blame; there was no sympathy meted out to him. His brother, who also worked on the drop-stamps, had been killed by a blow on the head with a piece of metal from the die only a short while before. They lay side by side in the little walled enclosure, for ever oblivious of the noise and din of the thunderous hammers and the grinding wheels of the factory.

There are several others, distinguished with titles of an expressive kind, working on the drop-stamps. Of these one answers to the nickname of 'Bovril,' one is 'Kekky Flapper,' one is 'Aeroplane Joe,' one 'Blubber,' and another is known about the shed as 'Wormy'. How they came to possess such inglorious appellatives cannot with certainty be told; a very little will suffice to brand you with an epithet in the work-shed. In addition to these, in the vicinity of the drop-stamps in the corner are an ex-groom, a grocer, a musical freak, a comedian, a photographer, a boy scout, a territorial, a jockey, a cowman, a pianoforte maker, and a local preacher.

Situated over the coal furnace that feeds the big drop-stamps is a boiler of the 'loco' pattern, one of those responsible for the tremendous din that is raised every day at meal-times when the steam is not required for the engines and hammers. These boilers have all served their time on the line – in passenger or goods traffic – and, after their removal from the engine frames, they have been distributed over the company's system and throughout the factories. The distance a boiler is required to travel under steam on the railway is about thirty thousand miles; after completing this it is superseded and removed from the active list on the permanent way. By the time the boiler and engine have travelled together so many miles they will be half worn out. The wheels, by reason of the frequent application of the brakes and 'skidding' on the rails, will be grooved and cut about, and the machinery will require new fittings and bearings. After the boilers have been removed from the frames they are overhauled and tested and then sold out to the different sheds and stations, wherever they may happen to be wanted.

The method of transacting business between the different sheds and departments at the works is exactly like that employed by outside firms and tradesmen. Bills and accounts are rendered, and the whole formula of hire and purchase is entered into by the different parties; everything, in fact, except the actual payment of money, is duly carried out. The sheds are required to show a balance on the right side at the end of each year; percentages are charged for working expenses, and all the rest is profit. Thus, some sheds will show profits of many thousands of pounds annually, though upon paper only; the surpluses do not exist in reality.

Although the new boiler costs £1,000 it is sold to the shed second-hand for £200, so that the cost of ten for the workshops was only £2,000. The charge for setting, and fitting, and also for repairs and cleaning, however, is very great; a big sum is needed to keep them in a fit condition for work. After they have been erected above the furnaces they are covered with a thick jacket of a compound of magnesia and fibre, to enable them to retain the heat, and they are afterwards painted black, so as to harmonise with the general environment. The steam pressure of the repaired boiler is usually fixed at about a hundred and twenty-five pounds per square inch. The capacity of each boiler is very great, and the composite power of the whole set formidable; if one of them should happen to explode the result would indeed be disastrous. A small staff of men superintends them by day and night, and greater care is taken of them than was the case formerly. I can remember when the shed was several times within a hair's breadth of being blown up and forty or fifty men hurled to perdition.

A few years ago, instead of trustworthy men being appointed to superintend the boilers, they were consigned to the charge of several youths, who were very careless and negligent in their work, and who seemed to have no idea whatever of the tremendous responsibility resting upon them for the safety and welfare of the life in the shed. Provided with mouth-organs and bones, or Jew's harps, they would play and skylark about for a long time and leave their boilers unattended at considerable risk. I have often known them to be away from their posts for an hour at a stretch, and to allow the water in the boilers to become almost entirely evaporated before they returned to fill them up again, which, as everyone knows, is an exceedingly dangerous practice. By the common regulation attaching to boilers, the water should never be permitted to fall below that point when it is visible in the gauge-glass. If it is allowed to do so the position becomes dangerous immediately, and, to obviate accident, the bars of the furnace fire should be withdrawn and no cold water admitted.

Once a youth – a wild, reckless fellow – was absent from the boiler an unusually long time in the middle of the morning before dinner. The stampers watched the water in the gauge-glass drop little by little and finally vanish, and still no one came to attend to it. Being a little anxious about it I sent several men and boys to try and find the boilerman, but without avail. His mates were nowhere to be found either, and the foreman was away from the shed at the time. From being anxious I soon felt alarmed. The matter was becoming serious, and we were not allowed, under any circumstances, to meddle with the injectors ourselves.

As I was warning all men in the locality of the danger the boilerman arrived, a little frightened, but in a desperate mood. I advised him to take the usual course in such a case, to have the fire withdrawn from the furnace and allow the boiler to burn, but as this would have meant certain dismissal for him he decided to risk everything and fill up the boiler or explode it. As he was determined in his foolhardy resolution we collected our mates and left the shed, retiring to a safe distance. By good fortune, however – by pure luck, and nothing else – the boiler received the water safely, though with a great deal of shuddering, and the danger was past. To make the best – or the worst – of it, there were three men on the back of the boiler at the time, laying on the coat of magnesia, for it had not been erected many days. Although we gave them warning of the danger they took not the slightest notice, but kept working away, in a hurry to get the job done, for it was piecework. If the boiler had exploded, packed as it was with terrific pressure and priming furiously, they would have been blown to atoms.

The bold and daring of the shed indulge in many jeers and uncomplimentary remarks, if some others, in the face of real danger, should adopt precautionary measures and take heed of their safety, but experience has taught me that it is better to be apprehensive and cautious and to take pains to safeguard oneself than to score a cheap victory by bravado and carelessness. When danger threatens in the factory, the best course is to stand quite clear at all costs; it is then no shame to put into practice the words of the old proverb, slightly amended: 'He that works and runs away will live to work another day.' By far the greater proportion of the accidents that happen daily at the works are the direct result of inattention, of not taking notice of warnings uttered by others, and the failure to exercise the instinct of self-preservation natural to each individual. It is not that the men are absolutely careless of themselves; it is rather that the care they do take is not considerable or sufficient.

CHAPTER XI

FORGING AND SMITHING – HYDRAULIC OPERATIONS – 'BALTIMORE' –
'BLACK SAM' – 'STRAWBERRY' AND GUSTAVUS – THE 'FIRE KING' –
'TUBBY' – BOLAND – PINNELL OF THE YANKEE PLANT

The drop-stamps and forgers, together with the plant known as the
Yankee hammers – so called by reason of their having been introduced
from the other side of the Atlantic – are the life and soul of the shed. The
hydraulic machines, through their noiseless and almost tedious operation
and the considerably less skill required on the part of the workmen in
carrying out the various processes, are dull and tame in comparison with
them. The steam-hammers, both by their noise, speed, and visible
power and by the alertness and dexterity of the stampers and forgers, are
certain to compel attention. There is a great fascination, too, in standing
near the furnace and watching the sparkling, hissing mass of metal being
withdrawn by the crane, or seeing the heated bars removed from the oil
forge and clapped quickly on the steel dies to be beaten into shape. No
one can withstand the attraction of the steam-hammers; even those who
have spent a lifetime in the shed like to stand and watch the stampers and
forgers at work.

Forging and smithing are, without doubt, the most interesting of all
crafts in the factory; other machinery, however unique it may be, will
not claim nearly as much attention. Visitors will pass by the most
elaborate plant to stand near the steam-hammers, or to watch the smith
weld a piece of iron on the anvil. The small boy who has just been
initiated into the shed, the youth, the grown-up man, and the grey-
haired veteran are bound to be attracted by the flashing of the furnace and
the white-hot metal newly brought out. They are greatly delighted, too,
with the long, swinging blow of the forging hammers, or the short,
sharp stroke of the stampers; to watch the metal being transposed and
conforming to the pressure of the dies, to see the sparks shooting out in

white showers, and the men sweating; to feel the earth shaking, and to hear the chains jingling, the steam hissing and roaring and the blows echoing like thunder all the time. To stand in the midst of it and view the whole scene when everything is in active operation is a wonderful experience, thrilling and impressive. You see the lines of furnaces and steam-hammers – there are fifteen altogether – with the monkeys travelling up and down continually and beating on the metal one against the other in utter disorder and confusion, the blazing white light cast out from the furnace door or the duller glow of the half-finished forging, the flames leaping and shooting from the oil forges, the clouds of yellow cinders blown out from the smiths' fires, the whirling wheels of the shafting and machinery between the lines and the half-naked workmen, black and bareheaded, in every conceivable attitude, full of quick life and exertion and all in a desperate hurry, as though they had but a few more minutes to live. And what a terrific din is maintained! You hear the loud explosion of the oil and water applied for removing the scale and excrescence from the iron, the ring of the metal under the blows of the stampers or of the anvil under the sledge of the smiths, the simultaneous priming of the boilers, the horrible prolonged screeching of the steam-saw slowly cutting its way through the half-heated rail, the roaring blast, the bellowing furnace, the bumping Ajax, the clanking cogwheels, the groaning shears, and a hundred other sounds and noises intermingled. There is the striker's hammer whirling round, this one pulling and heaving, the forgeman running out with his staff, the stamper twisting his bar over, the furnaceman charging in his fuel, the white slag running out in streams sparkling, spluttering, and crackling, the steam blown down from the roof through the open door, the thick dust, the almost visible heat, the black gloom of the roof and the clouds of smoke drifting slowly about, or hanging quite stationary like a pall, completely blotting out the other half of the shed, all which form a scene never to be forgotten by those who shall happen to have once viewed it.

The hydraulic work, on the other hand, though interesting, is not engrossing. There is a lack of life and animation in it; it is not stirring or dramatic. The huge 'rams' of the presses, though capable of exerting a pressure equal to two hundred tons weight, descend very slowly; the quick, alert steam-hammer could strike at least ten or a dozen blows while the ram is once operating. So rapid is the blow of the steam-hammer that the pressure raised in the metal by the impact of the dies is often still unspent when the hammer rebounds, so that, as the dies separate, if the metal is very hot, it explodes and flies asunder. The speed of the rebound may be gauged by the fact that the stamper can actually see the flow of metal in the dies from the blow after the hammer has left it. The metal, as the result of this, will frequently overflow the edge of the bottom die, and when the hammer descends again the top die will have to shear away a quarter, or half an inch.

It is instructive to note the effect of the blows on the hot metal. Continual beating it will quickly raise the temperature of the iron or steel; I have many times raised the heat of a piece in operation from a dull yellow to a brilliant welding pitch during the delivery of three or four blows. Hammers have recently been invented that, with continually beating on cold metal, will make it sufficiently hot to allow of drawing and shaping; but though such machinery is interesting, it is not of much use for serious manufacture. Compressed air, directed on metal of a dull yellow heat, will soon considerably increase its temperature; you may easily burn a hole quite through a six-inch steel bloom by the method.

The flying of sparks through the air will greatly intensify their heat; after travelling a few yards they will become very dazzling and brilliant and explode like fireworks. Sometimes a piece of this superfluous metal, an ounce or more in weight, forced out from the die with the blow, will shear off and fly to a great distance – often as much as sixty or seventy yards. This, at the moment of leaving the die, may be no more than a dull yellow, but by the time it falls to the ground it will be intensely hot and will throw off a shower of hissing sparks. The shearing-off of the bur is a source of great danger to the workmen. I have several times been struck with pieces and been brought to the ground in consequence; the effect is almost as though you had been struck with a bullet from a gun.

Nothing of this kind is ever possible with the hydraulic machines. If a weld is to be made it must be performed with one stroke of the ram; after the top die leaves the metal it will be too cool to receive any benefit from a second application of the power. Welding by hand or steam power is always preferable to that performed by hydraulic action; a joint that is made with six or ten small quick blows will be far more effective and durable than where the iron has been simply squeezed together by one operation of the ram. As soon as the hydraulic dies meet the metal is considerably chilled. Instead of intensifying the heat, as in the case of the steam-hammer, the cold tools greatly lessen it. The weld, when made, will most certainly be short and brittle.

Some portion of the personnel of the shed has already been given, but of the hundred and fifty comprising the permanent staff of the place several are conspicuous among the rest for strangeness of habit, queer characteristics, or strong personality. The men are a mixture of many sorts and of several nationalities – English, Scotch, Welsh, and Irish. There is the shabby-browed, fierce-looking son of Erin; the canny Scot from Motherwell over the border; the gruff and short-tempered old furnaceman from Dowlais; the doughty forger from Middlesborough; the cultured cockney with his superb nasal twang; the Lancastrian with his picturesque brogue; a representative of distant Penzance; an ex-seaman, nicknamed 'The Jersey Lily,' from the Channel Islands, and those hailing from nearly every county in the Midlands and south of England, from 'Brummagem Bill' to 'Southampton Charlie.' There are ex-soldiers and sailors with arms and breasts tattooed with birds, flowers, serpents, fair women and other emblems, and who have seen service in the East and West Indies, China, Egypt, or the Transvaal; those who constantly pride themselves on having once been in gentlemen's service – though they do not tell you how they came to leave it! – butchers and bakers, professional football players, conjurers, bandsmen, and cheap-jacks.

'Baltimore' works the middle drop-stamp, about halfway up the shed, and, in the line of smaller steam-hammers opposite to him, toils a mulatto known to everyone about the place as 'Black Sam,' or 'Sambo.' They are old hands, having both come to the premises as boys, where they have since been, except for the time when 'Balty' was absent for the annual training in the local Militia. It is not explained how he came to receive the nickname. Black Sam is so called from his very dark complexion, his short, black, curly hair and large, dark eyes. Baltimore is rather ordinary in appearance. His forehead is low, his cheek-bones high and his nose irregular. His lips are thick, he has a pointed chin and lantern jaws. He is of medium height, square and broad shouldered. As he walks his shoulders sway to and fro and up and down, keeping time with his footsteps; he is exceedingly unmilitary both in physique and movement.

It was by reason of these characteristics that Baltimore obtained the attention of his shopmates. They all laughed rudely to see him in the old-time Militia uniform – scarlet tunic much too big, with regulation white belt, baggy trousers too long in the legs, heavy bluchers on the feet and, instead of the swagger headgear worn in the Service today, the old Scotch cap with long streamers behind and a little swishing cane in the hand or under the arm. It is carefully handed down and passed from one to the other that when Balty was at home on furlough all the small boys of the street would gather round him, sniggering and jeering, and making fun of his cut and appearance, and it is said furthermore that he

used very unceremoniously to drive them away with his cane crying –
'Get out, you young varmints! 'Aven't you never see a sojer before?' In
the shed and at the furnace he continued to attract attention and be the
subject of jocular remarks made by his workmates. They never would
take him seriously, not even though he came in time to work one of the
biggest drop-stamps and be reckoned among the honourable company
of forgers.

To all the superfluous attentions and mock regard of his fellow-mates
Baltimore preserves a good-natured and even an indulgent attitude; he is
not at all disconcerted with their wit and sarcasm. Though not one of the
most skilful of workmen, he is very shrewd and painstaking; his whole
heart and soul are in the business. From morning till night he is toiling
and sweating over his blooms and forgings, and when he is off the
premises he is still concerned with his occupations at the hammer. He
will sometimes tell one of his mates how he lay awake the greater part of
a night working out in his mind some problem connected with a difficult
piece of forging and then came in the next morning and triumphantly
finished the job.

Sambo's father was an army veteran, a sergeant, who took for his wife
an Indian woman and became the parent of a family, of whom Samuel is
the eldest. He is of medium height, thin, but very erect, with low
shoulders and long neck. The forehead is sloping, the nose rather thick.
He has large dark eyes with tremendous whites, short woolly hair, high
cheekbones, skin very dark and sallow. The whole countenance is long
and the head angular; he has the clear characteristics of the half-cast. The
general opinion is that Sambo is out of place in the shed. He ought rather
to have been trained for a life on the stage; without doubt he would have
made a good pantomimist. Both his appearance and manner are comical;
he causes everyone to smile by reason of his ludicrous expressions and
grotesque facial contortions.

Sambo is quite aware of his own funniosity and readily lends himself
to the amusement of the small fry that sometimes comes to gaze upon
him. Snatching up a shovel, he claps it to his shoulder as though it were
the traditional nigger's instrument and, rolling his eyes and turning up
the whites of them, pretends to be fingering the banjo while he sings a
few lines of the 'Swanee River' or other coon song. Sambo has always
been the butt of the rougher section in the shed and has been forced to
suffer many indignities. It was a common thing for the bullies of the
place to throw him on the ground and disgrace him. This they continued
to do long after he had married and become the father of children.

Working just beyond Sambo, at the next furnace, is the very shadow of a man – a mere frame, a skeleton, which a good puff of wind might very likely throw down. He is stripped to the waist and hatless. His hair is long and it stands upright. His flannel shirt is thrown open; his trousers merely hang on him, and he is as black as a sweep with the smoke and grime of the furnace. This is 'Strawberry,' sometimes also known as 'Gooseberry.' His features are remarkably small and fine, and his neck is no bigger round than a span. He does not appear strong enough to do any work, but, for all that, he is very tough and wiry. Many a one laughs at him and tells him that he is melting away 'like a tallow candle,' but he answers them all boldly and tells them, with a merry twinkle in his tiny dark eyes, that he is all right. 'You look after yourself, mate, and don't fret about me,' says he.

Strawberry was at one time a cobbler, and used to get his living by the patching up and renovation of old soles. Long after he entered the shed he kept up the employment in his spare time, but by and by he discontinued the work and betook himself to the more genteel though less lucrative pursuits of flute-playing and photography. For a time he donned uniform and played in the local band, and then, after a while, that had to be discontinued. Now all his thought and care is to take photographs and make models of steam-engines, magic lanterns and cinematographic instruments. Mounted on a cycle, and provided with a camera, he scours the country round at week-ends for customers and comes home and does the developing and printing on Sundays. He is thoroughly versed in time exposures and the various mysteries of photographic development. Wherever he goes he carries a book of instructions in his pocket, and if you stop to speak with him for a moment he is sure to tell you of some new lens or snap-shot arrangement he has lately made, or wearies you nearly to death with an attempted explanation of the compounds in his home-made developers – 'Hypo-tassum' something or other, and the rest of it.

Another of Strawberry's hobbies is the blind poring over fusty books, several hundreds of years old, bought at auctions and usually fit for nothing but the fire or dust-heap. These he treasures with great care, and he is frequently trying to expound the contents of them to his work-mates, and to any others who will suffer to listen to him for a few moments. His latest passion is to seek out old caves, ruins and legendary sites; he is musician, artist, engineer, archæologist and antiquarian combined. I much fear, however, that he will suffer the furnaceman's fate in the end and perish of the smoke and heat of the fires.

Strawberry succeeded Gustavus, who died under very sad circumstances. Poor Gus was most unfortunate, though such cases as his are not of uncommon occurrence. He had been through the war in South Africa, and had fought there for his country. He had not been long on the furnace. His health was not good at the best of times. If regard for a man's health were had at the time of putting him on a job Gus would never have gone to the fires, but there is a ruthless, and very often a sinister, disregard of a man's physical condition when he is wanted to fill a difficult post. About a year before Gus's wife contracted milk fever, after confinement. This affected her reason and she had to be removed; her case was pronounced hopeless – absolutely hopeless. This came as a great shock to Gus; there were five little children, all babies, one of them new-born. He had no friends to come and take care of them and he was poor – very poor. Accordingly, with a little assistance from the neighbour, he determined to look after them himself. The oldest boy prepared the meals by day; Gus saw to the general needs at night and did the washing Sundays. Very soon one of the mites fell ill and had to go to the workhouse hospital. All the others but one suffered sickness, and Gus very soon followed suit. Worn out with the day's work at the furnace and obliged to toil and watch half the night over his infants, he soon fell a prey to ill-health, and was compelled to stop at home from work.

Then the little stinging insects of the shed began to cavil and sneer. 'He's oni shammin'. Ther's nothin' the matter wi' he. He's as well as I be. He oni wants to shirk the furnace. Kip un to't when a comes in.' By and by Gus started work again, but not till the overseer had played a treacherous trick upon him and tried to have him rejected at the medical examination through an innocent and incautious remark he had chanced to let fall concerning himself. The fact of the matter was, Gus was a broken, ruined man. His general health was gone. His sight was failing; his constitution was wrecked. For several weeks he dragged himself to work, in a last desperate effort to keep a home for his babes and supply them with food, though anyone might have seen that he was in positive torture all the while. At last he could bear up no longer. He came to work the fore part of the week, then stopped at home; in three days he was dead. His little boys and girls went to the workhouse, or to charities. One has to die before his mates in the shed think there is anything the matter with him. Then, in nine cases out of ten – especially if he happens to be one of the poorest and most unfortunate – he is mercilessly sneered over. Probably that was his own fault. They even blame him for dying; in three days he is almost totally forgotten. Cruel hearts and feelings are bred in the atmosphere of the factory.

There is one 'Fire King' and only one; all the others are mere apprentices – nobodies. He comes from 'The North,' from Middlesborough, of great iron fame. Without doubt he is a marvel. He is always talking about the 'haats' they used to draw 'way up there.' It was prodigious. There is nothing like it down south. 'Wales! I tell you Wales is a dunghill; they can't do it for nuts.' He looks at you with inexpressible scorn. Then he plunges the bar into the furnace hole and stirs up the coals, 'stops up' again, peers through the iron door and comes back mopping his face with the wiper. 'I tell you tha be a lot o' cowbangers about here. Tha never sin a furnace nor a haat afore. When I was at Sunderland' – here he gives an especially knowing wink, and scratches one side of his nose with his forefinger, drawing his head near to your ear and speaking in an undertone – 'when I was at Sunderland, though I says it myself, there wasn't a man on the ground as could hold a candle to Phil Clegg. The manager allus used to stop and talk to me about the haats, and slip a crown piece into mi hand for a drink. "Clegg," says he, "I've learned from you what I never knew before."' All this is accepted with reserve in the shed. It may or may not have been true; one is not compelled to believe all the extraordinary reports circulated by the forgers and furnacemen.

Some years ago the doughty one was set to do some initial forging in steel blooms and spoiled three parts of the material by overheating. 'Bad steel! damn bad steel! 'Twunt stand a bit o' haat,' said he. The matter was accordingly reported to the managers, and word was sent to the firm that had manufactured the blooms – 'Bad steel! Bad steel,' passed all along the line. Then the manufacturers' representative came to inspect the process and to report upon the quality of the metal. The Fire King scraped his leg and scratched his nose and talked much of 'kimicals,' winking at his mates and getting his metal to a fizzing heat. 'Too hot, too hot,' said the representative. 'Aye! man, but we must get it so hot or the hammer wunt bate it down,' the Fire King replied. 'Get a heavier hammer,' said the inspector, touching the spot immediately, and walking off in disgust. The steel was all right, it was merely overheated. Thereafter the Fire King's prestige visibly diminished. He became the scorn of the furnaces; he was humbled and disgraced for ever. He was subsequently put in charge of the damping-up of the furnaces, and he styled himself foreman of the night shift there, which was one, besides himself.

After all, 'Tubby' is the best furnaceman. He hails from Wales, 'the true old country, where the men comes from,' according to him. Tubby is short, fat and round, about the size of a thirty-six barrel, and he is extremely short-legged. His head is quite bald and shines well. His features are regular and well-formed. He has an aristocratic nose, thick neck, and shoulders shapeless with fat. At the fire he strips off his outer shirt and only retains his flannel vest. The sleeves of this are cut short to the shoulders and it is fastened at the neck by means of strings threaded with a bodkin. He drinks an enormous quantity of cold water, and it is singular that he never uses a cup but swallows it from the large two-gallon pot. To this habit he attributes his uncommonly good health and fine proportions.

He is a genius at the fire. Whether the furnace be in a good or bad condition he will soon have it as radiant as a star, and he is marvellously cool at it. His speech has a strongly Welsh accent and he talks with great rapidity, especially when he happens to become excited. At such times it is difficult to understand him; he pours out his words and sentences like a cataract.

Notwithstanding the old furnaceman's skill and general inoffensiveness, he could not escape a little practical joking at the hands of the youths. In the shed was an iron bogie, in the shape of a box, just big enough to contain his Falstaffian body. When he was on night duty he always seized upon this as a sleeping bunk for meal hours. Resting it upon the handles forward he sat in it, with his head at the back and his feet hanging over the front, and slept profoundly, with his arms folded and a coat drawn over his face. When he had fallen asleep several hard-hearted youths came up quietly and attached a strong rope to each handle of the bogie. They then raced off with it as fast as they could travel, going out of the shed and returning by a roundabout route to the furnace over bricks and stones, steel rails, and anything else that happened to be in the way. The jolting was terrific, but the bogie was drawn at such a rate that poor Tubby dared not attempt to get out and was forced to endure it as best he could. Arrived back at the furnace the youths speedily decamped and Tubby never knew for certain who had perpetrated the joke upon him in the darkness.

Dominus vobiscum. Et cum spiritu tuo. Domine sanctorum. The old ash-wheeler leans on his shovel and thus addresses you with profound gravity, as though he were the reverend Father himself ministering to his flock in the church. Boland is an Irishman and hails from far Tipperary. He brought his old mother over to England many years ago and has since dwelt in the railway town. He is a typical Hibernian. He is square-set and distinctive in feature, with heavy brows, thickish nose, strong eyes, and firm, expressive mouth. Notwithstanding the fact that he is slighted by the critical of the shed he has a good many virtues; underneath his rough exterior is concealed a wealth of kindness and good-nature. In common with the bulk of his race he is a Catholic in religion. If you should approach him on the subject you would be surprised at his interest in and affection for his Church and doctrine: he is immovable in his simple and childlike faith. In speaking of any matters connected with it his voice will be solemn and hushed; he is filled with reverence and awe. Though not a very constant church-goer he yet manages to attend at festival times and pays considerable attention to the sermon. He will always tell you the text, and in summing up the Father's oratorical abilities he tells you, as a climax, that he can 'go back in history two hundred years.'

The last and most important of all to be dealt with is Pinnell, of the Yankee Plant. He is by far the hardest working man in the stamping shed. In the first place he cannot help being a hard worker, for it is his nature so to be. Rest and he are most inveterate enemies. He *must* find something or other to do; he could not be idle though he tried never so hard. In the second place he is bound to work hard. The job requires it, or, at any rate, the 'super' requires it, which is a slightly different matter. Pinnell used to work one of the small drop-stamps and was always remarkable for his conscientiousness and dogged perseverance. He was the first to start work and the last to finish. He would never take a moment's spell. If there had been no work he would promptly have made some, and have kept plodding away at his forge and stamp. Accordingly, when the miraculous tools from the other side of the Atlantic – which, in the opinion of the Yankee innovator, were going to smash up the other section altogether and displace half the men in the shed – were introduced, Pinnell was the man selected to start the process and lead the way for others. He had to demonstrate what the machines were capable of doing, and upon his output would be based the standard of prices for those to follow after or work beside him.

The introduction of the Yankee hammers and the oil furnaces for heating was the beginning of hustle in the shed. Everything was designed for the man to start as early as possible, to keep on mechanically to and from the furnace and hammer with not the slighest pause, except for meals, and to run till the very last moment. His prices were fixed accordingly. Every operation was correctly timed. The manager and overseer stood together, watches in hand. It was so and so a minute; that would amount to so much in an hour, and so much total for the day. If Pinnell flagged a little – it is dreadful to have to keep hammering away for hours in an exhausted condition, with never a moment's pause – if he flagged a little, or checked the oil somewhat in the forge, the overseer promptly set it going again and pricked him on to greater effort, answering his words — if he ever dared utter any – with a wheedling and plausible excuse, and telling him it was not all hard; 'Just a busy little job,' and so forth. If nature required that he should leave the forge and walk across the shed, that was the subject of a note – 'One minute and three-quarters gone.' Did he think he could beat the records of all the other men at the stamps? The manager hoped he would try hard to do so, he wanted the machine to be quite first in output. The prices were weighed, chiselled, and pared with great exactness even to the splitting of a farthing: 'A halfpenny is too much for this job; I shall give you three-eighths.' Moreover, the overseers only timed him in the morning, after breakfast, which is the most active part of every day, and when all are fresh and fit for work, or never, so that the prices were fixed at a time when everything was going at its best. It is impossible to maintain the same speed in the afternoon, or even during the latter part of the morning towards dinner-time, that one is capable of after breakfast.

So Pinnell was little by little broken in to the new conditions. Whatever protests he made were of no avail. If the acute manager happened to make a slight misjudgment and give him a fair price for a job, one or other of the shed overseers – though always very flip with him to his face – rushed off privately and informed about it, and had it cut down to the dead level. Very often the overseers competed with each other to see which could make the lowest quotation in order to get into favour with the managers. Once, after playing an underhanded game in the fixing of prices, the foreman even induced Pinnell to leave his hammer and forge and go and protest to the manager himself, though he knew very well the matter was nothing but a farce. When the deluded one arrived at the office he was received with studied courtesy. A little arithmetic was entered into, and it was proved beyond all doubt that the job was well, and even generously paid for. Accordingly, feeling rather foolish for his boldness in going to the manager and his failure to succeed in the matter, Pinnell returned to his work, while the overseer stood in hiding and watched him back to his hammer, laughing at his simplicity.

When at last he found that there was no escape for him, he settled down in despair, and decided to bury himself at the toil. So exacting is the labour it admits of no interest whatever in anything else. It is a body-and soul-racking business, just that which keeps the whole man in a crushed and subdued state, and makes him a very part of the machinery he operates. It was nothing but the man's natural zeal for work and grit that kept him at the task. Night after night he went home to his wife and children as tired as a dog, too tired even to read the newspaper, or write a letter. He simply sat in the chair or lay on the couch till bed-time, completely worn out with the terrible exertions.

Very soon the abject misery of his condition found expression in words to his workmates. He was continually wishing himself dead. He said he should like to die out of it. Life was nothing but a heavy burden, and there was nothing better in sight in the future; only the same killing toil day after day. He often wondered *when* he should die. He had heart enough for anything, but somehow he felt he could never keep it up, and everyone told him he was 'going home sharp.' At the same time, nothing would prevent him from turning up at the hammer day after day; ill or well he was sure to be at his post. Sometimes, when his wife exhorted him to stay at home and recuperate and locked the doors against him, in the early morning he escaped to work through the window. There was no detaining him at all; he felt bound to come to the shed and endure the daily punishment. To intensify his sufferings everyone told him it was his own fault. He had no one to blame but himself; he should not have been such a fool as to lend himself so easily to it, they said.

So, eternally tired with the work – he has two forges to attend to, he heats all his own bars, drives his own hammer with the foot and operates the heavy trimmer by the side of it in the same manner – half-choked and blinded with the reeking smoke and fumes of the oil, sore-footed with using the treadle, his arms blistered and burnt with the scale and hot water from the glands and valves – they are very often in bandages – his hands cut and torn with the sharp ends of the bars, or burned with the hot ones that sometimes shoot out from the die and slip white-hot through his palm and fingers, beaten and distressed with the heat, the gazing-stock of everyone that passes through the shed and who look upon him as a freak and a marvel, he keeps plodding away, a much be-fooled and over-worked individual, the utter victim of a cruel and callous sytem.

CHAPTER XII

FIRST QUARTER IN THE FORGE

'Hey-up!'

'What's up?'

'Wake up!'

'What's the matter?'

'Get up!

'Go to hell!'

'You-u-u! Tell me to go to hell, will you? I'll smash you. I'll – I'll ——'

'Come on, then! Try it on! I'm not afraid of you! You're nobody!'

'Well, wake up! and jump about when I tell you.'

'Wake up yourself, whitegut!'

'Who are you calling whitegut, eh? Who are you calling whitegut?'

'Who shot the sheep and had to pay for it?'

'Blast you! I've had enough of your jaw. I'll put your head in that bucket of oil.'

'*Will* ya? You got to spell able first.'

Scuffle, in which the younger is thrown down to the ground, after which he gets up and runs away, crying:

'Baa-a-a!'

'I'll give you "Baa-a-a!" Wait till I get hold of you!'

'Baa-a-a! Baa-a-a!'

'Take that! you-u-u!' throwing a lump of coal that misses him and goes flying through the office window.

'Ha! ha! ha! ha! ha!'

'Everybody's doing it, doing it, doing it;
    Everybody's doing it now.'

'Yes, and you'll be doing it directly! 'Tis all your fault. If you was to look after your work instead of acting about so much that wouldn't have happened. Blasted well light that fire up!'

'Here's the gaffer comin'.'

'A good job too! I don't trouble.'

'What the hell's up this end? Ya on a'ready this mornin'? I'll send the pair of you home directly.'

''Tis my mate here. He's the cause of everything. He's no good to me. He won't do nothing.'

'D'ye hear this?'

'I allus does mi whack.'

'Don't talk to me. Hello! What's this 'ere? Who bin smashin' the window? Ther'll be hell to pop over this. If I reports ya you'll be done for, both on ya.'

'Please, sir, I kicked a piece of coke and it went through the pane.'

'Hey?'

'The hammer fled off the shaft and went through the window.'

'Why the devil don't you look after the shaft then, and keep the wedges tight. You'll knock somebody's head off presently. I daresay you was at that blasted football again. The first I ketches at it I'll sack. Have un clean off the ground. I'll give un football!'

'Light that fire up, Laudy!'

'Got a job on over 'ere, gaffer.'

'Wha's the trouble?'

'Top cylinder busted, ram cracked, and the crown of the furnace fell in.'

'How did that happen?'

'Night chaps, I s'pose. 'Twas done when we got here this mornin'.'

'You're out for the rest o' the wik then. Set yer mind at rest on that. Damn it! Everything happens on nights. This blasted night work's a nuisance. Go and tell Deep Sea and fetch the brickies, and get they on to't. Wher's yer mates?'

'Waitin' instructions.'

'They can go home, and stop ther' if tha likes. Got nothin' for 'em to do. Go and tell 'em.'

'Sign this order, sir.'

'Come on then, quick! No time to mess about with you. Hello! Bailey's Best! Wha's this for?'

'Leg irons.'

'You don't want best for them. Cable's good enough for they. What ya thinkin' about?'

'Have a look at this 'ere die, guvnor?'

'Wha's up wi' he?'

'Wants dressin' out, or else re-cuttin'.'

'Spit in him, and get yer iron hot!'

'Wanted on the telephone, quick! Number fifteen shop.'

'Got no coke out at the hip, gaffer!'

'The water tank's half empty.'

'The glass on the boiler's smashed.'

'Please, sir, the chargeman's out, and he got the key of the box.'

'And my mate bin an' squished the top of his finger half off.'

'Damn good job, too! How many more on ya?'

'Are you coming to answer number fifteen?'

'Oh, be God!'

'Another day doin' nothin'. You can never start till the middle o' the wik.'

'Steady on with that oil, Laudy! Steady on I tell you! He'll go off directly.'

BANG!

'There! What did I tell you!'

'Oh, Christ! My eyes got it.'

'Serves you damn well right! I told you on it. You got the front half out now. Get some oily waste.'

'There's plenty here.'

'You haven't got the back stopped up yet. Get some wet sand and stop that hole up. Now then! Be quick with you!'

'Steady on a bit, then! I don't want to get burned to death.'

'Serve you right if you was to!'

'Steady on, I say! Damn well do it yourself then! I'm not going to get myself burned.'

'I shut him off. Make haste with you. Ya ready?'

'Right.'

Foo-oo-oo-oo-oo.

'What a blasted smoke! Shut some of that oil off.'

'Let it alone! That won't hurt. We wants to get on.'

'It gets down my inside. I shall spew in a minute.'

'That'll do you good.'

'Shut some of it off.'

'Let it alone, I tell you!'

'I'm not going to be pizened.'

''Tis no worse for you than 'tis for me.'

'I can't see two yards.'

'Hello! Hello! What the hell's on there?'

'Sweep! Sweep! Sweep!'

'Steady on with that oil, mate! We gets all the smoke here.'

'I can't help it.'

'Yes you can help it, too! Shut some of that oil off.'

'That won't make no difference.'

'Wind off, mate! and hammer down. This is a bit too thick. Hey! Gaffer! Are we expected to work in this?'

'That'll kill the worms in yer guts.'

'I can't stand this. My head aches splittin'. I'm half-smothered.'

'We don't care a damn about the smoke, mate, as long as we can get the iron hot. 'Tis no worse for you than 'tis for the rest. If you don't like it you can stop out. There's plenty more to take yer place.'

'That's all you get for your trouble! Wants the inspector in here. It's worse than bein' up the chimmuck. Go on, mate! Hammer up, Jim.'

'He'll be all right directly, old man. He ain't got hot yet.'

'Hot, be hanged! He ought to be dropped in the middle of the sea, and you along with him! The pair of you ought to be down with the *Titanic*.'

'Don't talk wet!'

'Come on, Laudy! and put some pieces in the fire.'

'I ain't filled the lubricators yet.'

'Ain't filled the lubricators! What ya bin at this half-hour?'

'God! Give us a chance.'

''Twill be breakfast-time before we makes a start.'

'I wish 'tood be! I wants mine.'

'What the hell a' ya talkin' about?'

'Baa-a-a!'

'Now then! You knows what I told you! Get and put some pieces in the fire.'

'Can't find my tongs now.'

'Where did you leave 'em last night?'

'Chucked 'em down.'

'What's this here?'

'That en' them.'

'Damn well go and look for 'em then. You'll lose your head directly.'

'Strike a light, mate! That key's in there tight.'

'Look out! Hold that bar up.'

'I wants the tongs first.'

'I shan't hit you.'

'I don't know so much.'
'Come on! A couple o' blows'll do the trick.'
'Not in these trousers!'
'Old Ernie's thinkin' about the Tango.'
'The tangle, more likely.'
'Don't you worry, mate!'
'Ya got him?'
'Right!'
Slap, slap, slap.
'Whoa! Wait a minute. That hammer's comin' off.'
'Hold him up.'
'Is he shifted?'
'He's gone a bit, I think.'
'Hold your hand the other side, and feel him.'
'Now go on. Steady, mate!'
Slap, slap.
'Ho! Hooray!'
'What did I tell you?'
'Everybody's doin' it, doin' it, doin' it.'
'Our mate's strong this mornin'. He bin eatin' onions.'
'Give us a bit of that packing. That thin piece! Now get the pinch bar, and prise the monkey up.'
'How's that?'
'A bit higher. Right! That'll do.'
'Key in?'
'Ah! Slap him in.'
'Give us the sledge.'
'Get that big un.'
'Shaft's broke in two.'
'Get the furnace one, then.'
'How about packing?'
'Same as before.'
'Look out, then!'
'Blow up, mate?'
'Right away with you.'
'How tight do you want him?'
'As tight as you can get him. Slip him in. That'll do now.'
'Hey-yup! Hammer-up. He's burned a bit, mate.'
'Be hanged! You only got half a piece.'
'Can't help it. That was stoppin' to get the key out.'

'Go on. Hit him!'
Bang, bang, bang.
'Whoa! That'll do.'
'What's the dies like, chum?'
'All right now.'
'Blow up?'
'Ah! Let's have you.'
'Tool up, mate!'
'The chain's twisted.'
'Can't you see it's upside down! D'you want to smash the bounder?
Now go on.'
Bang.
'Light again.'
Bang.
'That'll do. Oil up.'
'Pi, Pi, Balli!' (Greek for 'Boy! boy! whack 'em along) 'Let's have you!
whack 'em along there!'
'Hullo!'
Whizz.
'As quick as you like, mate! We've got to move today. Hit him, there!'
Bang, bang, bang.
'Whoa! Tool up, quick! Light, now!'
Bang.
'One more. Light!'
Bang.
'That got him.'
'Pi, Pi, Balli! All hot! All hot! Let's have you!'
Whizz.
'Hooray!'
'Not much afore breakfast, but look out aater!'
'Wormy's makin' some scrap on the next fire. Look at 'im!'
'Rat, O! Rat, O! Get that rat out o' the fire, old man.'
'Don't burn 'em! Don't burn 'em!'
'Another snider, O!'
'The blasted jumper won't work.'
'Oil they tongs a bit.'
'Pizen that rat in the fire.'
'Go to the boneyard and dig Smamer up, and fetch he back.'
'What the hell are ya talking about? Don't you never spile one?'
'Hair off! Hair off!'

'Don't get your bracers twisted.'

'Tell him off, kid.'

'I'll put my hand in your mouth directly.'

'You're the finest worm I've ever seen.'

'Come on here, and not so much of your old buck!'

'Get out of the road, and let Pep have a try.'

'Damn well get away from here! Who the hell can hot iron with you about? Your face is enough to spoil anything.'

'Get 'em hot! Get 'em hot!'

'Get hold of that lever, you reptile!'

'I've seen better things than you crawling on cabbages.'

'How's that? Will that do for you?'

Whizz. Slap.

'Get that muck out o' your fire.'

'Hit him hard! Right up.'

Bang, bang, bang. Knock.

'Keep off the top!'

'You said right up.'

'Shut some of that steam off.'

'Steam's all right.'

'Shut it off, I tell you!'

'Shut it off yourself! Mind the tongs, or you'll get it.'

Bang, bang, bang, bang.

'Don't answer me back or I'll flatten you out.'

'Nothing's never right for you. You ought to be in a bigger town.'

'Tool up, there!'

'Rope's off the wheel, mate!'

'Shut the blasted wind off.'

'He's cut all to pieces.'

'Tha's knockin' the top. I told you of it. I shall ast the gaffer for another mate. This'll take us till dinner-time. Go and get the spanners, and ast Sid for a new rope, and look sharp about it!'

'Now, Laudy! Wake up with you! We shan't earn damn salt.'

'I don't trouble. I can't help it.'

'Well! Come on, then.'

'Tongs won't hold 'em.'

'Get another pair.'

'Which uns?'

'There's plenty more about.'

'I'm sick o' this job.'

'You don't like work.'

''Cause you're so fond of it!'

'Don't waste them ends off. They won't fill up as it is.'

'I reckon the fella as started work ought to come back and finish it.'

Crack.

Boom.

Bump.

'Don't burn the damn things! Look at that! All over me.'

'My clothes is afire.'

'What's yer little game there, eh? Med as well kill a fella as frighten him to death.'

'Oo! My grub got it!'

'Get these others out first.'

'What O! I'm not goin' to see *my* grub burn. What do *you* think?'

'All the damn lot'll be spoiled.'

'I don't care a cuss! I got some tiger in there.'

'Steady that oil a bit.'

'God! Doan it stink!'

'Shut some of it off, I tell you. It's running all over the place.'

'Half on it's water.'

'That second one there, and keep to the top row.'

'Hey-up!'

Crack.

'Why don't you be careful?'

Snap. Bump.

'Back tool's jammed now.'

'The safety bolt's broke.'

'Shut the belt off.'

'Look out, then!'

'Stop the oil, and pull them others out.'

'Let 'em alone! We shan't be a minute.'

'Well! Jump about then.'

'Here's Calliper King comin'!'

'Tell him to clear off. We can do very well without him. That fellow makes me bad.'

'If you was to put the spanner on the nuts sometimes you wouldn't get half the trouble.'

'All right, mate! There's no damage done. We can't think of everything.'

'Your bearings are hot.'

'They'll get cold directly.'

'You might get them seized.'

'Damn good job! Shove some oil into 'em, kid!'

'Who are you calling kid?'

'Look out, there!'

'I shall report you, mind!'

'You can please yourself. 'Twon't be the first time. If you'll only keep out o' the road we shall be all right. Blow up, Laudy!'

Foo-oo-oo-oo-oo.

'Pull the belt over.'

'Right?'

'I'm ready.'

'Take him, then.'

Crack.

Click, clack. Bump.

'How's that?'

'That got him. Now we shan't be long!'

'Yip ho! All new uns!'

'I got that pistol in my pocket.'

'Is he any good?'

'Kill at hundred and twenty.'

'What? Inches?'

'Inches be damned! Yards, man!'

'You never killed anything with him.'

'Ain't he, though? I know he have.'

'What have you killed? A dead cat?'

'Dead cat! You're afraid to let me try him on you.'

'You couldn't hit a barn door.'

'I tell you what I done.'

'What's that? Oh! I know. Who shot the sheep? Baa-a-a!'

'Shut your blasted head!'

'Pride o' the Prairie! Got any cartridges?'

'Half a boxful.'

'Slugs or bullets?'

'Slugs.'

'Let's have a look!'

'Get this work done first. 'Twill be breakfast-time directly.'

'Hey-up! He's slightly wasted.'

'I should blasted well think so.'

Crack.

Boom.
'Hello! There's another snider!'
Bang.
'Keep him there! We don't want your scrap.'
'Pi, Pi, Balli! Tha's a good heat, mate!'
'We haven't done anything yet.'
'What! Tell somebody else that yarn! Hear that, Jim?'
'Wha's up?'
'Chargeman says we ain't done nothin' yet.'
'More we ain't, have us?'
'Have us not! Tha's only a rumour.'
'I didn't think we had.'
'You bin asleep an' only just woke up. All good uns, too.'
'We shall want 'em, bi what I can see on it.'
'What d'ya mean?'
'Look at the next hammer! They won't start today.'
'How's that, mate?'
Whizz.
'Mind my toe.'
'Good shot, that!'
'Cool your tongs out.'
'Have a drink.'
'Put it on the anvil.'
Bang, bang, bang.
'Whoa! Tool.'
'Ain't he slippy!'
'Light blow.'
Bang.
'That takes a bit of doing, one hand!'
'Come on, Lightning!'
'Unknown swank!'
'All hot! All hot!'
'You'll get the price cut directly.'
'Come and see the boys!'
'I'm a-lookin' at ya!'
'Ain't a burned one yet.'
'Don't make a song about it.'
'You got a good mate on the hammer.'
'Fifty without stoppin' the wind. All new uns!'
'See who you are!'

'Stand back, and mind the mallet! There's one for you, Wormy!'
'Take a couple, mate?'
'Come on with 'em.'
Slap, slap.
Bang, bang, bang.
Bang, bang, bang.
'Fire's gettin' low. Wants some more coke up.'
'Wher' d'ye want thase few pieces, Willums!'
'Tip 'em up anywhere, Mat!'
'All you'll get today.'
'You're talking wet. They won't last five minutes.'
'You'll hef to see gaffer, then. We got to change knives.'
'Get out of the road, or you'll get your whiskers singed.'
'Dossent thee fret thy kidneys. This is too damn hot for me. You got no room to mauve.'
'Somebody got to do a bit.'
'Thee dossent do't all.'
'You'd have to go home if I did.'
'Top hammer's stopped now. Middle un's ready.'
'What's up a-top? Going to start, there? See that rope's all right! Have the sharp edges took off the wheel.'
'We be done for.'
'What's the matter?'
'Top bloke broke. Only had forty more to do.'
'Ram up, and get your dies out. Give a hand there, mates.'
''Tis the chaps as make the luck. What do *you* think? We get on all right.'
'Here's the bummer in a tear.'
'Why the hell don't you be careful! You'll break all the tackle in creation. First one thing and then another. Ropes and wheels and dies. You wants to go home for a month. That 'ood teach 'e a lesson. You don't trouble a damn for nothing.'
'I asked the fitters to see to it, and they wouldn't come.'
'That block was never strong enough for the job.'
'Go an' fetch Moses. What ya goin' to put in next?'
'Pull-rod levers. Die seventy-two.'
'Don' want them. Put in hunderd an' one.'
'Chargeman says levers. Wanted urgent. Chaps bin up after 'em.'
'Let 'em wait. I'm the foreman. You knows that.'
'All right. Don' make no difference to me.'

'Did you send for me?'
'I did. Get on wi' new blocks for piston rods.'
'Any alterations?'
'Not as I knows on.'
'We've had complaints about the others.'
'I don't care. Let 'em file 'em. The devils be never satisfied.'
'Better have 'em a bit stiffer?'
'They'm stiff enough. They wasn't set level.'
'They was as level as a billiard table, gaffer!'
'I could a' shoved my finger underneath 'em.'
'I had 'em packed tight everywhere.'
'Then you didn't have yer iron hot. 'Tis no good to arg' the point. Take care wi' the next lot, mind!'

'Let him go to hell! He'd make anybody a damn liar. Key out. Hang on to that spanner. Damp up, and shut the blower off. Fetch the iron trucks. We shall want some help to get these out o' the way.'

'Billy, sing that song,
That good old song to me!'

'Now, Jacko! Give us a hand here.'
'I can't. My leg's bad.'
'That won't hurt your leg, will it? I wants your hand, not your leg. 'Tis all in the gang.'
'I got one stuck on the jumper.'
'All right. Blind you! We'll do it ourselves. This *is* a show! Come on, mates! Keep the handles down, and mind he don't tip.'
'Give him a blow on that bar to get him off the jumper, can't ya; and don't stick up there doin' nothin'. You ain't heard our mate's new nickname, have you, Wormy?'
'No. What's that?'
'Flannel. Know why that is?'
'No.'
'Cos water allus makes him shrink. Look at him! The only curly-headed boy in the family!'
'You hump-backed, monkey-faced baa-boon! You broke loose from the Zoo, you did. I won't hit another stroke for nobody, now, damn if I do!'
'Get out! I'll spiflicate you!'
'I'll bash the tongs across your head.'

'What ya goin' to do? Take that! *Now* what ya goin' to do? I've had enough of your jaw.'

'Let the kid alone, can't you!'

'I'll get my own back on him, before night, see if I don't. I'll drop the hammer on his head.'

'Fetch him out, Wormy!'

'Hey-yup!'

Whizz-z-z.

'Keep that hammer still, will ya! Hit him if you dares! Now go on. Steady!'

Bang, bang, bang, bang, bang.

'Whoa! whoa! steady! steady! Light when I tell ya!'

Bang, bang, bang, bang, bang, bang.

'Blast you! What a' you doin'? You smashed him all to pieces.'

'I told you I'd do it.'

'Workin' your breakfast-time, there?'

'Goin' to keep on all day?'

'Ain't you goin' to chuck up?'

'How's the balance?'

'What! only just started?'

'Whack 'em along!'

'How many more?'

'Work 'em out!'

'What time is it?'

''Ere's old Sid with the checks!'

'What's up, Flannigan?'

'Only wants two minutes!'

'Flatfoot's gone by.'

'You're on late, mate!'

'What's going to happen?'

'Got a book-ful?'

'Tool up, there!'

'Put him up yourself!'

'Put that tool up, Wormy, and catch hold o' that lever.'

'Light blow!'

Bang.

'Whoa! That'll do.'

'What cheer, Sid!'

'Stand back, here, and let's get by.'

'Wants a lot o' room for a little un, don't ya?'

'Not so much as you. Not so much as you. My time's precious, not like yourn. We got summat to do, we have.'

'Ah! Sit on your backside an' count they checks out, that's all.'

'Goin' to have your bit o' brass when I offers it to you?'

'Put him on the anvil.'

'Shan't! Take him in your hand. Lose him, and then blame me.'

'My hand's oiley!'

'Don' matter! Wipe him in your breeches, can't you? Come on, kidney bean-stick!'

'Little fat maggot!'

'Go on, bones!'

'Pimple on a cabbage!'

'Alpheus!'

'Sideus!'

'*Nemo mortalium omnibus horis sapit!*'

'σφραγιδοννχαργοκομήτης.'

'Lend my father your wheelbarrow!'

'Using your knife breakfast-time, kid?'

'No! I got bread and scrape.'

'Who got the frying-pan?'

'You can have him for a fag.'

'I got a bit o' dead dog, I have.'

'What d'ya call it? Looks like a bit of Irish.'

'That never died a natural death!'

'That drove many a man up a tree!'

'Lend us that catalogue of firearms, Dick!'

'He's underneath the bucket.'

'How much longer ya going to keep on?'

'I wants to get my blocks right afore breakfast.'

'Laudy! You left that rotten stinking oil on.'

'No, I didn't!'

'Yes you did! Stop it off, and put that board in the hole!'

'I tell you it's shut off. That's only the stink you can smell.'

'It makes me feel rotten. I shan't want any grub.'

'Ain't it damn hot! We shall be dead afore night.'

'Hit him, Wormy!'

Bang, bang, bang.

'Whoa!'

'What's the die like?'

'Wants to go over a bit yet.'

'Chuck it up!'

'Lie down, can't you!'

'Mind your own business!'

'Put him through the tool.'

'Got the coke ready for after breakfast, Jim?'

'Ah!'

'I'm going to put you through your facings, by and by.'

'I don't trouble! I ben' a-goin' to work no harder for nobody.'

'Look out for Ratty! He's peepin' about. He's going to report the first one as puts his coat on afore the hooter goes.'

'He's worse than old Wanky!'

''Tis all damn watchmen here!'

'How's the minutes?'

'It's quarter past.'

'There's the buzzer!'

'There he goes!'

'Tools down, mates!'

'Whack 'em down!'

'Hooter!'

'Hoo-ter-r!'

'Hoo-oo-ter-r-r!'

CHAPTER XIII

THE NIGHT SHIFT – ARRIVAL IN THE SHED – 'FOLLOWING THE TOOL' –
THE FORGEMAN'S HASTE AND BUSTLE – LIGHT AND SHADE –
SUPPER-TIME – CLATTER AND CLANG – MIDNIGHT – WEARINESS –
THE RELEASE – HOME TO REST

Whatever the trials of the day shift at the forge may be, those of the night turn are sure to be far greater. For the daytime is the natural period of both physical and mental activity. The strong workman, after a good night's rest and sleep, comes to the task fresh, keen, vigorous, and courageous. Though the day before him be painfully long – almost endless in his eyes – he feels fit to do battle with it, for he has a reserve of energy. In the early morning, before breakfast, he is not at his best. He has not yet 'got into his stride,' he tells you. His full strength does not come upon him suddenly, it develops gradually. He can spend and spend and spend, but cannot exhaust. Nature's great battery continues to yield fresh power until the turn of the afternoon. Then the rigid muscles relax, and the flesh shows loose and flabby. The eyes are dull, the features drawn; the whole body is tired and languid.

But this is with the day shift, working in the natural order of things. A great change is to be observed in the case of the night turn. There nature is inverted; the whole scheme is reversed. The workman, unless he is well seasoned to it, cannot summon up any energy at all, and he cannot conquer habit, not after months, or even years of the change. When, by the rule of nature, he should be at his strongest and the exigencies of the night shift require that he should sleep, that strength, bubbling up, keeps him awake, dead tired though he be, and when he requires to be active and vigorous just the reverse obtains. The energy has subsided, the sap has gone down from the tree. Nature has retired, and all the coaxing in the world will not induce her to come forth until such time as the day dawns and she steals back upon him of her own free will. That is what, most of all, distinguishes the night from the day shift, and makes it so wearisome for the pale-faced toilers.

There is a poignancy in preparing for the night shift, the feeling is really one of tragedy. This is where the unnaturalness begins. Everyone but you is going home to rest, to revel in the sweet society of wife and children, or parents, to enjoy the greatest pleasure of the workers' day – the evening meal, the happy fireside, a few short hours of simple pleasure or recreation and, afterwards, the honey-dew of slumber. As you walk along the lane or street towards the factory you meet the toilers in single file, or two abreast, or marching like an army, in compact squads and groups, or straggling here and there. The boys and youths move smartly and quickly, laughing and talking; the men proceed more soberly, some upright with firm step and cheerful countenance, others bent and stooping, dragging their weary limbs along in silence like tired warriors retreating after the hard-fought battle.

There is also the inward sense and knowledge of evening, for, however much you may deceive your external self, you cannot deceive Nature. Forget yourself as much as you please, she always remembers the hour and the minute; she is far more painstaking and punctual than we are. The time of day fills you with a sweet sadness. The summer sun entering into the broad, gold-flooded west, the soft, autumn twilight, or the gathering shades of the winter evening, all tell the same story. It is drawing towards night; night that was made for man, when very nature reposes; night for pleasure and rest, for peace, joy, and compensations, while you – here are you off to sweat and slave for twelve dreary hours in a modern inferno, in the Cyclops' den, with the everlasting wheels, the smoke and steam, the flaring furnace and piles of blazing hot metal all around you.

Within the entrance the place seems almost deserted. The huge sheds have poured out their swarms of workmen. The black-looking crowds have disappeared, and the great, iron-bound doors are closed up and locked. The watchmen, who have been patrolling the yard and supervising the exodus of the toilers, are returning to their quarters. Only the rooks are to be seen scavenging up the fragments of bread and waste victuals which the men have thrown out of their pockets for them.

Arrived at the shed you are greeted with the familiar and dreadful din of the boilers priming, the loud roar of the blast and the whirl of the wheels. The rush of hot air almost overpowers you. You feel nearly suffocated already, and half stagger through the smoke and steam to reach your fire and machine standing under the dark, sooty wall. As you thread your way in and out between the furnaces and among the piles of iron and steel you receive a severe dig in the ribs with the long handle of the man's shovel who is cleaning out the cinders and clinker from beneath the furnaces, or the ash-wheeler, stripped to the waist and dripping with perspiration, runs against you roughly with his wheelbarrow and utters a loud 'Hey-up!' or otherwise assails you with 'Hout o' the road, else I'll knock tha down,' and hurries off up the stage to deposit his load and then comes down again to get in a stock of coal from the waggon for the furnaces. Here the smith is preparing his fire, while his mate breaks up the coke with the heavy mallet; the yellow flames and cinders are leaping up from the open forge by the steam saw. The oil furnaces are puffing away and spitting out their densest clouds of pitchy smoke, filling the shed, while the stamper fixes his dies and oils round, or half runs to the shears in the corner and demands his stock of iron bars to be brought forthwith. The old furnaceman, sweating from the operation of clinkering, shovels in the coal and disposes it with the ravel. The forging hammers glide up and down, clicking against the self-act, while the forger and his mates manipulate the crane and ingot, or charge in the blooms or piles. Everyone is in a desperate hurry, eager to start on with the work and get ahead of Nature, before she flags too much. It is useless to wait till midnight, or count upon efforts to be made in the hours of the morning.

All this is during your entry to the shed and often before the official hour for starting work. On coming to your post you, too, strip off hat, coat, and vest, and hang them up in the shadow of the forge, then bind the leathern apron about your waist, see to your own fire and tools – tongs, sets, flatters, and sledges – obtain water from the tap by the wall, shout 'Hammer up!' to your mate, and prepare to thump away with the rest. The heat of the shed in the evening, from six o'clock till ten o'clock, is terrific in the summer months. For hours and hours the furnaces and boilers have been raging, fuming, and pouring out their interminable volumes of invisible vapour; the sun without, and the fires within have made it almost unbearable. The floor plates, the iron principals, the machine frames, the uprights of the hammers – everything is full of heat; the water in the feed-pipes is so hot as to startle you. As the hour draws on, towards nine or ten o'clock, this diminishes somewhat. The cool night air envelops the shed and enters in through the doors, restoring the normal temperature, though, if the night be muggy, there will be scarcely any diminution of the punishment till the early morning, when there is always a cooling down of the atmosphere.

Now the general toil commences in every corner of the smithy. The brawny forger pulls, tugs, or pushes the heavy porter; the stamper runs out with his white-hot bar, spluttering and hissing, and poises one foot on the treadle while he adjusts it over the die, then *Pumtchu, pom-tchu, ping-tchu, ping-tchu*, goes the hammer, and over he turns it deftly, blows away the scale and excrescence with the compressed air, and *pom-tchu, ping-tchu*, again replies the hammer. Here he claps the forging in the trimmer, click goes the self-act, and down comes the tool. The finished article drops through on to the ground; the stamper thrusts the bar into the furnace, turns on more oil and off he goes again. The sparks swish and fly everywhere, travelling to the furthest wall; he wipes away the sweat with the blistered back of his hand, looking half-asleep, and rolls the quid of tobacco in his cheek.

Hard by the smith is busy with his forge and tools. His mate is ghastly pale and thin in the yellow firelight, though he himself looks fat and well. He sets the blast on gently till the iron is nearly fit, then applies the whole volume, to put on the finishing touch and make the iron soft and 'mellow.' This lifts up the white cinders in clouds and blows them out of the front also, so that now and then they lodge on the blacksmith's arms and in his hair, but he shakes them off and takes little notice of them. He jerks the jumper up and down once or twice, turns the heat round quickly, then shuts off the blast, and with a lion-like grip of the tongs, brings it to the anvil and lays on with his hand-hammer, while his mate plies the sledge. Presently he throws down his hammer, grips the 'set tool' or 'flatter,' and his mate continues to strike upon it till the work is completed. If the striker is not proficient and misses once or twice, he jerks out, in a friendly tone – 'On the top, or go home,' or, 'Go and get some chalk' – *i.e.* to whiten the tool – or, 'Follow the tool, follow the tool, you okkerd fella.' Once, when a smith had a strange mate – a raw hand – with him, and bade him to 'Follow the tool,' when he put that down the striker continued to go for it till it flew up and nearly knocked out the smith's eye, but he excused himself on the ground that he thought he had to 'follow the tool.'

Here is a skinny, half-naked fellow, striving with all his might to draw a heavy bogie piled up with new blooms, half a ton or more in weight. His head is thrown far forward, about a yard from the ground. His arms, thin and small, are strained like rods of iron behind his back; only his toes grip the ground. He shouts out to someone near for help.

'Hey! Gi' us a shove a minute.'

'Gi' thee tha itch! Ast the gaffer for a mate. I got mi own work to do,' the other replies, and keeps hammering away.

Next is a belated stamper in want of tools. 'Hast got a per o' tongs to len' us a minute, ole pal?'

'Shove off wi' thee and make a pair, or else buy some, like I got to. Nobody never lends I nothin',' is the answer he receives.

This one wants a blow. 'Come an' gi' I a blow yer.'

'Gi' thee a blow on the head. I got no time to mess about wi' thee.'

Another is concerned as to the hour – there are those whose thoughts are always of the clock, anxiously awaiting the next stop. 'What time is it, mate?'

'Aw! time thee wast better,' or 'Same as 'twas last night at this time. Thee hasn't bin yer five minutes it.'

Perhaps the steam pressure is low. 'Wha's bin at wi' the steam, matey? We chaps can't hit a stroke.'

'Got twisted in the pipes, I 'spect. Go an' put thi blower on, an' fire up a bit, an' run that slag out.'

This one cannot obtain his supply of bars from the shears. 'Now Matty! Hasn't got that iron cut? I can't wait about for thee.'

'Dwunt thee be in sich a caddle. Thee ootn't get it none the zooner. Other people got to live as well as thee, dost naa!'

'All right! I shall go and see *he*,' (the overseer).

'Thee cast go an' do jest whatever thee bist a-mine to. 'Twunt make a 'appoth o' difference.'

By and by the overseer comes up and shouts – 'Hey! Can't you let these chaps on, Matthews?'

'No, I caan't! Tha'll hef to woite a bit. Ther's some as bin a-woitin' all night, ver nigh. 'Tis no good to plag' I, else ya wunt get nothin' done at all.'

Here is the forger bellowing at his driver. 'Go on! Go on! Hit him! Hit him! Hit him! Light, ther'! Light! 'Old on! 'Old on! Whoa, then! Castn't stop when I tells tha? Dost want to spile the jilly thing? Gi' us up they gauges. A's too thick now. Up a bit, ther! Hit un agyen! Light now! Light! Light! That'll do! Whoa! Take 'old o' this bar, an' gi' us that cutter. Now, Strawberry! turn 'e over in the fire, an' don' stand ther' a-gappatin'. 'Aaf thi 'ed 'll drop off in a minute. Ther's a lot to do yet, else ya won't get no balance. Hout o' the road, oot!'

'Haw-w-right. Kip yer wool on. 'Tis a long time to mornin' it. Thee bist allus in a caddle,' the other answers.

'Shet thi 'ed, an' mind thi own business, else I'll fetch the gaffer to thee! Pull up ther', an' le's 'ev un out on't. We be all be'ind agyen! Everybody else ull a done afore we begins! Hang on to that chayn, Fodgy! Now then! ALL together! UGH!'

So the ingot is brought out with shouts and cries, the rattling and jingling of chains and the loud roaring of steam in the roof outside. The blaze of the furnace and the spluttering, white-hot metal make it as light as day in the shed. The forger and his mates stagger under the weight of the ingot and porter-bar and incline their heads to escape the fierce heat. Their faces and necks are burnt red and purple – of the colour of blood-poisoning. Their shirt sleeves are hanging loose to protect their arms; they wear thin, round calico caps on their heads and leathern aprons about their waists. At the first blow or two the sparks shriek around, and especially if the ingot is of steel and happens to be well-heated. The smiths yell out at the top of their voice and rush to save their clothes hanging up beside the forge. The men's faces look transfigured in the bright light. Their shadows, huge, weird, and fantastic, reach high up the wall, even to the roof. The smallest object is thrown into relief and the shafts of the sledges cast a shadow as sharp and clear as from the sun at mid-day. As the mighty steel monkey descends, half covering the white mass, the shadow falls on the roof, walls, and machinery around, and rises as the smooth, shapely piston glides upwards into the cylinder; up and down, up and down, it goes, like the rising and falling of a curtain. This continues till the heat of the forging diminishes and the rays of the metal are no longer capable of overpowering the light cast out from the fireholes and the smoky, sleepy-looking gas-jets hanging in lines down the smithy.

As the iron becomes cooler the hammer beats harder and harder. The oscillation is very great and the sound nearly approaches a ring. The steam roars overhead and leaks and hisses through the joints of the pipes and glands. The oil in the stamper's dies explodes with a cannon-like report. The huge hydraulic engines *tchu-tchu* outside; the wheels whirr and hum away in the roof, and the smith's tools clang out or ring sharply on the anvil. Without, through the open doors, the night shows inky black; the smoke and steam beat down and are blown in with the wind, or the fog is sucked in quickly by the currents. Now the rain beats hard on the roof and runs through in streams, while the wind clatters between the stacks and ventilators overhead with a noise like thunder; or, if it is mid-winter, the light, feathery snowflakes are wafted in from above and sway to and fro and round and round, uncertain where to lodge, until they are dissolved with the heat and finally descend in small drops like dew upon the faces and arms of the forgers.

At the end of every hour the watchman with his lamp passes through, like a policeman on his beat, and stands a moment before the furnace to warm himself or to watch the shaping of the ingot. The old furnaceman views him askance, or ventures to address him with a 'How do?' or 'Rough night out,' to which the other responds with a nod, or a 'Yes; 'Tis!' and takes his departure into the blackness outside. At frequent intervals the overseer walks round and takes his stand here and there, with his hands behind him, or twisting his fingers in front, or with his thumbs thrust into the arm-holes of his waistcoat, and glares at the men, spitting out the tobacco juice upon the ground or on the red-hot forging. Presently he shouts: – 'Ain't ya done that thing yet? How much longer ya going to be? He'll want a bit o' salt directly. Wher's Michael? Ain't he in tonight? Wha's up wi' he?'

'He's a-twhum along o' the owl' dooman tonight,' someone answers. The grimy toilers curse him under their breath and wish he would soon clear off, which he presently does, slipping quickly away into the shadows or climbing up the wooden stairway into the well-lit office.

The first spell is at ten o'clock – that is, after four hours of terrific hammering and sweating. This is the supper-hour. Here the engines cease and the wheels stop their grinding. The roar of the blast has ceased, too; there is not a flicker from the coke fires. The old furnaceman is still shovelling away, for the forger was on till the last moment. Now he 'stops up,' lays a little coal dust along the furnace door, shuts off his blower, puts down the damper, and proceeds to rinse his hands in the water bosh. All the while he was attending to his fire he had the wiper about his neck and held one corner of it in his mouth. After drying his hands with it he gives his grimy face a good rub, goes to his clothes hanging up by the wall, slips on his waistcoat, stirs his tea in the can with the blade of his pocket-knife, takes his food from the peg and comes and sits down near the furnace, or in the sand-bunk. The one in charge of the steam walks from boiler to boiler, setting on the injectors. They admit the cool water with a murmurous, sleepy sound – there is no priming yet. The furnace fire glitters through the chinks of the door or grate like the stars on a frosty night. The old furnaceman does not eat much. He tastes a little and bites here and there, then he wraps the whole up again.

'What! Bistn't agwain to hae thi zupper, then?' someone enquires.

'No-o! Can't zim to get on wi't tonight,' he answers.

'Well! Chock it out for they owld rats, they'll be glad on't. Yellacks is a girtun ther' now, in atween they piles!'

Try how you will you cannot enjoy your food on the night shift. I have carried mine home again morning after morning, or thrown it out for the birds in the yard. I have seen men – and especially youths – go to sleep with the food in their mouths. You are too languid to eat much, and what you do eat has no savour. It is remarkable, also, that while you continue working you do not feel the fatigue so much, but as soon as you sit down you are assailed with increased weariness; you feel powerless and exhausted and have no strength or energy left. Many, in order to keep awake and fresh, go out into the town, deserted at that hour. Some walk outside in the yard and bruise their shins against this or that obstruction in the darkness. Others, again, after partaking of a few mouthfuls of food, go on making up their fires, not only to keep themselves awake, but also to help the work forward and earn their money for the shift. I have many times worked all night – through both meal-hours – in the attempt to earn my wages, and then have been deficient.

Here and there a small party will sit together and chat the meal-time away, or a few will endeavour to read. Very soon, however, the newspaper or book slips from the fingers. The tiredness and heat together prevail; the eyes close and the mouth opens – the toiler is fast asleep. Presently someone comes on the scene with a loud shout: 'Hey-yup! What! bist thee vly-ketchin' agyen? Get up and check, else tha't be locked out,' or another staggers around with half-closed eyes and bawls out, ''Ow beest bi tiself, Bill?' the reply to which usually is, 'Thee get an' laay down,' or 'None the better for thy astin'.' Occasionally several will start singing a song, or hymn, and be immediately assailed with loud cries of 'Lay down, oot!' or 'Yeow! Yeow! Kennul! Kennul!' or a large lump of coal is thrown against the roof to break and fall in dust upon the choristers. Some spread rivet bags in front of the furnace and lie upon them and others lie down upon the bare bricks or iron of the floor. A few minutes before eleven o'clock the stragglers arrive back from the town. The old furnaceman bestirs himself, lifts the damper, sets on the blower, routs the coals of the fire and shouts, 'Come on, yer,' to his mates. The steam-hammer man opens the valve and raises the monkey, making it glide up and down to work the water out of the cylinder, the forgemen and smiths bustle about again and the terrific din recommences.

So the furious toil proceeds hour by hour. *Bang bang, bang. Pum-tchu, pum-tchu, ping-tchu, ping-tchu. Cling-clang, cling-clang. Boom, boom, boom. Flip-flap, flip-flap. Hoo-oo-oo-oo-oo. Rattle, rattle, rattle. Click, click, click. Bump, bump. Scrir-r-r-r-r-r. Hiss-s-s-s-s-s. Tchi-tchu, tchi-tchu, tchi-tchu. Clank, clank, clank, clank, clank.* The noises of the steam and machinery drown everything else. You see the workmen standing or stooping, pulling, tugging, heaving, dragging to and fro, or staggering about as though they were intoxicated, but there is no other sound beyond the occasional shouting of the forger and the jerking or droning of the injectors. It is a weird living picture, stern and realistic, such as no painter could faithfully reproduce. If the oil in the stampers' forges is worse than usual the dense clouds of nauseating smoke hang over you like a pall so thickly that you cannot see your fellows a few paces away, making it intensely difficult to breathe and adding a horrible disgust to the unspeakable weariness. Then the bright flashing metal and the white gas-jets show a dull red. Even the sound seems deadened by the smoke and stench, but this is merely the action of the impurity upon the sense organs; they are so much impaired with the grossness of the atmosphere as to fail in their functions. By and by, when the air has cleared a little, it all rushes back upon you with increased intensity. Everything is swinging and whirling round, and you seem to be whirled round with it, with not a thought of yourself, who you are, where you are, or what you are doing, but keep toiling mechanically away. Oft-times you would be quite lost, but the revolutions of the machine, the automatic strokes of the hammer, and the *habit* of the job control you. And if this should fail, your mate, half asleep, whacks his heat along and casts it upon your toe, or sears you with the hot tongs, or he misses the top of the tool at the anvil and strikes your thumb instead. There are many things to keep you alive, and always the fear of not earning your money for the turn and having to be jeered at and bullied by the chargeman or overseer and so have your life made miserable. The faces and fronts of the smiths and forgers, as they stand at the fires or stoop over the metal, are brilliantly lit up – yellow and orange. Here are the piles of finished forgings and stampings upon the ground – white, yellow, bright red, dull red, and almost black hot; the long tongues of fire leap up from the coke forges,and every now and then a livid sheet of flame bursts out from the stamper's dies. There is plenty of colour, as well as animation, in the picture, which obtains greater intensity through contrast with the blackness outside.

The greatest weariness assails you about midnight, and continues to possess you till towards three o'clock. Then Nature struggles violently, demanding her rights, twitching, clutching, and tugging at your eyelids and striving in a thousand ways to bring you into submission and force her rule upon you, but the iron laws of necessity, circumstance, and system prevail; you must battle the power within you and repel the sweet soother, struggling on in the unnatural combat. The keen eye of the overseer is upon you, who is always whipping you to your task, or the watchman is striving to take you loitering and so bring himself into notice; it is useless to give way. Necessity urges; the body must be clothed and fed. There are the wife and children at home, and you must live. I have felt it, and I know what it is. There, in the smoke and stench, the heat and cold, draught and damp of midnight I have slaved with the rest, not harder or with greater pains than they, though perhaps I have noted the feelings whereas they have not. The eyes ache, the ears ache, the arms ache, the legs ache, the feet ache, and the heart aches. I have many times wished, in those dark, awful hours, that the hammer would smash my head; that I might be suddenly caught and hurled into eternity, and I have heard others express the same wish openly and sincerely. Sometimes I have stolen out of the great doors to stand for a moment in the open in the cold dark or starry night, and looked out towards the hills, or away over the town with the whirl of the shed behind me. There was the great red moon showing through the clouds low down, or the fiercely glittering Mars setting in the west, or inky blackness above, with a few tiny lights twinkling in the far-off streets of the town and a silence as deep as death out beyond. If I could but have heard the old barn owl hooting in the farmyard, the cow lowing in the meadow or stall, the fox yelping in the little wood, or even the bark of a dog, I should have been strengthened and relieved, but there was never a sound of them – nothing but the black outlines of the sheds around, the small distant lights of the town and the great white blaze and crash of noises within. Even to pause there is but to intensify the torture and the cold air soon chills you to the bone. The only course open is to keep toiling away with the rest and wear the night out.

The second stop is at two o'clock and is of brief duration – twenty minutes or half an hour at the outside. It is merely a break in order to have a mouthful of food, a something, so that it shall not be said that the men have to toil for seven consecutive hours in that unspeakable weariness. Here the huge engines become silent again and the heavy pounding stops. The wheels and machinery under the wall look as inert and innocent as though they have never moved; it would be difficult to imagine that they were capable of such noise and uproar if you had not heard it yourself but a few minutes before. The boilers, relieved of the strain upon their resources, begin to prime again with a continued crashing, shattering sound which the boilerman tries in vain to subdue with cold water through the injectors. The furnace glitters and the oil forges smoke. The air is laden with the peculiarly nauseous fumes of the water-gas that make the toilers feel sick and ill and destroy the appetite.

This time the men are unusually silent and mopish. Each selects a place for himself and sits, or lies down, apart from the others. Only the tough, wiry forgeman, the strong smith, or the hardy coalies and ash-wheelers can attack the food. The rest usually go to their jackets, open their handkerchiefs, look at the contents, eat a little perhaps, half-heartedly, and wrap them up again. The constitution of the forgeman is almost like iron itself. He and the smith can usually manage their meal, and the coal-wheelers, from being constantly out in the fresh air, are not quite as weary as are the others, and so can relish the food better. On Friday nights – when the men are more than usually drowsy – the food may be a little more tempting and tasty. At six o'clock the wages were paid, and at supper-time a few, at least, will have gone or sent out into the town for an appetizing morsel: some sausages, rashers, a mutton chop, a pound of tripe, a bloater, or a packet of fried fish and chipped potatoes – the youth's favourite dainty. Then, in the early hours, amid the din of the boilers, the black frying-pan or coal shovel is produced and the savoury odour is wafted abroad. The greatest pleasure, however, is usually in the anticipation of the meal. The food itself is seldom eaten – or no more than a small part of it, at least – the other is cast out for the rats and rooks. Years ago, in the autumn, we boys used to gather mushrooms in the fields on our way to work and cook them for 'dinner' in the early morning and suffer severely for it afterwards. Nature, disorganized with the exigencies of the night shift, refused the proffered dainties. It is difficult to digest even ordinary food taken in the unwholesome air of the shed at such an unearthly hour.

Punctually to the moment, if not before time, the engines begin to throb again; the piston rods, gliding slowly at first, soon attain a rapid speed. The huge crank, flashing in the bright gas-light, leaps over and over. The big belt strains and creaks as though it would avoid its labour and the turning of the shaft overhead, but the heavy fly-wheel spins round, and the little pulleys and cogs go with it; they must all obey the urging of the mighty steam wizard lurking in the green-painted cylinder. The donkey engines, forcing the blast, are coughing and spitting out the white vapour and labouring painfully under the wall in the lean-to outside. Within the fires are flashing and the flames leaping, and the toil goes on as before.

About three o'clock, or soon after, the weariness begins to diminish somewhat, and the old habit of the body reasserts itself. The natural hour of repose is passing, and the fountain of energy begins to bubble up within you; you feel to be approaching the normal condition again. The fatigue now gives place to a feeling of unreality and stupidity; you seem to be dazed and irritable, as though you had been aroused from sleep before the accustomed time. Now you experience deep pains in the chest, resulting from loss of sleep. The head aches as though it would burst and the eyes are very painful and 'gritty,' but you feel cheered, nevertheless, with the thought of daylight, the coming cessation from toil, and the opportunity of obtaining a breath of fresh, pure air again. The overseer slips to and fro quickly about this time in order to keep the men well on the move, pricking here and prodding there, and visiting those whom he knows will tell him all the news of the night's work – such as may have escaped him. The toilers pay him but little attention, however, and keep plodding languidly away.

Steadily, as the day dawns, the light within increases, red, white, or golden, stealing through the thick glass of the roof or by the wide open doors, and soon after one appears with a long staff and turns off all the gas. It is really day once more, and there is not much longer to go. At twenty minutes past five the hooter sounds loudly, calling up the men of the day shift, and the pace flags visibly. A few, however, who have not done any too well in the middle hours of the night, hammer away with increased energy right up to the last, for they know the day overseers and the chargemen will go round and feel the forgings to see how late the others were toiling. If the iron is cool they know that their mates have been dilatory and the tale is told around.

A few minutes before six o'clock the engines slow down and stop and the roar of the blast ceases. The steam-hammers are lowered with a loud thud and the furnace fires are banked up; the mighty toil is over, for this turn, at any rate. Now the forgers and stampers unbind their aprons and roll them up; the smiths stow their tools, placing these in the iron box and those in the boshes of water to soak the shafts and tighten the handles of the sledges. After that they swill their hands at the tap, put on muffler, jacket, or great-coat, and file out of the shed – dirty, dusty, tired and sleepy-looking. Not for them the joy of morning, the vigour, freshness and bloom, the keen delight in the open air, the happy heart and elevated spirit. They slouch away through the living stream of the day toilers now arriving as black as sweeps, half-blinded with the bright daylight, blinking and sighing, feeling unutterably and unnaturally tired, out of sorts and out of place, too, and crawl home, like rats to their holes, to snatch a little rest, and recuperate for new efforts to be made on the following turn.

Few of the men's wives or parents in the town will be up to welcome them at that early hour and provide them with warm tea and a breakfast.

Accordingly, some go home and straight to bed without food at all, a few walk about the streets or out towards the country for an hour or so till the home fire is lit, while others go home and get the breakfast themselves. Perhaps, if trade in the shed is brisk, they will be required to work overtime till eight or nine o'clock. I have done this for months at a stretch and afterwards walked home to the village, oft-times sitting down on the roadside to rest, reaching home at about ten o'clock and getting to bed an hour before noon, to be awakened by every slight noise without the house. At one time I was aroused by the old church clock striking, at another by the sound of the school bell, or the children at play underneath the window, or by the farm waggon. At four in the afternoon, rested or not, you must rise again, wash and dress, snatch a hasty meal, and plod off to the town, four miles distant, forgetful of everything behind you – the gentle peace of the village, the long line of dreamy-looking hills, the haymakers in the field, the sweetly sorrowful sound of the threshing machine by the ricks in the farmyard, the eternal pageantry of the heavens, the whole natural life and scenery of the world. The knowledge of the loss lies like lead at the heart and fills one with a keen regret, a poignant sense of the cruelty of the industrial system and your own weakness with it; yet one must live. But there is real tragedy in working the night shift at the forge.

CHAPTER XIV

INFERIORITY OF WORK MADE BY THE NIGHT SHIFT – ALTERING
THE GAUGES – THE 'BLACK LIST' – 'DOUBLE STOPPAGE CHARLIE' –
'JIMMY USELESS' – THE HAUNTED COKEHEAP – THE OLD VALET –
THE CHECKER AND STOREKEEPER

The work produced on the night turn is greatly inferior to that made by
the men of the day shift. It is impossible to do good work when you are
tired and weary. One has not then the keenness of sense, the nerve, nor the
energy to take the requisite pains. You are not then the master of your
machinery and tools, but are subject to them; even where the work is with
dies and performed mechanically, there will be depreciation. Perhaps the
stamper's tools have shifted a little. The keys want removing, the dies re-
setting and then to be rammed up tight again. But he is too weary to do
much with the sledge, so he keeps dragging along with his dies a-twist and
makes that do, whereas, if he were working by day he would rectify them
immediately and bang away at top speed.

It is the same with the forger. He, too, tough as he is, cannot maintain
the precision he would exercise by day. The pile or ingot on the porter-bar
seems to him to have doubled in weight. The flash of the blazing metal half
blinds him. He cannot stand the heat so well; it is all against turning out
good work. Unless the bloom is kept exactly square under the stroke of
the hammer it lops over on one side and obtains an ugly shape, which it
will be impossible to rectify; there is nothing more unsightly to the eye of
the careful smith or hammerman than a shabby piece of forging. Very
often, too, a portion of slag or sand from the bed of the furnace has
adhered to the pile and, falling away, has left a hole in the metal. Although,
in the uncertain light, the forger may think that he has hammered it quite
out, when he views the piece by daylight he finds it rough and untidy and
perhaps worthless. It may be too small now; there is not enough metal to
clean up under the tools of the slotting- or shaping-machine.

Then there is the smith's weld or bend to be considered. In the first place, the smith is liable to mistake the heat of his parts by gaslight, for then they appear brighter and hotter than they really are, and when he brings them out to the anvil, the metal, instead of shutting up well, will be hard and glassy under the tools. It will, consequently, go together badly and leave a mark or 'scarf,' which is not at all desirable, though the weld may be strong enough inside. In such a case resort will be had to 'nobbling'; that is, covering up and concealing the scarf with the small round ball of the hand-hammer. This must be done secretly, for no foreman would tolerate much of it. It is looked upon as a mark of bad workmanship, though the bluff old overseer of the regular smiths' shed may condone it in a few cases with: 'Hello! You be at it agen then! But ther', you be no good if you can't do't. I allus said any fool can be a smith but it takes a good man to nobble.' The smiths, under ordinary circumstances, are not allowed to use a file. They must finish their job manfully with the sledge and tools, otherwise they might fake up a bad forging, with nobbling and filing, and make it look as strong as the best.

There are more cases of ill-health among men of the night than of the dayshift, but the reason of this will be obvious to any. It is evident that the unnatural conditions of all-night toil must weaken and wear down the body and render it unfit to bear the strain put upon it, and especially to withstand the cold draughts from the doors and roof, which are the most fruitful source of sickness among the workmen – a large number is always absent with chills and influenza. Small regard for a man's health is had at any time in the factory. It is nothing to the officials that he is out on the sick list, unless he happens to be drawing compensation for an injury. I remember once, when work was slack in the shed, the day overseer left orders for the night boss to send the men outside in the yard and keep them there for two or three hours shifting scrap iron, in order that they might 'catch cold and stop at home, and give the others a chance.'

Accidents, too, are frequent on the night shift; the greater part of the more serious ones happen on that turn. Then the men, by reason of the fatigue and dulness, are unable to take sufficient care of themselves; they lack the quick presentiment of danger common to those of the day shift. There is also the matter of defective light and carelessness in the use of tools, and very often, the mad hurry to get on in the first part of the night – the wild rush and tear of the piecework system. It was not long ago that 'Smamer's' brother was killed at the drop-stamps with a blow on the head, shortly after starting work. A jagged piece of steel, ten or twelve pounds in weight, flew from the die and struck him between the eye and ear knocking out half his brains. As things go, no one was to blame. The men were all hurrying together to get the work forward, but he was murdered, all the same, done to death by the system that is responsible for the rash haste and frenzy such as is common on the night shift.

Nearly all whitewashing and painting out the interiors of the sheds is done by night, when the machinery is still. This is performed by unskilled hands – youths, for the most part; from one year's end to another they are employed at it, taking the workshops by turn. The work is very unhealthy and extremely dangerous. The men construct a little scaffolding and work upon single, narrow planks, or crawl like flies along the network of girders in and out among the shafting, with a single gas-jet to afford them light. One false step or overbalancing would bring them down to the ground, thirty feet below, amid the machinery; death would be swift and certain for them if they should miss their footing on the planks. Their wages, considering the risks they take, are very low; 18s. or 19s. a week is the amount they commonly receive. Several of the men, whom I know personally – steady fellows and good time-keepers – had been getting 18s. a week for twenty years till recently; then, after persistent applications for an advance, they were granted the substantial rise of 1s. a week! One sturdy fellow, braver than the rest, on meeting the manager one day, complained to him of the low wages, but was unsuccessful. His overseer, upon hearing of it, promptly told him to clear out, which he afterwards did, and went to Canada and saved £150 in less than a year. When the small boys asked Bill Richards, the old smiths' foreman, for a rise, he used jokingly to tell them to 'Get up a-top o' the anvul.'

The running expenses of much of the 'labour-saving' plant is truly enormous and very often so great as entirely to counteract the much boasted profit-making capacity of the machine, but the managers do not mind that in the least as long as they can show a reduction of hands. If, by any means at all, they can get one man to do what formerly required the services of two or three, they do not trouble about machinery or fuel expenses; the losses incurred by these they make good by speeding up the workman and getting a bigger share out of him. They would rather pay fabulous sums for plant and running expenses than allow the workman to get a few shillings more in wages.

The wholesale waste of material, fuel, and energy, in many of the sheds, is appalling; many thousands of pounds are annually thrown away in this direction. Walk where he will the keen observer will detect waste; no one seems to trouble about the real economy. I have seen it daily for years and have made numerous suggestions, but to no purpose; the overseers are too stupid and ignorant, or too haughty and jealous, to carry out ideas, and the managers are no better. They squander thousands of pounds in experiments and easily cover up their short-comings, but if the machineman happens to break a new tool, or spoil metal of a few pence in value, he is suspended and put on the 'black list.'

If a workman sees a way to make improvements in processes and the like, he immediatey falls into disfavour with the overseers. Some years ago I, as chief stamper, was anxious to improve the process of making a forging, and also the forging itself, and waited on the overseer with a view to having the alteration made, but I could not obtain his sanction for a long time. At last, as new dies were to be made, I succeeded, after some difficulty, in obtaining his consent for the improvement. Happening to enter the die shed while the job was in the lathe I was told by the machineman that no alteration had been authorised. Grasping the situation, I took a bold course, carried out the suggested alteration myself, and set the dies in the steam-hammer. The improvement was a complete success. I was cursed and abused by the overseer, and he was highly congratulated by the staff in my own presence and hearing. The improvement was not to be permanent, however. Shortly afterwards the dies were re-cut, and made in the old way again. At another time, when I had assisted the overseer with an idea, he would not speak to me for a fortnight.

Many times after that I stood for improvements, and was rewarded with the cutting of my prices and the threat of dismissal, and I had the mortification of being 'hooted' by my shop-mates into the bargain. The fact of the matter is, workmen and overseers, too, want to run along in the same old grooves, at any rate, as far as processes are concerned. The foreman and manager think they have done enough if they merely cut a price; they are blind to see that improvements in the process of manufacture is the first great essential. There are many jobs in the sheds which have been done in the same old way for half a century. It is painful to contemplate the ignorance, stupidity, and prejudice of the staff in charge of operations.

Every shed has an institution called 'The Black List.' This list is filed in the foreman's office and contains the names of those who have been found guilty of any indiscretion, those who may have made a little bad work, indifferent time-keepers, and, naturally, those who have fallen into disfavour with the overseer on any other account, and perhaps the names have been added for no offence at all. When it is intended to include a workman in the list, he is sent for to the office, bullied by the overseer before the clerks and office-boy, and warned as to the future. 'I've put you on the black list. You know what that means. The next time, mind, and you're out of it. I give you one more chance.'

Not long ago an apprentice – a fine, smart, intellectual youth – was asked by a junior mate to advise him as to a piece of work in the lathe and went to give the required assistance. While thus engaged he was sent for to the office and charged with idling by the overseer. He tried to explain that he was helping his mate, but the foreman would not listen to it. 'Put him on the black list,' he roared to the clerk. The lad's father, enraged at the treatment meted out to his son, promptly removed him from the works, and sacrificed four or five years of patient and studious toil at his trade. It is useless to continue in the shed when you have been stigmatised with the 'black list.' You will never make any satisfactory progress; you had better seek out another place and make a fresh start in life.

A favourite plan of the overseer's is to catch a man in a weak state and force him to undergo a strict medical test. As a matter of fact, the 'medical test' is a farce; it is merely an examination by one of the staff. Even if the workman passes the test satisfactorily it is recorded and tells against him. Quite recently one of the forgers came to work with a black eye, as the result of a private encounter, and the overseer, after jesting with him concerning it, communicated with the examiner and hustled him off to pass the 'medical test.'

'What have you been at with the hammer?' said I to little Jim one day, finding the lever working very stiffly.

'I dunno. The luminator's broke,' answered he.

'The what broke?' I inquired.

'That there yu-bricator, the thing what you puts the oil in,' he replied.

Most of the articles stamped seemed to suggest something or other to Jim's childish mind. One job, made three at a time, looked like 'little bridges'; something else resembled great butterflies. This was like an airgun, and that 'just like little pistols.' Jim's opinion of factory work is interesting – he is a little over fifteen years of age. Coming up to me one day, cap, waistcoat, everything cast aside, his shirt unbuttoned, his face soot black, and with the sweat streaming down his nose and chin, he said naively – 'This is what I calls a weary life. This place is more like a prison than anything else.' After that he wished to know if I had any apples in my garden, or, failing that, would I bring him along some crabs in my pocket?

'Double Stoppage Charlie' was well-known at the works. He first of all used to keep his wife short of cash, telling her each pay-day it was 'double stoppage this week.' He often figured in a public place, too, and invariably made the same excuse. It was always 'double stoppage week' with him, so he came to be honoured with the nickname of 'Double Stoppage Charlie.' There was also 'Southampton Charlie,' who had seen service with the Marines, and who was for ever talking about the 'gossoons' and telling monstrous yarns of things – chiefly of blood fights and shipwrecks. He took pride in informing you that he had been told he would have made a capital speaker of French, by reason of his wonderful powers of 'pronounciation.'

Jimmy Eustace – better known as 'Jimmy Useless' – was full of poaching adventures and midnight tussles with the gamekeepers and police. He was delighted to tell you of how they dodged the men in blue and waded half a mile, up to their necks in water, along the canal in the dark hours in order to keep out of their clutches. This happened in his young days, in the neighbourhood of Uffington. He was always somewhat of a rake, though he was a very clever constructor of all kinds of iron work. Everyone called him 'an old fool,' however, when Queen Victoria's new Royal Train was made, and the workmen went out in the yard to see it. 'He go to see that thing? Not he! He could make a better one than that standing on his head, any day.' His long grey hair hung down as straight as candles and his grey beard had the true lunar curve. He chewed half an ounce of tobacco at a time, and spat great mouthfuls of the juice about everywhere.

A little humour is occasionally in evidence in the life that is lived by the grimy pack of toilers in the factory sheds. There is, for instance, the story of the young man engaged to be married to a smart lass, and who gave himself certain unjustifiable airs, representing himself as holding a position in the drawing office. After the wedding took place, at the end of the first week, he took home 18s. in wages and was severely taken to task by his spouse and mother-in-law. It transpired that he was employed pulling a heavy truck about; that was the only 'drawing office' to which he was attached.

One young fellow was subjected to the ridicule of his mates by reason of an accident that befell him on his wedding-day. He lived far out in the country, and, on the morning of the ceremony, just before the appointed hour, happening to give an extra specially good yawn, he dislocated his jaw and had to be driven twelve miles to a doctor. Another artless youth, newly brought into the shed, when he was put to withdraw the white-hot plates from a vast furnace, finding the iron rake much too short, tied a piece of tar-cord on the end in order to lengthen it!

The riveter and his mates occasionally practise the ludicrous. One day, when 'Dobbin,' the 'holder-up,' who was short-sighted, was sitting underneath the floor of the waggon with his head against the plate, dozing perhaps, the riveter began to beat on the floor with his hand-hammer and severely hurt his mate's cranium. Shortly afterwards Dobbin unconsciously took his revenge. It is usual to 'drift' the holes with a steel tool in order to make them clear to admit the rivet, and on this particular occasion the riveter thrust his finger through instead and Dobbin, seeing it in the dim light and thinking it was the drift, gave it a mighty ram upwards with the dolly and smashed it.

Then there is 'Budget,' who works one of the oil furnaces, with only half a shirt to his back and hair six or seven inches long and as straight as gunbarrels; whose face, long before breakfast-time, is as black as a sweep's; who slaves like a Cyclops at the forge and is frequently quoting some portions of the speeches of Antonio and Shylock in 'The Merchant of Venice,' which he learnt at school and has not yet forgotten. He sprang out of bed in a great fright, seized his food and ran at top speed, and only partly dressed, half through the town in darkness to discover finally that it wanted an hour to midnight: he had only gone to bed at ten o'clock. His father is a platelayer on the railway receiving the magnificent sum of 16s. a week in wages, and his mother, after suffering five operations, was lately sent home from the hospital as incurable; it is a struggle to make both ends meet and to keep the home respectable. It is no wonder that Budget's shirt is always out of repair and that he himself is racked with colds and influenza.

There is romance in every walk of life, and legends of ghosts and spirits that frequent desolate ruins and dark places, but few would think to find such a thing as a haunted forge or coke heap, though they were believed to exist by the credulous among the night-men at the factory. 'Sammy,' the cokewheeler, had a mortal dread of the cokeheap at midnight, by reason of strange, weird noises he had heard there in the lone, dark hours, and the men at the fires often had to wait for fuel, or go and get it in for themselves. Accordingly, certain among them determined to frighten the old man still further. For several nights in succession, at about twelve o'clock, someone scaled the big high heap at the back and waited for Samuel's return from the shed with his wheelbarrow. When he arrived the hidden one set up a loud, moaning noise and started to clamber down the pile. The coke gave way and fell with a crash, and Sammy, stuttering and stammering with a childlike simplicity and in a paroxysm of fear, rushes off and told how the 'ghost' had assailed him.

The haunted forge was in the smith's shed, adjoining the steam-hammer shop. There a simple fellow was by a waggish mate first of all beguiled into the belief that a treasure was hidden beneath the floorplate and anvil, and then induced to go alone during the supper-hour in the hope of obtaining a clue from the 'spirit' as to its exact whereabouts. Accordingly he went fearfully in through the darkness and up to the fire, while his mate, concealed in the roof, moaned and spoke to him in a ghostly voice down the chimney, telling how, many years before, he had been murdered on that spot and his body buried there together with the treasure, and promising to discover it to the workman if he would come secretly to the fire a fixed number of nights and not communicate the matter to any outsiders. This went on for some time, until the unhappy dupe was made ill, and driven half out of his mind with crazy fear, and things began to get serious. Suddenly the noises stopped, and the midnight visit to the forge was discontinued.

Cases have occurred in which a man has actually been driven out of his mind by continual and systematic trading on his weakness, and by a downright wicked and criminal prosecution of the unscrupulous game. Teddy, the sweeper-up, who was a young married man, and highly respectable, but who discovered a trifling weakness, was assailed and befooled with disgusting buffoonery and drivelling nonsense to such an extent that he became a perfect mental wreck, to the complete amusement of the clique who had brought it about, and who indulged in hysterical laughter at the unfortunate man's antics and general condition. To such a point was the foolery carried that Teddy had to be detained, and he fell seriously ill. In a fortnight he died, and those who had been the chief cause of his collapse went jesting to his funeral. It was nothing to them that they had been instrumental in his death; a man's life and soul are held at a cheap rate by his mates about the factory.

Jim Cole is considerably out of place in the factory crowd; ill-health and other misfortunes were the cause of his migration to the railway town. He is a Londoner by birth, and was first of all a valet in good service; afterwards he bought a cab and plied with it about the streets of the metropolis. As a valet he lived with a sister of John Bright, and was often in attendance upon the famous statesman and orator. John Bright's faith in the Book of Books is well nigh proverbial; the old valet says whenever he went to his room in the morning he was always sitting up in bed reading the Bible.

As a cabman Jim was brought into contact with many celebrities, and it is interesting to learn in what light great men appear to those who are at their service about the thoroughfares. He knew Tennyson well by sight. The famous poet was never a favourite with the 'men in the street.' His testiness of manner and severity were well-known to them; to use Jim Cole's words: 'They hated the sight of him.' 'There goes the miserable old d——l,' they would say to each other.

Carlyle was not a favourite with the cabmen either. They said he was 'hoggish,' and 'too miserable to live.' Everyone was in his way, and everything had to be set aside for him. His brilliant literary fame was no recommendation in the face of his stern personal characteristics.

Oscar Wilde was 'a very nice man.' There was not a bit of pride in him; he would talk to anyone. He would not walk a dozen yards if he could help it, but must ride everywhere. He often gave cabby a shilling to post a letter for him. One day Jim Cole was driving him, and they met Mrs Langtry in her carriage. Thereupon Oscar Wilde stopped the cab, got out, and stood with one foot on the step of the popular actress's carriage, remaining in conversation with her for nearly an hour. At the end of the journey Oscar stoutly denied the time, declared he was not talking to Mrs Langtry for more than ten minutes, and refused to hand over the fare demanded. Ultimately, however, he admitted he might have been mistaken, and so came to terms and paid the extras.

Once James was engaged to drive the celebrated Whistler and Mrs Whistler to Hammersmith, and came very near meeting with disaster. That night he was driving a young mare of great spirit, and she took fright at something on the way and bolted. Poor Jim was in great suspense, fearing an accident at every crossing. The mare flew along at a terrific speed, but the hour was favourable and the traffic thin; there was a fair, open road all the way. He strained every nerve to subdue the animal and slacken the pace, but for over two miles he had not the slightest control of the vehicle. Whistler was quiet and apparently content within; he had not the faintest idea that anything was wrong. At last, after a great race up Hammersmith Broadway, the pace began to flag; by the time they reached their destination Jim was able to 'pull her up' successfully. Whistler was delighted with the journey and waxed enthusiastic about it. He clapped and patted the animal fondly on the neck, several times exclaiming – 'You splendid little mare!' Whistler was a great favourite with the cabmen and he often chatted with them, and made them feel quite at their ease.

Mr Justin M'Carthy and his son were other celebrated fares. They were very quiet and unassuming and earned the great respect of the cabmen. Ill-health dogged the old-time valet. He is now forced to do the work of a menial, lost and swallowed up in the crowd of grimy toilers at the factory.

There is one in every shed who stands at the ticket-box and checks in the workmen at the beginning of each spell; *i.e.* at six A.M., at nine o'clock, and two in the afternoon. It is his duty also to carry off the box to the time office and bring back the tickets to the men before they leave the shed. At the time office the metal tickets are sorted out and placed on a numbered board; this the checker receives and carries round to all the men and hands them their brasses. It is a favourite plan of the man on the check-box to allow the workmen to drag a little by degrees until they get slightly behind the official moment, and then to close the box sharp and shut out forty or fifty. This causes the men to lose half an hour, or they may possibly be compelled to go home for the rest of the morning or afternoon. For some time afterwards they are very punctual at the box, but by and by they are allowed to drag again and the act of shutting out is repeated. The checker, as well as officiating at the ticket-box, acts as a kind of shop watchman, and supplies the overseer with information upon such points as may have escaped his notice.

Besides the checker, there is the regular shed detective, who locks up the doors and cleans the office windows, and his supernumerary who guards the doors at hooter-time and completes the custody of the place: there is little fear of anything transpiring without its becoming known to the foreman. As those selected to watch the rest are invariably the lazy or the incompetent they are sure to be heartily contemned by the busy toilers; there is nothing the skilful and generous workman detests more than to have a worthless fellow told off to spy upon him.

The storekeeper is another who, by reason of his extreme officiousness and parsimonious manner in dealing out the stores, is not beloved of the toilers in the shed. He treats every applicant for stores with fantastic ceremony, examining the foreman's slip half-a-dozen times or more, and turning it round and round and over and over until the exasperated workman can stand it no longer, and sets about him with, 'Come on, mate! Ya goin' to mess about all day? We got some work to do, we 'ev. Anybody'd think thee'st got to buy it out o' thi own pocket!' If the applicant wants a can of oil the vessel is about half-filled; if a hammer is needed the storekeeper searches through the whole stock to find out the worst, if nails, screws, or rivets are required they are counted out with critical exactness, and if the foreman is not at hand to sign the order – no matter how urgent the need is – the workman must wait, perhaps for an hour, till he returns to initial the slip. The time necessary for an order to reach the shed after it has been issued from the general stores, fifty yards away, is usually a week, and the workmen are forbidden to begin a job until they have actually received the official form.

The political views of the men in the shed are known to the overseer and are – in some cases, at any rate – communicated by him to the manager; there is no such thing as individual liberty about the works. He whose opinions are most nearly in agreement with those of the foreman always thrives best, obtains the highest piecework prices and the greatest day wages, too, while the other is certain to be put under the ban. In brief, the average overseer dislikes you if you are a tip-top workman, if you have a good carriage and are well-dressed, if you are clever and cultivated, if you have friends above the average and are well-connected, if you are religious or independent, manly, and courageous; and he tolerates you if you creep about, are rough, ragged, and round-shouldered, a born fool, a toady, a liar, a tale-bearer, an indifferent workman – no matter what you are as long as you say 'sir' to him, are servile and abject, see and hear nothing, and hold with him in everything he says and does: that is the way to get on in the factory.

CHAPTER XV

SICKNESS AND ACCIDENTS – THE FACTORY YEAR – HOLIDAYS – 'TRIP' –
MOODS AND FEELINGS – PAY-DAY – LOSING A QUARTER –
GETTING MARRIED.

Sickness and accidents are of frequent occurrence in the shed. The first-named may be attributed to the foul air prevailing – the dense smoke and fumes from the oil forges, and the thick, sharp dust and ashes from the coke fires. The tremendous noise of the hammers and machinery and the priming of the boilers have a most injurious effect upon the body as well as upon the nervous system; it is all intensely painful and wearisome to the workmen. The most common forms of sickness among the men of the shed are complaints of the stomach and head, with constipation. These are the direct result of the gross impurity of the air. Colds are exceptionally common, and are another result of the bad atmospheric conditions; as soon as you enter into the smoke and fume you are sure to begin sniffing and sneezing. The black dust and filth is being breathed into the chest and lungs every moment. At the weekend one is continually spitting off the accretion; it will take several days to remove it from the body. As a matter of fact, the workmen are never clean, except at holiday times. However often they may wash and bathe themselves, an absence from the shed of several consecutive days will be necessary in order to effect an evacuation of the filth from all parts of the system. Even the eyes contain it. No matter how carefully you wash them at night, in the morning they will be surrounded with dark rings – fine, black dust which has come from them as you lay asleep.

A short while ago I was passing through a village near the town, and, seeing a canvas tent erected in a cottage garden I made it my business to inquire into the cause of it and to ask who might be the occupant. Thereupon I was told that the tent was put up to accommodate a consumptive lad who slept in it by night and worked in the factory by day. On asking what were the lad's duties I was informed that he *worked on the oil furnaces*. The agonies he must have suffered in that loathsome, murderous atmosphere may easily be imagined. Strong men curse the filthy smoke and stench from morning till night, and to a person in consumption it must be a still more exquisite torture. Reading the Medical Report for the county of Wilts recently I noticed it was said that greater supervision is exercised over the workshops now than was the case formerly. From my own knowledge and point of view I should say there is no such supervision of the factory shops at all; during the twenty odd years I have worked there I have never once heard of a factory inspector coming through the shed, unless it were one of the company's own confidential officials.

The percentage of sickness and accidents is higher at the stamping shed than in any other workshop in the factory. The accidents are of many kinds, though they are chiefly scalds and burns, broken and crushed limbs, and injuries to the eyes. It is remarkable how so many accidents happen; they are usually very simply caused and received. A great number of them are due, directly and indirectly, to the unhealthy air about the place. When the workman is not feeling well he is liable to meet with an accident at any moment. He has not then the keen sense of danger necessary under such conditions, or, if he has this, he has not the power in himself to guard against it. He has a vague idea that he is running risks, but he is too dazed or too ill fully to realise it, and very often he does not even care to protect himself. He is thus often guilty of great self-neglect, amounting to madness, though he is ignorant of it at the time. When he is away from the shed he remembers the danger he was in, and is amazed at his weakness, and vows resolutions of taking greater pains in the future, but on coming back to the work the old conditions prevail, and he is confronted with the same inability to take sufficient precautions for his safety and well-being. Where the air is good, or even moderately pure, the workmen will be more keen and sensible of danger. Both their physical and mental powers will be active and alert and accidents will consequently be much more rare.

As soon as a serious accident happens to a workman a rush is made to the spot by young and old alike – they cannot contain their eager curiosity and excitement. Many are impelled by a strong desire to be of service to the unfortunate individual who has been hurt, though, in nine cases out of ten, instead of being a help they are a very great hindrance. If the workman is injured very severely, or if he happens to be killed, it will be impossible to keep the crowd back; in spite of commands and exhortations they use their utmost powers to approach the spot and catch a glimpse of the victim. The overseer shouts, curses, and waves his hands frantically, and warns them all of what he will do, but the men doggedly refuse to disperse until they have satisfied their curiosity and abated their excitement.

Immediately a man is down one hurries off to the ambulance shed for the stretcher, another hastens to the cupboard for lint and *sal volatile*; this one fetches water from the tap, and the 'first-aid men' are soon at work patching up the wound. In a few moments the stretcher arrives and the injured one is lifted upon it and carried or wheeled off to the hospital. Some of the men inspect the spot at which the accident occurred and loiter there for a moment; afterwards they go on with their work as though nothing had happened.

If the injured man dies word is immediately sent into the shed. A notice of the funeral is posted upon the wall and a collection is usually made to buy a wreath, or the money is handed over to the widow or next-of-kin to help meet the expenses. There are always a few to follow the old comrade to the grave, and the bearers will usually be the deceased man's nearest workmates. Occasionally, if the funeral happens to be that of a very old hand, and one who was a special favourite with the men, the whole shed is closed for the event. Within two or three days afterwards, however, the affair will be almost forgotten; it will be as though the workman had never existed. Amid the hurry and noise of the shop there is little time to think of the dead; one's whole attention has to be directed towards the living and to the earning of one's own liveli-hood. For a single post rendered vacant by the death of a workman, there are sure to be several applicants; a new hand is soon brought forward to fill the position. Though he does not wish to be unnatural towards his predecessor, he thanks his lucky stars, all the same, that he has got the appointment; it is nothing to him who or what the other man was. It is an ill wind that blows nobody good, and that, for the most part, is the philosophy of the men at the factory.

There is one other point worth remembering in connection with the matter of pure or impure air in the shed, and that is, that the quality of the work made will be considerably affected by it. The more fit a workman feels, the better his work will be. If he is deficient in health it will be unreasonable to expect that his forging will be of the highest quality; there is bound to be a depreciation in it. The same may be said of the workman's relations with his employers – his satisfaction or dissatis-faction with existing conditions. If he is treated honestly and fairly the firm will gain greatly thereby, in many ways unknown to them. The workman, in return, will be conscientious and will use his tools and machinery with scrupulous care. But if he is being continually pricked and goaded, and ground down by the overseer, he will naturally be less inclined to study the interests of the company beyond what is his most inevitable duty, and something or other will suffer. In any case it is as well to remember that in such matters as these the interests of all are identical; where there is mutual understanding and appreciation, gain is

Caricatures of Trip were popular as post-cards. This: 1904. Destinations included Weymouth, Weston-super-Mare, South Wales, London and North of England

bound to accrue to each party. No general has ever won a battle with an unhealthy or discontented army, and the conditions in a large factory, with ten or twelve thousand workmen, are very similar; the figure is reasonably applicable.

The year at the factory is divided into three general periods; *i.e.*, from Christmas till Easter, Easter till 'Trip' – which is held in July – and Trip till Christmas. There are furthermore the Bank Holidays of Whitsuntide and August, though more than one day's leave is seldom granted in

Overleaf: Start of Railway Works' annual holiday: Trip, 1910. Locomotives in steam, *County of Monmouth* and *County of Somerset*, wait to take workers and families to sea-side

connection with either of them. Sometimes there will be no cessation of labour at all, which gives satisfaction to many workmen, for, notwithstanding the painfulness of the confinement within the dark walls, they are, as a rule, indifferent to holidays. Many hundreds of them would never have one at all if they were not forced to do so by the constitution of the calendar and the natural order of things.

Very little travelling is done by the workmen during the Easter holidays. Most of those who have a couple of square yards of land, a small

Trip Train, 1912. Mechanics' Institute established the Trip, 1849, for 500 people. In 1905, 24,500 people, about half Swindon's population, left in 22 special trains in little over 2 hours

back-yard, or a box of earth on the window sill, prepare for the task of husbandry – the general talk in spare moments now will be of peas, beans, onions, and potatoes. The longest journeys from home are made by the small boys of the shed, who set out in squads and troops to go bird's-nesting in the hedgerows, or plucking primroses and violets in the woods and copses. Young Jim was very excited when Easter came with the warm, sunny weather; it was pleasant to listen to his childish talk as he told us about the long walks he had taken in search of primroses and violets, going without his dinner and tea in order to collect a posy of the precious flowers. Questioned as to the meaning of Good Friday, he was puzzled for a few moments, and then told us it was because Jesus Christ was born on that day. Though he was mistaken as to the origin and signification of the Festival, there are hundreds of others older than he at the works who would not be able to answer the question correctly.

At Whitsuntide the first outings are generally held. Then many of the workmen – those who can afford it, who have no large gardens to care

Trip Train, 1912. A week's pay was lost through Trip till 1913, when mid-week holiday dates provided half-pay for two consecutive weeks instead

for, and who are exempt from other business and anxieties – begin to make short week-end trips by the trains. The privilege of a quarter-fare for travel, granted by the railway companies to their employees, is valued and appreciated, and widely patronised. By means of this very many have trips and become acquainted with the world who otherwise would be unable to do so.

When the men come back to work after the Whitsuntide holidays they usually find the official noticeboard in the shed covered with posters

containing the preliminary announcements of the annual Trip, and, very
soon, on the plates of the forges and walls, and even outside in the town,
the words 'Roll on, Trip,' or 'Five weeks to Trip,' may be seen scrawled
in big letters. As the time for the holiday draws near the spirits of the
workmen – especially of the younger ones, who have no domestic
responsibilities – rise considerably. Whichever way one turns he is
greeted with the question – often asked in a jocular sense – 'Wher' gwain
Trip?' the reply to which usually is – 'Same old place,' or 'Up in the
smowk;' *i.e.*, to London, or 'Swindon by the Sea.' By the last-named
place Weymouth is intended. That is a favourite haunt of the poorer
workmen who have large families, and it is especially popular with the
day trippers. Every year five or six thousand are conveyed to the
Dorsetshire watering-place, the majority of whom return the same
evening. Given fine weather an enjoyable day will be spent about the
sands and upon the water, but it if happens to rain the outing will prove a
wretched fiasco. Sometimes the trippers have left home in fine weather
and found a deluge of rain setting in when they arrived at the seaside
town. Under such circumstances they were obliged to stay in the trains
all day for shelter, or implore the officials to send them home again
before the stipulated time.

'Trip Day' is the most important day in the calendar at the railway
town. For several months preceding it, fathers and mothers of families,
young unmarried men, and juveniles have been saving up for the outing.
Whatever new clothes are bought for the summer are usually worn for
the first time at 'Trip'; the trade of the town is at its zenith during the
week before the holiday. Then the men don their new suits of shoddy,
and the pinched or portly dames deck themselves out in all the glory of
cheap, 'fashionable' finery. The young girls are radiant with colour –
white, red, pink, and blue – and the children come dressed in brand-new
garments – all stiff from the warehouse – and equipped with spade and
bucket and bags full of thin paper, cut the size of pennies, to throw out of
the carriage windows as the train flies along. A general exodus from the
town takes place that day and quite twenty-five thousand people will
have been hurried off to all parts of the kingdom in the early hours of the
morning, before the ordinary traffic begins to get thick on the line.
About half the total number return the same night; the others stop away
till the expiration of the holiday, which is of eight days' duration.

The privilege of travelling free by the Trip trains is not granted to all
workmen, but only to those who are members of the local Railway
Institute and Library, and have contributed about six shillings per annum

to the general fund. Moreover, no part of the holiday is free, but is counted as lost time. The prompt commencement of work after Trip is, therefore, highly necessary; the great majority of the workmen are reduced to a state of absolute penury. If they have been away and spent all their money – and perhaps incurred debt at home for rent and provisions beforehand in order to enjoy themselves the better on their trip – it will take them a considerable time to get square again; they will scarcely have done this before the Christmas holidays are announced.

Caricature post-card, 1910. At their peak, Trip trains took about 26,500 people by special trains from within the works

At the end of the first week after the Trip holiday there will be no money to draw. When Friday comes round, bringing with it the usual hour for receiving the weekly wages, the men file out of the sheds with long faces. This is generally known at the works as 'The Grand March Past,' because the toilers march past the pay-table and receive nothing that day. The living among the poorest of the workmen will be very meagre, and a great many will not have enough to eat until the next Friday comes round, bringing with it the first pay. The local tradesmen

Overleaf: Brass Foundry, 1907. A model of workshop layout, it housed thirty-three crucibles, three air furnaces, four moulding machines. Annual output, about 1,700 tons

and shopkeepers look upon the Trip as a great nuisance because, they say, it takes money away from the town that ought to be spent in their warehouses; they do not take into consideration the fact that the men are confined like prisoners all the rest of the year.

Work in the sheds, for the first day or two after the Trip, goes very hard and painful; everyone is yearning towards the blue sea or the fresh open country, and thinking of friends and kindred left behind. This feeling very soon wears off, however. Long before the week is over the

Brass Foundry Outing, August 17, 1907

spirit of work will have taken possession of the men; they fall naturally into their places and the Trip becomes a thing of the past – a dream and a memory. Here and there you may see scrawled upon the wall somewhere or other, with a touch of humour, '51 weeks to Trip'; that is usually the last word in connection with it for another year.

There are three general moods and phases of feeling among the workmen, corresponding to the three periods of the year as measured out by the holidays. The period between Christmas and Easter is one of hope and rising spirits, of eager looking forward to brighter days, the long evening and the pleasant week-end. The dark and gloom of winter has weighed heavily upon the toilers, but this has reached its worst point by the end of December; after that the barometer begins to rise and a more cheerful spirit prevails everywhere.

From Easter till Trip and August Bank Holiday – notwithstanding the terrible trials of the summer weather in the case of those who work at the furnaces – the feeling is one of comparative ease and satisfaction. A series of little holidays is included in this period. The men are encouraged to bear with the heat and fatigue through the knowledge that it will not be for long; a holiday in sight goes far towards mitigating the hard punishment of the work in the shed. The summer sunshine and general bright weather, the occupations of gardening, and the prevalence of herbs and salads, fresh, sweet vegetables, flowers, and fruits all have a beneficial effect upon the workman and tend to distract his attention from the drabness of his employment and make the weeks go by more easily. The period is one of lightness. It is the time of realization, the fulfilling of dreams dreamed through the long, dark winter.

From August till Christmas the feeling is one almost of despair. Five whole months have to be borne without a break in the monotony of the labour. The time before the next holiday seems almost infinite; a tremendous amount of work must be done in the interval. Accordingly, the men settle down with grim faces and fixed determinations. The pleasures of the year are thrust behind and forgotten; day by day the battle must be fought and the ground gained inch by inch. The smoke towers up from the stacks and chimneys, the hammers pound away on the obstinate metal, the wheels whirl round and the din is incessant. Day after day the black army files in and out of the entrances with the regularity of clockwork; it is indeed the period of stern work – the great effort of the year. Whatever money the workmen save must be put aside now or never; the absence of holidays and lack of inducement to travel will provide them with the opportunity. Now is the time for purchasing new clothing and boots and for getting out of debt – if there is any desire to do that; it is in every sense of the word the great productive period.

It is also interesting to note the various moods and feelings common to the workmen during the passage of the week. Monday is always a flat, stale day, and especially is this true of the morning, before dinner-time. It might reasonably be supposed that the workmen, after an absence of a day, or a day and a half, would return to the shed rested and vigorous, and fit for new efforts, but this is far from being the actual case. As a matter of fact, Monday is an extremely dull day in the shed. Everyone seems surly and out of sorts, as though he had been routed up from sleep before time and had 'got out of bed on the wrong side.' The foreman comes on the scene with a scowl; the chargeman is 'huffy' and irritable; the stampers and hammermen bend to their work in stony silence, or snap at each other; even the youngsters are quiet and mopish. Work seems to go particularly hard and against the grain. It is as though everything were under a cloud; there is not a bit of life or soul in it. This feeling is so general on the first day of the week that the men have invented a term by which to express it; if you ask anyone how he is on that day he will be sure to tell you that he feels 'rough' and 'Monday-fied.' By dinner-time the cloud will have lifted some-what, though not till towards the end of the afternoon will there be anything like real relief, with a degree of brightness. By that time the tediousness of the first day will have worn off; the men's faces brighten up and a spirit of cheerfulness prevails. Now they speak to each other, laugh, whistle and jest, perhaps; they have won the first skirmish in the weekly battle.

Tuesday is the strong day, the day of vigorous activity, of tool- and also of record-breaking. The men come to work like lions. All the stiffness and sluggishness contracted at the week-end has vanished now. There is a great change, both in the temper and the physical condition of the men, visible about the place; they move more quickly, handle their tools better, and appear to be in perfect trim. The work made on Tuesdays is always the greatest in amount and usually the best in quality. Everyone, from the foreman to the office-boy, seems brighter and better, more fit, well, and energetic – great things are accomplished on Tuesdays at the works.

Wednesday is very similar to Tuesday, though the men are not quite as fresh and vigorous. The pace, though still smart and good, will fall a little below that of the day previous. Three days' toil begins to tell on the muscles and reserve of the body, though this is counterbalanced by the increase of mental satisfaction and expectation, the knowledge of being in mid-week and of getting within sight of another pay-day and cessation from work.

Thursday is the humdrum day. As much work will be done as on the day preceding, but more effort will be required to perform it. An acute observer will perceive a marked difference in the general behaviour of the workmen and in the manner in which they manipulate the tools. They will begin to look tired and haggard. When they leave the shed at mealtimes they do not rush headlong out, pushing and shouting, but file away soberly and in comparative silence.

By Friday morning the barometer will have risen considerably. Notwithstanding the tiredness of the individual, he is nerved to fresh efforts and induced to make a final spurt towards the end of the weekly race. His manner is altogether more cheerful, and he becomes quite affable to his mates. If the manager or overseer passes through the shed more frequently than usual and comes and times him at his work, he takes but very little notice of him. Those who are by nature gruff and surly melt a little and show a more genial disposition on the Friday. The secret of all this lies in the fact that Friday is both the last whole day to be worked at the shed, and it is pay-day, too. The men's faces brighten considerably at the approach of that happy and eagerly-awaited hour. When they collect together around the pay-table they indulge in jocular remarks with one another, and the majority bubble over with good-nature. As they pass the table in single file they grab up the box containing the money with commendable determination. If the pay is a full one there will be a broad smile, or a grin, on the faces of most of the men as they remove the cover and pocket the coin; that is about the happiest and most triumphant moment of all for them.

To draw the wages each man is furnished with a metal check having a number, corresponding with his name in the register, stamped upon it. The check is issued to the men as they enter the shed after dinner, and is a guarantee that they have wages to receive on that day. Each man's wages are put up in a tin box, which is also stamped with his number. The foreman takes his position at the head, and two clerks stand behind the table. Of these, one calls out the number upon the box and the other takes it and claps it sharply on the table. The men are waiting ready and take it as they walk past; two hundred may be paid in about five minutes by this method. Extras for piecework are paid fortnightly. Whatever stoppages and contributions are due for the local Sick and Medical Fund, coal, wood, and other charges, are deducted on the normal week, and this is called 'stoppage week.' Accordingly, the day of great good-humour comes fortnightly, and that week is known among the men as 'balance week.'

Saturday is the day of final victory, the closing up of the weekly battle, though a great part of the eagerness evinced a day or two before will have vanished now that the time to take the hebdomadal rest is really at hand. It is strikingly true, even here, that expectation is better than realization. Notwithstanding the fact that the men are tired and worn out they do not

Overleaf: The Cash Office, 1911

appear to be as keen for the rest as might be imagined; they now seem to have recovered their normal powers and work away quite unconcernedly up to the last moment. The boys and youths, however, will be restless; they whistle and sing and rush off like shots from a gun as soon as the hooter sounds.

Sunday is the day of complete inactivity with most of the workmen, and it is possibly the weakest and the least enjoyed of all. If the weather is dull and wet a great number stay in bed till dinner-time, and sometimes

Swindon Amateur Bicycle Club (the town's oldest) 1907. Tom Hamblin, front row, third from left (see illustration on pp. 24–5). Club's headquarters: The Eagle Hotel

they remain there all day and night, till Monday morning comes. This will not have done them much harm; they will feel all the more refreshed and the better able to face the toil and battle of the coming week.

Every day, as well as the year and week, has its divisions and a temper and feeling on the part of the men corresponding with each of them. In the morning, before breakfast, nearly everyone is sober and quiet, very often surly, and even spitefully disposed. During that time the men in the shed rarely speak to each other, but bend down to the labour in silence.

After breakfast the tone improves a little, and continues to do so till dinner-time, when the tempers of the men will have become about normal; they are restored to their natural humour and disposition. When they return after dinner a still greater improvement is discernible, and by five o'clock in the afternoon they are not like the same beings. In the evening, after tea, greater good-fellowship than ever prevails, and if a man meets his mate in the town he is quite cordial. By the next morning, however, he is metamorphosed again; the old conditions

Amateur Gymnastic Society, Swindon, was not exclusively male: Ladies Gymnastic Team, 1911–1912

obtain, and so on day after day and month after month. The best work of the day is always made in the morning, between the hours of nine and eleven.

If a workman oversleeps in the morning and is too late for admittance before breakfast, he may start at nine o'clock. This is called 'losing a quarter.' There are those at the works who are noted for losing quarters; they are usually absent from the shed before breakfast once or twice a week. Such as these, by the frequency of their absence, are not noticed very much, but if one who is habitually a good timekeeper happens to be out unexpectedly before breakfast, means are taken to celebrate the event. When he arrives there will be a little surprise awaiting him. He will find an effigy of himself standing near the forge, and will receive a salute composed of hammers knocking on steel plates, and the rattling of any old pot that chances to be at hand. During the meal-time the workmen obtain several coats, a hat, and a pair of boots, and fix them on the handles of the mallets and broom, and then chalk out the features of a man upon the coke shovel. Afterwards they assemble in a gang and greet their comrade with an overpowering din. If he is wise he will take it all in good part and join in with the fun, and the din will soon cease; but if he loses his temper – as is sometimes the case – he is assailed more loudly than ever, and driven half mad with the uproar.

A somewhat similar reception is given to a workman who has just been married. As soon as it is known that the banns are published – and this is certain to leak out and news of it be brought into the shed – he becomes the object of very special attention. The men come to him from all quarters and offer him their congratulations, sincere and otherwise, very often accompanying them with advice of different kinds, sometimes of a highly sarcastic nature. Many insist upon shaking hands with him and, with mock ceremony, compliment him on his decision to join the 'Big Firm,' as they call it, assuring him, at the same time, that they shall expect him to 'stand his footing.' Occasionally, if their mate is poor, the men of a gang will make a small collection and buy him a present – a pair of pictures, a piece of furniture, or a set of ornaments. Perhaps this may be carried out ridiculously, and the whole thing turned into a joke, whereupon the prospective bridegroom loses his temper and soundly lashes his mates for their unsolicited patronage.

If the workman divulges the time and place of the wedding there will certainly be a few to witness it, in order to see how he behaves during the ceremony. Very often they wait outside the church with missiles of several kinds, such as old shoes and slippers, rice, barley, Indian corn, and even potatoes, ready to pelt him. Occasionally, however, it happens that the wily mate has deceived them with regard either to the time or the place, and if they turn up at the church they will have to wait in vain, the laughing-stock of all passers-by. When the newly married man recommences work he is received with a loud uproar. This is called 'ringing him in.' A crowd of men and boys beat upon

Above: W. Veal, Jeweller, 87 Regent Street, about 1910: 'The Noted House for Wedding Rings'. *Overleaf:* Brides may have worked in Compton's Factory, one of Swindon's main places of employment for women. Uniforms were made here for GWR. About 1910

Family group outside house in Jennings Street. In window, notice of an anniversary service. 'Every denomination', from Plymouth Brethren to Roman Catholics, 'had their place of worship.' (Jefferies)

any loose plate of metal that will return a loud clang – such as lids of tool-chests, steel bars, anvils, and sides of coke bunks – and make as much noise as possible. This is all over by the time the hooter sounds. With the starting of the shop engine the men fall in to work, and the marriage is forgotten by the crowd.

CHAPTER XVI

COLD AND HEAT – MEALS – FAT AND LEAN WORKMEN – WAYS AND MEANS – PRANKS – ALL FOOLS' DAY – NEW YEAR'S EVE

Two kinds of weather go hard with the toilers in the shed; they are – extreme cold and extreme heat. When it is very cold in the winter the men will be subjected to a considerable amount of draught from the doors and roof; on one side they will be half-baked with the heat, and on the other chilled nearly to the bone. The furnacemen and stampers will be drenched with perspiration day after day, in the coldest weather. When they leave the shed to go home at meal-times and at night they will run great risks of taking cold; it is no wonder that cases of rheumatism and lumbago are very common among those who toil at the furnaces and forges. The workmen, for the most part, wear the same clothes all the year round, winter and summer; they make no allowance for cold and heat with warm or thin clothing.

Very few wear overcoats, or even mufflers, in the coldest weather, unless it is wet. They are often numbed with the cold, for they feel it severely, and they commonly run up the long yard in order to keep themselves warm in frosty weather on their return to the shed after meals. If you ask them why they do not wear a cravat or muffler they tell you it is 'no good to coddle yourself up too much, for the more clothes you wear the more you will want to wear.' A great many – of the town workmen especially – do not possess an overcoat of any kind. Whatever the weather may be they journey backwards and forwards quite unprotected. I have known men come to the shed drenched to the skin, many a time, and be forced to work in that condition while the garments were drying on their backs. Now and then, though not often, a bold and hardy workman will remove his shirt or trousers and stand and dry them at the furnace door. If he does this he is certain to be shied at and made the target for various lumps of coke and coal. Amusement is sometimes caused by the shirt taking fire; I have more than once seen a workman reduced to the necessity of borrowing an overcoat to wrap around him in lieu of upper garments. Sometimes the clothes of half the gang are set alight with sparks from the hammers, and burnt to ashes.

The heat of the summer months, for those who toil at the furnaces and forges, is far more painful to endure than are all the inconveniences of cold weather. This is especially the case in close and stuffy sheds where there is a defective system of ventilation, or where the workshop is surrounded by other buildings. The interior of these places will be like a hot oven; it will be impossible for the workmen to maintain any degree of strength and vigour at their labour. In the early morning, before eight o'clock, the air will be somewhat cooler, but by the time of re-starting, after breakfast, the heat will be deadly and overpowering; the temperature in front of the furnaces will be considerably over 100 degrees. Where there is a motion of air the workmen can stand a great amount of heat on all sides, but when that is quite stagnant, and thick and heavy with the nauseous smoke and fumes from the oil forges, it is positively torturous. The exigencies of piecework will admit of no relaxation, however; approximately the same amount of work must be made on the hottest day of summer as on the coldest day of winter.

There is one inevitable reason of all this – the work made under such conditions will be inferior in quality, for the men cannot spend the time they should over the hot metal. If you stand and watch the stampers you will see, from their very movements, how wretchedly tired and languid they are; one-half of them are scarcely able to drag their weary limbs backwards and forwards – they are truly objects of misery. At the same time, they do not complain, for that would be fruitless, and they know it. Lost to everything but the sense of their own inexpressible weariness, with grim necessity at their elbows, they spend their last effort on the job, having no interest available for the work, only longing for the next hooter to sound and give them a temporary rest. Those who work out of doors in the extreme heat of the sun, though they perspire much, yet have pure air to breathe, so that there will be a minimum of fatigue resulting from it. In the dust and filth of the shed, however, the perspiration costs very much more. It seems drawn from the marrow of your bones; your very heart's blood seems to ooze out with it.

The change from cold to heat, and also the shifting of the wind, is immediately felt in the shed; there is no need of a weather-vane to inform you of the wind's direction. Even when there is air moving, only one half of the place will benefit from it. Entering the shed at one end, it will pile up all the smoke and fume at the other. This, instead of passing out, will whirl round and round in an eddy, and tease and torment the workmen, making them gasp for breath.

The toilers have resort to various methods in order to mitigate the heat during the summer months. The furnacemen, stampers, and forgers usually remove their shirts altogether, and discard their leathern aprons for those made of light canvas, or old rivet bags. The amount of cold water drunk at such times is enormous. It is useless to advise the men to take it in moderation: 'I don't care, I must have it,' is the answer made.

Swimming, washing and Turkish baths, beyond Swindon Book Market, Faringdon Road. Water from GWR source at Kemble was heated at works and supplied to baths

Occasionally the officials issue oatmeal from the stores, to be taken with the water. This removes the rawness from the liquid, and makes it much more palatable, and less harmful to the stomach. The boys are especially fond of the mixture; they would drink it by the bucketful, and swallow grouts and all. They do not believe in wasting anything obtained gratis from the company.

One plan, in very hot weather, is to wrap a wet towel or wiper about

the head, cooling it now and then with fresh water. Some hold their heads
and faces underneath the tap and let the cool water run upon them; and
others engage their mates to squirt it in their faces instead. Such as do this
tie an apron close around the neck under the chin, and receive the volume
of water full in the face. It is delicious, when you are baked and half-
choked with the heat in midsummer, to go to the big tap under the wall
and receive the cold water on the inside part of the arm, just below the
shoulder, allowing it to run down and flow off the finger tips. This is very
cooling and refreshing, and is a certain restorative.

Now and then, during the meal-hour, a hardy workman will strip
himself and bathe in the big bosh used for cooling the furnace tools. In the
evening, after a hard sweating at the fires, many of the young men will pay
a visit to the baths in the town. Little Jim and his mates, who have no
coppers to squander upon the luxury of a dip under cover, betake
themselves to the clay-pits in a neighbouring brick-field. There they dive
down among the fishes and forget about the punishment they have
suffered today, and which is certainly awaiting them on the morrow.

The majority of the workmen go out of the sheds to have their food. In
very many workshops they are not permitted, under any consideration, to
remain in to meals. On the score of health this is as it should be; it forces the
workman, whether he likes it or not, to breathe a little fresh air. It also
removes him from his surroundings for the time, and affords him some
refreshment in that way. The sheds in which the men are allowed to have
their meals unmolested are the smiths' shops, the steam-hammer shops,
and the rolling mills shed. In all these places the men perspire considerably,
and they would be very liable to take a chill, especially in the winter
months, if they were forced to go out into the cold air to meals. Mess-
rooms are provided for the men of some shops, and tea is brewed and food
cooked for as many as like to repair to them. Very many will not patronise
them, however, because they do not like eating their food in public; they
say it is 'like being among a lot of cattle.' Such as these take their food in
their hand and eat it as they walk about, or perhaps they visit a coffee
tavern or an inn of the town. During fine weather a large number have
their meals in the recreation field underneath the trees. Their little sons or
daughters bring the food from home, with hot tea in a mug or bottle, and
meet them outside the entrances. Then they sit down together in the shade
of the elm-trees and enjoy the repast.

The forgers and furnacemen do not eat much food in the shed during the
summer months. The heat of the fires and the fumes from the oil furnaces
impair their appetites, and large quantities of bread and other victuals are

thrown out in the yard for the rats and birds. Rooks and sparrows are the only regular feathered inhabitants of the yard, if, indeed, the rooks can be so called, for they have their nests a long way off. They merely obtain their food about the yard during the day and go home to bed at night. The sparrows build their nests almost anywhere, though their favourite place seems to be in the sockets made in the walls for containing the lamp brackets. As the lamps are removed during the summer months, the holes afford a convenient resting-place for the ubiquitous *passeres*.

No starlings frequent the yard; they prefer a quieter and more natural habitation. A robin, even, is an unusual visitor, while martins and swallows never visit the precincts of the factory. The sweet *chelidon* – the darling stranger from the far-off shores of the blue Mediterranean – shuns the unearthly noise and smother of the factory altogether; her delight is in places far removed from the whirling of wheels and the chu-chuing of engines.

The rooks seem perfectly inured to the smoke and steam and the life of the factory yard; at all hours of the day they may be seen scavenging around the sheds, picking up any stray morsel that happens to be lying about. Four of these frequent the yard regularly. Summer and winter they are to be seen strutting up and down over the ashes of the track, or perched upon the tops of the high lamps. Once, during a gale, I saw a rook try to alight upon the summit of a lamp, eighty feet high – on the small curved iron stay that crowns the whole like a bow. Although it secured a footing on the top, it could not balance itself to rest there, but was forced to keep its two wings entirely expanded in order to maintain any equilibrium at all. This it did for nearly two minutes, but the force of the wind was so great that it could not keep its balance and was presently blown away. To view it there, with wings outstretched, brought to mind a bird of a much nobler reputation than that of Master Rook; it was worthy of the traditions of the eagle.

It is instructive to note the various types of men and to consider how they compare with one another. Big, fat workmen invariably make better mates than do small, thin ones. Their temper is certain to be more genial, and they are usually more open and simple, hearty and free; everything with them, to use a time-honoured phrase, seems to go 'as easy as an old cut shoe.' Even Cæsar, though very thin himself, wished to have about him men who were fat and sleek – he was suspicious of the lean and hungry-looking Cassius. Fat workmen, as a rule, seem incapable of much worry. If anything goes amiss they look upon it with the greatest unconcern and lightly brush it aside, while the thin, small individual is forever fretting and grieving over some trivial thing or other. It is noteworthy that hairy men, as well as being considerably stronger, are usually better-tempered than are those who are lacking in this respect. The little person is proverbially vain and conceited and 'thinks great things' of himself, as the Greeks would have said, while the words of the old rhyme are uniformly true and applicable:–

> 'Long and lazy,
> Black and proud,
> Fair and foolish,
> Little and loud.'

Small pride is discovered in the individual of sixteen or seventeen stone weight. Nor are size and bulk in a workman always indicative of the greatest prowess. Very many men of no more than five feet or less in stature, and of correspondingly small proportions, are veritable lions in strength.

Of all styles of workmen soever the dandy, or, as he is vulgarly called, the 'swanker,' is usually the least proficient at his trade. There is another who would delight to stand with his hands behind him, or perhaps to walk about like it: he is certain to be of the self-conscious type, one not extra fond of making unnatural exertions. This one, whenever an opportunity presents itself, would stand with his thumbs thrust in the armholes of his waistcoat and complacently look upon all around him; you may know him for one who would rather see you do a job than do it himself. That one yonder is fond of standing with his arms folded, and another would thrust his hands deep into his trousers pockets at every stray opportunity. Such as these may come in time to draw as much wages as the best workmen on the premises, or they may even obtain more, but they will never be experts themselves; they are too choice, and too dilatory. Your capital workman never adopts any of these attitudes. Walking or standing, pausing, resting, or viewing any other operation, his hands are down by his sides – free, and in the most advantageous position for rendering assistance to himself, or to others, as the case may be.

The men of one department or shed – except in the case of a fire – never help those of another, no matter how great the difficulty may be, unless they have been officially lent, and this is of extremely rare occurrence. One might think that where two sheds stand side by side, help would occasionally be given, when it was required, but such is the

---

Overleaf: Men leaving railway works, Rodbourne Road, about 1905. Tram waits until crowd has gone

condition of things, and so rigid is the system imposed at the works, that this is completely out of the question. The men of two contingent sheds, though they may have been working close together for twenty or thirty years, are almost total strangers. They may see each other now and then, and recognise one another by sight, but they do not think of exchanging conversations.

There is one matter, however, in which, notwithstanding the many facilities at hand for perfect equipment, the works resembles most other establishments, and that is in the frequently defective supply of proper tools for the workmen and the too great tendency to use anything that may be lying about for makeshift. When I came into the factory as a boy I expected to find everything of this sort in perfect arrangement. In the rough and ready trade of agriculture I had been accustomed to making the best use of old, worn-out tools. The farmer, if he is not blessed with abundant capital, is often forced to have recourse to crude means and expedients in order to tide himself over a difficulty. He must bind up this and patch that, and sometimes set his men to work with tackle that is broken and antiquated. One looks for this, naturally, out on the farm, and is surprised if he does not find it so. But in the factory, thought I, there will be none of it. I supposed that all the machinery would be in perfect trim, that tools would be very plentiful and of the best description, and that everything would be ordered for the men's convenience in order to expedite the work.

A short acquaintance with matters in the shed soon dispelled this illusion, however. I found that the same condition of things obtained in the factory as was the case on the far away, deserted farm. There something ailed the chaffcutter, the mowing- or reaping-machine, the plough, the elevator, or the horse-rake. Some links were missing from the traces and had to be replaced with stout wire; many things were in use that were heavy, cumbersome, and primitive. Here something is wrong with the steam-hammer, drill, lathe, or hydraulic machine. The wheel-barrows are broken, the shovels are without handles, the besoms are worn out; hammers and chisels, tongs, sets, and other tools are almost as scarce as pound pieces. You seldom have any decent tools to work with unless you can make them yourself, or pay the smith for doing it out of your own pocket. Then, in nine cases out of ten, if the machinery breaks down, the same means are resorted to as were adopted by the farmer or haulier; any patching up will do until such time as someone or other can make it convenient to carry out the necessary repairs. As long as the parts hang together and the wheels go round, that will be considered sufficient. This kind of procedure, in the case of a famer or other, who has no very great convenience for equipping himself with every desirable apparatus, may be condoned, but in a large and professedly up-to-date factory there is no excuse at all for it – it is pure misdemeanour and slovenliness.

Many pranks are played upon one another by the workmen, though it is significant of the times that skylarking and horse-play are not nearly as common and frequent as they were formerly. The supervision of the sheds is much more strict, and the prices are considerably lower than they used to be; there is not now the time and opportunity, nor even the inclination to indulge in practical jokes. Under the new discipline the men are generally more sober and silent, though they are none the happier, nevertheless. The increased efforts they are bound to make at work and the higher speed of the machinery has caused them to become gloomy and unnatural, and, very often, peevish and irritable. It is a further illustration of the old adage —

'All work and no play
Makes Jack a dull boy.'

There is one matter for congratulation, however, and that is that the youngsters are not to be deprived of their sports and amusements on any pretext whatever. Though you set them to do almost impossible tasks they will find the time and the means to exercise their natural propensity to playfulness.

It is a bad sign when there is a total absence of play in the shed. It is bad for the individual and for the men collectively; it indicates too great a subjection to working conditions – the subjugation of inherent nature. It is of far greater value and importance to mankind that spirit and character should be cherished and maintained, than that the trifling and petty rules of the factory should be scrupulously observed and adhered to. At the same time, no sane person would recommend that an unrestricted liberty be allowed the workmen. There is bound to be a certain amount of law and order, but where everything is done at the piece rate and the firm is not in a position to lose on the bargain, it is stupid obstinately to insist upon the observance of every little rule laid down. Piece-rated men seldom or never work at a perfectly uniform speed; there are dull and intensely active periods depending sometimes upon the physical condition of the workman and sometimes upon the quality known as 'luck' in operation. Give the workman his head and he will fashion out his own time-table, he will speedily make up for any losses he has incurred before. The feeling of fitness is bound to come; he revels in the toil while it possesses him. There never was, and there never will be, a truly mechanical man who shall work with the systematical regularity of a clock or steam-engine; that is beyond all hope and reason, beyond possibility and beyond nature. What is more, it is absolutely unnecessary and undesirable.

One prank that used to be greatly in vogue in the shed was that of inserting a brick in the sleeve of a workmate's jacket as it was hanging up underneath the wall or behind the forge. This was sometimes done for pure sport, though occasionally there was more than a spice of malice in the jest. Perhaps the owner of the garment had been guilty of an offence, of tale-bearing, or something or other to the prejudice of his fellow-mates, and this was the means adopted for his punishment. Accordingly, a large brick was quietly dropped into the sleeve from inside the shoulder and well shaken down to the cuff, and the jacket was left hanging innocently in its position. At hooter time all those in the secret congregated and waited for the victim of the joke to come for his coat. Suddenly, as the hooter sounded, he rushed up in a great hurry, seized his coat and discovered the impediment, while all the others speedily decamped. He had considerable difficulty in dislodging the brick from the sleeve. After trying in vain for ten minutes or more he was usually forced to cut away the sleeve, or the lining, with his pocket-knife.

Another favourite trick was to place some kind of seat under a wall in order to entice the unwary, and to fix up above it a large tin full of soot, so arranged as to work on a pivot, and operated by means of a string. The soot was also sometimes mixed with water, and stirred up so as to make an intensely black fluid. By and by an unsuspecting workman – usually an interloper from the yard or elsewhere – would come along and sit down upon the improvised seat. Very soon one of the gang shouted out 'Hey up!' sharply, and as the victim jumped up someone pulled the string and down came soot, water, and very often the pot, too, upon his head. If the joke was successful the dupe's face was as black as a sweep's; a loud roar of laughter went up from the workmen and the unhappy victim very quickly got outside. Sometimes, however, he did not take it so quietly, and I have seen a free fight as the outcome of this adventure.

The water-pipe plays a great part in practical joking in the shed, though this is more usually the juvenile's method of perpetrating a jest or paying off an old score. There is also the water-squirt, which is another juvenile weapon. It is sufficient to say that the use of this, whenever it is detected, is rigidly put down by the workmen themselves; it is universally looked upon as a nuisance. Great injuries to health have been done, in some cases, by senseless practical joking with the water-pipe. I have known instances in which a workman has thrust the nose of a pipe up the trouser leg of another as he lay asleep on the floor in the meal-hour, during night duty, and he has been awakened by it to find himself quite drenched with the stream of water and most wretchedly cold. One lad, who used to drive the steam-hammer for me, was often treated to this by some roughs of the shed, and, as a consequence, was afflicted with chronic rheumatism. Finally he had to stop away from work altogether, and he lay as helpless as a child for nine years, with all his joints stiff and set, and died of the torture.

There is a touch of humour in the situation sometimes, however, as when, for instance, upon breaking up for the Christmas holidays, a group of workmen were singing 'Let some drops now fall on me,' and a wag, in the middle of the hymn, shot a large volume of water over them from the hose-pipe. Another trick is to fill a thin paper bag with water and throw it from a distance. If it happens to strike its object the bag bursts, and the individual forming the target receives a good wetting.

All Fools' Day is sure to be the occasion for many jokes of a suitable kind. A common one at this time is to take a coin and solder it to the head of a nail, and then to drive the nail into the sill of a door, or into the floor in a well-frequented spot where it is bound to be noticed. As soon as it is spied efforts will certainly be made to detach the coin, and, in the midst of it, the party of youths who prepared the trap rush forward and bowl the other over on the floor, at the same time greeting him with boisterous laughter and jeers. Even the chief manager of the works' department has been the victim of this jest. In this case an old sixpence was strongly soldered to the nail, which was then well driven into the floor. Presently the manager came along, saw the coin, and made several attempts to pick it up. It needs not to be said that the jest itself was witnessed in respectful silence; the bowling over a chief might have been attended with certain undesirable consequences.

New Year's Eve was always suitably observed and celebrated by those on the night-shift. When the men came in to work they set about their toils with extra special celerity, and the steam-hammers thumped away with all possible power and speed. This effort was maintained till towards midnight, and then everyone slowed down. At about one o'clock a general cessation of hostilities took place. The steam-hammers were silenced, the fires were damped, and the tools were thrown on one side. All that could be heard was the continual 'chu-chu' of the engine outside forcing the hydraulic pumps, and the exhaust of the donkey engine whirling the fan. In one corner of the shed a large coal fire was kindled on the ground, and around it were placed seats for the company. Then an inventive and musical-minded workman stretched a rope across from the principals and came forward with two sets of steel rods, of various lengths and thicknesses, and capable of emitting almost any note in the scale. These were tied about with twine and suspended from the rope in a graduated order, from the shortest to the longest. Someone else fetched a big brass dome from a worn-out boiler, while others had brought several old buffers from the scrap waggon. Two were trained to strike the rods, and the others were instructed to beat on the dome and buffers.

Shortly before midnight, when the bells in the town and the far-off villages began to peal out, the workmen commenced their carnival. Bells were perfectly imitated by striking the bars of steel suspended from the rope; the buffers contributed their sharp, clear notes, and the brass dome sounded deeply and richly. This was called 'Ringing the changes.' When the noise had been continued for a sufficient length of time food was brought out and the midnight meal partaken of. Although strictly against the rules of the factory, someone or other would be sure to have smuggled into the shed a bottle or jar of ale; this would be passed round and healths drunk with great gusto. When supper was over a melodeon or several mouth-organs were produced, and selections were played for another hour. After that the majority had a nap; they seldom started work any more that morning. The foremen and watchmen were usually missing on New Year's Eve, or if they should happen to arrive upon the scene they never interfered. For once in their lives they, too, became human, and accepted the situation, and perhaps the old watchman sat down with the men and drank out of their bottle and afterwards puffed away at his pipe. If the high officials at the works had only known of what was going on at the time they would have sacked half the men the next day, but even they, sharp as they are, do not get intelligence of everything.

All this happened some twenty years ago and would not be possible today. The shed in which it took place has been deserted by the forgers and transformed into a storehouse for manufactures. The kindly disposed old watchmen are dead, or have been superseded, and a new race of foremen has sprung up. Of the workmen some are dead and others have retired. A great number are missing, and many of those who remain have altered to such an extent under the new conditions that I have sometimes wondered whether they are really the same who worked the night shift and jested with us in the years ago. So striking is the change that has taken place, not only in the administration, but in the very life and temper of the men of the factory during the last decade.

GWR veterans, 21 June, 1924, each with fifty years service or more at Swindon. Alfred had worked with these men

CHAPTER XVII

GETTING A START – THE NEW HAND – TOWN AND COUNTRY
WORKMEN – PROMOTION – DISCHARGING HANDS – LANGUAGE OF
THE SHED – EDUCATION – THE EDUCATED MAN NOT WANTED –
GREASING THE FORGE

Formerly, when anyone was desirous of obtaining a start in the factory, he tidied himself up and, arrayed in clean working costume, presented himself at one or other of the main entrances immediately after break-fast-time so as to meet the eyes of the foremen as they returned from the meal. Morning after morning, when work was plentiful, you might have seen a crowd of men and boys around the large doorways, or lining the pavements as the black army filed in, all anxious to obtain a job and looking wonderingly towards the opening of the dark tunnel through which the men passed to arrive at the different sheds. The workmen eyed the strangers curiously, and, very often, with contempt and displeasure: it is singular that those who are safely established themselves dislike to see new hands being put on. They look upon them as interlopers and rivals, and think them to be a menace to their own position.

Those in want of a start were easily recognisable from the rest by reason of their clean and fresh appearance. Many of them were clad in white corduroy trousers, waistcoats of the same material, with cloth jackets and well-shone boots, and they wore a plain red or white muffler around the neck. Some of them were very modest and bashful, and quite uneasy in face of the crowd; the boys especially were astonished to see so many workmen at once passing by like an army.

As soon as the men had disappeared within the entrances the hooter sounded and the great doors were shut. Shortly afterwards the staff clerks came along, the foremen walking between them at the same time. Very often the two classes were not to be distinguished; in such a case the overseers passed by unchallenged. It usually happened, however, that the foremen were known to one or other of the crowd. As they came up the word was sent round and there was a rush to see who should be the first to put the usual question – 'Chance of a job, sir?' This was sometimes accompanied with an obsequious bow, or the applicant merely raised his forefinger to his forehead. If the foreman was not in need of hands, he simply said 'No' to each applicant and pushed by them all. If he required any he asked them where they came from and what they had been doing, and furthermore questioned them as to their age. If the answers were satisfactory he merely said, 'Come along with me,' and conducted the men off, and they followed with alacrity.

The boys hardly ever had the courage to address the foremen. If they could summon up the necessary resolution, however, they said, 'Please, sir, will you give me a job?' and if the reply was favourable they followed off in high glee, wondering all the way at the strange surroundings, the busy workmen, and the vast array of machinery. Boys usually had but little difficulty in obtaining a start; they were soon taken on and initiated into the mysteries of the sheds. When the foreman saw them outside he went up to them and asked them if they wanted a job and promptly told them to 'Come along.'

When an applicant was taken in hand by the foreman he was conducted to the shop office. From that place he was sent, in company with the office-boy, to the manager's department, where he had to submit to a whole code of formal questions, and was also required to read the rules of the factory and to subscribe his name to them, pledging himself to their observance. After that he was required to undergo a strict medical examination, though one not so severe as that now in vogue. If he was successful in this he was told to present himself at the shed, and was there informed when he might begin work. This might be at any hour of the day, though it was usually fixed for the early morning – getting a start commonly occupied one day entire. Sometimes it happened that a man's references were unsatisfactory; in that case, after working for several days, he was discharged and another was brought forward to fill the vacancy.

The boys were always frightened at the thought of one painful ordeal which they were told they would have to undergo. They were seriously informed by their new mates in the shed that they would have to be branded on the back parts with a hot iron stamp containing the initials of the railway company, and very many of the youngsters firmly believed the tale and awaited the operation with dreadful suspense. As time went on, however, and they were not sent for to the offices, they came to discredit the story and smiled at their former credulity.

Different methods are now employed in engaging new hands. They are now seldom taken up from the entrances, but must apply at the works' Inquiry Office and begin to pass through the official formula in that way, or the foreman is supplied with names from private sources. This is another indication of the times, a further development of system at the works. By reason of it many good and deserving men and boys are precluded from the chance of getting a start in the factory, and many less competent ones are admitted; it affords an excellent opportunity for the exercise of favouritism on the part of the overseer. Whoever now has a mate he would like to introduce into the shed approaches the foreman. If he is a favourite himself room will be made for his friend, somehow or other, but if he is a commoner, and not reckoned among the 'lambs,' he will be met with a curt refusal, or his application will be put off indefinitely. The officials do not gain anything by the method; they will not be able to exercise as great a choice in the selection of hands, but must have what is sent them.

Another tendency at the works is that to keep out all those who do not live in the borough or within a certain area around the town, or, if they are given the chance of a start, it is only upon condition that they leave their homes and come and live under the shadow of the factory walls. It is said that this rule was first introduced chiefly in deference to the tradesmen and shopkeepers of the town, because they are under the impression that all wages earned in the town should necessarily be spent there, either in the payment of rent or the purchase of provisions and clothes.

When a new hand enters the shed he attracts considerable attention; all eyes are immediately fixed upon him. If he has worked in the factory before he will go about his duties in a very unconcerned manner, but if he is a total stranger to the place he will be shy and awkward, and will need careful and sympathetic instruction; it will be some time before he is entirely used to the new surroundings. If he is rustic in appearance, or seems likely to lend himself to a practical joke, the wags of the place soon single him out and play pranks upon him. It sometimes chances, however, that they have mistaken their man; they may meet with a sudden and unlooked for reprisal and be beaten with their own weapons.

The workmen who come from the villages are usually better-natured and also better-tempered than are those who are strictly of the town, though there are exceptions to the rule. On the whole, however, they make the more congenial mates, and they work much harder and are more conscientious. They dress much more roughly than do their

Right: Commercial Road, 1913–14. Railway wives bought basic commodities from little shops at terrace corners, very near home. *Below:* Regent Street, main shopping street of town. Railway wives only shopped here when they had extra money to spend. About 1908

Overleaf: Regent Street, from the other direction. County Electric Pavilion Cinema (opened 1910) right, first word of film title: 'Colonels . . .' Tramlines in middle of road. About 1912

Tradesmen's turnout for some special occasion such as Bath and West Show.
Mr Rimes, butcher, in striped apron. About 1906, year of tram-car disaster

Bridge Street, before 1905. GWR men returning to work

confrères of the town; the last-named would not think of wearing corduroys in the shed. There is often a great temperamental difference between the two, and they differ widely in their ideas of and adaptability for work in the shed. The country workman is fresh and tractable, open to receive new ideas and impressions of things. He brings what is practically a virgin mind to the work; he is struck with the entire newness of it all and enters heart and soul into the business. He is usually more active and vigorous, both in brain and body, than is the other, and even where he falls short in actual intelligence and knowledge of things, he more than makes up for it with painstaking effort; he is very proud of his new situation.

The town workman, on the other hand, is often superior, disdainful, and over-dignified. There is little in his surroundings that is really new and strange to him. He has always been accustomed to the crowds of workmen, and if he has not laboured in the shed before he has heard all about it from his friends or parents. His mind has often become so full of the occupations and diversions of the town that it is incapable of receiving new ideas; it is like a slate that has been fully written over and is impossible of containing another sentence or word. Instead of exhibiting shyness or reserve he immediately makes himself familiar and causes his presence to be felt. Before he has been in the shed many days he knows everything and can do everything, in his estimation, and if you attempt to reason with him, or offer any advice as to how to proceed, he will inform you that he 'knows all about it without any of your telling.'

Many of the town workmen, and especially those of the more highly skilled classes and journeymen, though village-born themselves, show considerable contempt for the country hand newly arrived in the shed, and even after he has worked there many years and proved himself to be of exceptional ability. They consider him at all times as an interloper and a 'waster,' and make no secret of their dislike of and antipathy to him. They often curse him to his face, and tell him that 'if it was not for the likes of him' they would be getting better wages. 'If I could have my way I'd sack every man of you, or make you come into the town to live. All you blokes are fit for is cow-banging and cleaning out the muck-yard; you ought to be made come here and work for ten shillings a week,' they say. All this has but little effect upon the countryman, however, and he seldom deigns to reply to it. Whether his coming to the factory to work was really better for him or not, prudent or otherwise, he does not attempt to argue. There is no law that prohibits a man from changing his occupation and taking another place when he feels inclined so to do.

Faces of young and old at annual Children's Fête, organised by Mechanics'
Institute from 1868 in GWR Park, second Saturday in August.
By 1890, crowd numbered 20,000

The same, about 1919–20. Touring showmen set up prize-fighting galleries
and side-shows on Friday evening. Wilders' firework display
illuminated Saturday's dusk

Detail of illustration bottom left. Children brought their own mugs on string tied round neck. Huge urns dispensed 680 gallons of tea. Red-Cross nurse's costume, typically post-war; right

When the average boy of the town first enters the shed he is not long in finding his way about and taking stock of the other juveniles and men; he is here, there, and everywhere in a few moments. With his shirt-sleeves turned up to the elbow he walks round, whistling or humming a tune, and greeting all indiscriminately with a wink or a nod, and a 'What cheer?' or 'Pip! pip!' If the men beckon to him – with a sly wink at their mates, intending to ask some ridiculous question or take a rise out of him – the youngster shakes his hand at them and retires straightway with a knowing nod and the expression, 'I don't think,' laying great stress upon the don't. By and by, however, as he becomes a little more proficient and 'cheeky,' the men get hold of him and treat him to a little rough play. They will either twist his arm round till he cries out with the pain, and nearly crush him in a vice-like grip, or dip his head in the nearest bosh of water.

The country lad behaves in a manner quite the reverse of this. He remains strictly near his machine or steam-hammer, and is usually too bashful to speak, unless it be to his immediate mates. He is afraid of strangers, and it will be some weeks before he ventures to walk to the other end of the shed. Even when he does this it will be not to converse with the other boys and men, but in order to watch the machines, the furnaces, and steam-hammers. There he will stand with great attention and view the several operations, and if anyone shouts out at him he will move quietly away and watch something else with the same earnestness, or go back to his own place. His conduct is altogether different from that of the other, and he is often singular in turning up his shirt-sleeves *inside*, and right up to the very shoulders. Before the town boy goes home from the shed he is careful to wash off the black from his face, comb his hair, and tidy himself up. The country boy, on the other hand, wears his livery home with him; he likes everyone to see that he has been engaged at a hot, black job. In a word, town boys are ashamed of the badge of their work, while country boys are proud of it.

Perhaps, when the village boy starts in the shed, one or two kindly disposed workmen will immediately take notice of him, and, calling him to them, will ask him where he comes from, and upon what kind of work he was before engaged, and all about himself, and so win him over with their friendliness; no matter how long he remains in the shed he does not forget their former kindness to him. In contradistinction to this the wags of the shed make him a ready mark for their diversions, running away with his cap, or sending him on many ridiculous errands and confounding him with stupid questions and conundrums. One favourite jest was to send him to the engine-house after a 'bucket of blast,' and another was to despatch him for the 'toe punch.' The 'toe punch' consisted of a vigorous kick in the posterior, which the youngster, if he obeyed the instructions given, was most certain to receive; but he very soon came to know what was intended and sturdily refused to run any more errands.

A great alteration, physically and morally, usually takes place in the man or boy newly arrived from the country into the workshop. His fresh complexion and generally healthy appearance soon disappear; his bearing, style of dress and all undergo a complete change. In a few weeks' time, especially if his work is at the fires, he becomes thin and pale, or blue and hollow-eyed. His appetite fails; he is always tired and weary. For the first time in his life he must go to the surgery and obtain medicine, or stay at home on the sick list. His firm carriage – unless he is very careful of it – leaves him; he comes to stoop naturally and walks with a slouching gait. His dress, from being clean, tidy, and well-fitting, partakes of the colour of soot and grease and hangs on his limbs; I know cases in which men have lost ten pounds in weight in a fortnight and regained it all in a little more than a week's absence from the shed.

The change in character and morals is often as pronounced as is the physical transformation; the newcomer, especially if he is a juvenile, is speedily initiated into the vices prevalent in the factory and taught the current slang phrases and expressions. Some of the workmen are greatly to blame in respect of this, and are guilty of almost criminal behaviour in their dealings with young boys. They use the most filthy language in their presence, purposely teaching them to swear, and sometimes also producing obscene pictures and books for their perusal. The foremen are not free from blame and responsibility in this matter. Many of them use the most foul language, and curse the men openly before the youngsters upon the slightest provocation. There is a species of Continental picture card that is far too popular in some of the offices; where the example is set by superiors it is small wonder that the rank and file are affected with the contagion. The managers themselves are guilty of coarse language and vulgar expressions. Certain remarks of theirs are frequently repeated and circulated in the sheds, and do not tend to improve the morals of the workmen, or to increase respect for those who made them.

Promotion among the workmen is very slow and tedious, unless there happens to be an influence at work somewhere behind, which is often the case. It is superfluous to say, moreover, that the cleverest man is not the one usually advanced; that would be contrary to all precedent at the factory. He is more usually the very individual to be kept under; the foreman will be sure to keep him in the background and hide his light underneath the bushel, or try his best to snuff it out altogether. The only material advancement possible to a workman, besides being appointed overseer, is that of being raised to the position of chargeman. A few privileges attach to the post of chargeman, especially if there is a big gang; his wages are higher, and he draws a sum called percentage, equal to 10 per cent. of his own weekly wages, deducted out of the 'balance' earned by the gang.

The system of paying percentage is very unpopular with the rank and file of the workmen; whether the chargeman's behaviour is good or bad, he is heartily hated by most of the men in consequence of it. Foremen they must tolerate, but a chargeman they fully despise. They do not like to think that any of their earnings go to pay for his supervision, although in most cases he is quite a necessary individual. In times past the chargeman used to pay the piecework 'balance' to the men, having received the money in bulk from the company, and he was often guilty of scandalous robbery and cheating. The chargeman could and did pay the gang what amount he pleased, and kept several pounds a week extra for himself. All that is past and done with now. The 'balance' is paid to the man with his day wages; no opportunity of cheating him is given to the chargeman.

As soon as it becomes known that it is intended to discharge a number of hands considerable anxiety is evidenced by the rank and file, and especially by the unskilled of the shed. They begin to quake and tremble and to be full of apprehension, for it is usually men of their class who are chosen to go, together with any who may be old and feeble, those who are subject to periodical attacks of illness, who have met with an accident at some time or other, those who are awkward and clumsy, dwellers in country places, and those whom the foreman owes a grudge. It can generally be surmised beforehand by the men themselves who will be in the number of unfortunates. Groups of workmen gather and discuss the situation quietly; there is great suspense until the notices are actually issued. Sometimes as many as a hundred men of the same shed have received their notices of dismissal on one day. The notices are written out upon special forms and the clerk of the shed, or the office-boy, carries them round to the men; it is a dramatic moment. Although fully expecting to receive the dreaded 'bit of paper,' the men hope against hope; they are quite dazed when the clerk approaches and hands it to them, for they know full well what it means. The young men may not care a scrap. To them all the world is open. They have plenty of other opportunities; but to those who are subject to illness – contracted on the premises – or who are getting on in life and are becoming old and grey and unfit for further service, it is little less than tragedy. One day's notice is served out to the men; they are quickly removed from the shed and are presently forgotten.

Of the number discharged a great many loiter about the town for several weeks, unable to find any sort of employment. These scatter about among the villages and try to obtain work on the farms; those are assisted by their relatives and kindred in various parts of the country to leave the locality altogether. Some find their way into the workhouse and end their days there, and others develop into permanent loafers and outcasts and beg their food from door to door, picking up stray coppers around the station yard or in the market-place.

Great relief is felt in the shed when the discharging is over. A common remark of the workman who is left is, 'Ah well! 'Twill be better for we as be left. 'Tis better to sack a few than to keep us all on short time here.' That is invariably the view of the well-established in the factory. Occasionally, when a workman knows he has been selected for dismissal through spite, or personal malice, he may go to the overseer and 'have it out with him,' but there is no remedy. The foreman has had the whole batch in his eye for some time past. Whatever little indiscretion is committed he records it and the man is marked. The overseer boasts openly that he shall 'get his own back,' sooner or later. 'We don't forget it, mate, you bet, not we! His time'll come all right, some day.' After the last great discharge of hands at the factory, in the year 1909, when a thousand men were dismissed in order to 'reduce expenses,' it was reported that every manager at the works was granted a substantial increase in salary. In less than a month, for some inscrutable reason, a number of new hands, equivalent to those who had been discharged, were put on again.

The speech of the workmen in the sheds necessarily varies according to the country or locality which gave them birth or to the part in which they were settled before coming to the railway town, and to the degrees of culture existing among them. The majority, including foremen, fitters, smiths, and other journeymen and labourers, speak a common language, plain, direct, and homely; there is little pretence to fine words and 'swell' phrases. The average workman detests nothing more than to be bound to a mate who is always giving himself airs, who lays stress upon his claim to superior knowledge of grammar and other matters, and who makes use of affected or artificial language and 'jaw-breakers,' as the men call them. Sometimes a new-comer to the shed may attempt to make an impression with a magnificent style of diction, though he is only mocked and ridiculed for his pains, and he soon conforms to the general rule and habit of the workshop. Even if he really possesses culture, it is soon effaced and swallowed up amid the unsympathetic environment of the shed. Occasionally one meets with an individual – it may be a workman or a clerk – who can never speak simply, but tries to express everything in ridiculous and fantastic language, and who at all times looks upon himself as a perfect hero. The blunt and matter-of-fact workmen take an entirely different view of him and his jargon, however; they look upon him as a perfect fool or an idiot.

One habit of speech is particularly noticeable amongst the men, that is the adding of the suffix 'fied' to a number of words; you often hear them make use of such expressions as 'Monday-fied,' 'sweaty-fied,' 'bossy-fied,' 'silly-fied,' and so on. Another peculiarity is the adding the letter y to a surname, usually a monosyllable, and especially to those ending in dentals and labials, such as Webb-y, Smith-y, Legg-y, Lane-y, Nash-y, Brooks-y; you never find the termination used with such words as Fowler, Foster, Matthews, Jerrom, or Johnson. This is no more than an extension of the rule which is responsible for such forms as Tommy, Annie, Betty, Teddy, or Charlie.

If one workman asks another how he is feeling, he usually receives for an answer – 'Rough and ready, like a rat-catcher's dog,' or 'Passable,' or 'Among the Middlings,' or 'In the pink, mate!' as the case may be, with the common addition of 'Ow's you?' A few are still to be found, and these among the town dwellers, too, who can neither read nor write. I especially remember one youth, of a very respectable family, of good appearance and fairly well-to-do, who could not write his name or read a letter. Such cases as this are happily rare now. Where there is an illiterate workman, if the cause of his deficiency be carefully sought out, it will usually be found to have been entirely through his own fault.

As for the fruits of education exhibited among the men in the sheds generally, that is rather a difficult and delicate matter to touch upon. One thing, however, is obvious to any who care to pay the sightest attention to it: extremely little of those subjects taught with such assiduity at school remains with the individual in after life – such things as grammar, composition, history, geography, arithmetic, and chemistry are universally forgotten. The boys of the town are especially remarkable for shortness of memory and general forgetfulness; they have few powers of mental retention, and are almost incapable of concentrating upon a matter. You have often to instruct them upon each trivial detail half-a-dozen times, and before you can turn round they have forgotten it again. The least occurrence is sufficient to distract their attention. Scolding will not help matters, it is really a natural defect. When I have had occasion to reprove boys for apparent carelessness and neglect they have more than once replied – 'I can't help it. I forgot it.' There is great truth in the first of those sentences.

Sport and play, and especially football, claims the attention of the juveniles. The love of the last-named pastime has come to be almost a disease of late years – old and young, male and female, of every rank and condition, are afflicted with it. Whatever leisure the youngsters have is spent in kicking about something or other amid the dirt and dust; from one week's end to another they are brimful of the fortunes of the local football team. Many a workman boasts that he has denied himself a Sunday dinner in order to find the money necessary for him to attend Saturday's match. Politics, religion, the fates of empires and govern-ments, the interest of life and death itself must all yield to the supreme fascination and excitement of football.

There is an almost total lack of spontaneous interest in anything – with the exception of sport and politics – that happens in the world without the factory walls and the immediate vicinity of the town. The great business of life is entirely ignored; small inclination is discoverable – even if there were opportunities – to pay attention to anything but the ordinary duties and routine of the shed. The beauties of wood and field, or hill and down, scarcely appeal to the average working man. Though magnificent downland and historical relics are within easy reach of the town's-people, few are tempted to walk so far from the smoky atmosphere of the factory as to visit them; a great indifference to the compelling attractions of Nature apparently exists. Yet, on the other hand, if you should happen to enter the shed with a handful of common wild flowers – willow-herb, rosebay, bell flower, oxeye, and so on – you would immediately be surrounded by a crowd of boys, and men, too, full of admiration for the lovely stranger, and all eagerly inquiring after their names, thereby discovering an innate passion for them, though lack of opportunity and other circumstances had almost obliterated it. Every man, woman, and child, though they may not be well aware of it, is a nature-lover at heart; they all have a fond regard for the simple, natural things of the earth – birds, plants, and flowers. The men of the shed are always eager to listen to and take part in political discussions, but they

Football, 1908. Swindon Town play Crystal Palace at Swindon: big crowd of men, women and children. Feb 2nd: Swindon Town 0, Crystal Palace 0; Oct 17th: Swindon Town 4, Crystal Palace 0

West End Workmen's Football Club, 1903–4: another of the many local football clubs

are, as a rule, totally indifferent to the interest of literature. At the same time, if you have anything to tell them of birds, flowers, and animals, life on the farm, haymaking, reaping, threshing, ploughing, and so on, they are full of attention: they evidently derive great pleasure from the relation of these simple matters and occupations.

As for general culture, it may at once be said that the educated man is not wanted at the factory. What is more, the managers will not have him if they can by any means avoid it; there is a great antipathy to him

IN MEMORY OF

Manchester

CITY.

WHO FELL AT

The County Ground, Swindon

FIGHTING FOR THE

ENGLISH CUP.

MARCH 5TH, 1910.

AGED 4TH, ROUND.

Bury Manchester City
Their day is over and done,
Sing them a little sad ditty
And cheer for the team that won,
Oh don't you think 'twas rather a pity
You came to Swindon, Manchester City

Funeral arrangements by G.W.R.

Caustic memorial to Manchester City footballers, 1910, topped by an elegant hearse

on the part of the staff in and out of the shed. Where a workman is known to possess any intellectual abilities above those commonly found and has the courage to raise his voice in any matter or to interest himself in things pertaining to the town, or if he has in any way access to the ear of the public, he is certain to be marked for it; at the first convenient opportunity he will be shifted off the premises. Every workman who desires to improve himself in any direction other than in that which tends to promote the interests of the company is looked

Coate Reservoir provided natural pleasures: the WEA paid an annual visit here,
1911. Alfred discussed with Reuben George a WEA subsidy for
Poems in Wiltshire – fruitlessly

Fishing at Coate Reservoir 1905. Jefferies (1848–87) sailed his home-made boat
on this deep, fish-shaped pond. It contained large pike and tench

upon with suspicion; he is immediately included in the number of 'undesirables.'

Several years ago the manager of a department who was at the time Chairman of the local Educational Authority, sent for me in order to see whether I might be of any use to him in his office. After a lengthy interview he expressed his disappointment at being unable to offer me any position, and took care to point out to me the folly of my ways. My intellectual qualifications were beyond his consideration, said he. I was

Whit Monday 27 May 1912, Coate Reservoir. Only the young men are dressed informally. This reservoir, constructed in a marshy hollow, 1822, is now called Coate Water

so full of many matters as to be quite worthless to him. He must have certificates. What was the use of my trying, anyhow? He would quote two words to me – *Cui bono*? The world was full of better men than I. What was the good of literature? His advice to me was to go back to my furnace, look after my wife and family, and trouble no more about it.

At the forge, however, the steady persistence of my efforts towards self-improvement was not appreciated. Day after day the foreman of the shed came or sent someone with oil or grease to obliterate the few words of Latin or Greek which I had chalked upon the back of the sooty furnace in order to memorise them. Even my tool-boxes and cupboard, always considered more or less private and sacred, were periodically smeared with fat and the operation was often carried out in a very offensive manner. The plan was not successful, however, and I was often more amused than annoyed, though it was most seriously intended by the overseer, who always said he was acting under the manager's orders. At one time he had caused the furnace back to be tarred. Before the tar had

completely dried I innocently chalked upon it several words that figured in my studies for the day. By the next morning the characters had become permanent. The colour of the chalk had set, and as often as the overseer or his agent came with the oil-pot and removed the dust and soot, thinking to baffle me, he was confronted with the Horation precept, *Nil desperandum*, a quotation from the *Hecuba*, and Σταύρωσον αὐτόν (Crucify him) from the New Testament. The one most appreciated at the works is he who remains silent and slavishly obeys every order, who is willing to cringe and fawn like a dog, to swear black is white and white is black at the bidding of his chief, to fulfil every instruction without ever questioning the wisdom or utility of it, to be, in a word, as clay in the potter's hand, a mere tool and a puppet.

Where the cultured person does exist in the shed he must generally suffer exquisite tortures. There can be no culture without a higher sensibility, and he will be thereby rendered less able to endure the hardships of the toil, and the otherwise brutal and callous environments of the place. As for the view, held in some quarters, that education will make a man happier at work and better satisfied with his lot and condition, that is pure myth and fallacy, and the sooner it is dispensed with the better. On the other hand, it will most certainly produce dissatisfaction, but such, perhaps, as will speedily wake him up to his real needs and requirements – a larger freedom, and the attainment of a fuller and better life. Any kind of education that tends to make the workman at all subjective to his lot is worthless and retrograde; he must be roused up to battle towards perfection of conditions and must himself be prepared to make some sort of sacrifice towards the accomplishment of that end, unless he is content to occupy the same level for ever. Nor will it be sufficient for him to have obtained higher wages and greater leisure if he does not attempt to derive something more than a mere physical or material benefit from them. Whatever advantage is gained in the future must be turned to sterling account – to the acquisition of useful knowledge and the increase of mental strength and fitness, otherwise the battle will have been fought greatly in vain.

CHAPTER XVIII

SHORT TIME AND OVERTIME – 'BACK TO THE LAND' – THE TOWN
INFLUENCE – CHANGES AT THE WORKS – GRIEVANCES – THE
POSITION OF LABOUR – ILLS AND REMEDIES – THE FUTURE OUTLOOK

Frequent spells of short time occur at the works, which are most certain
to be followed by brisk and busy periods, as though the officials were
anxious to make up for every moment of the previously lost time. It
usually happens that the change is made direct from prosperity to
adversity and *vice versa*. One week the machinery in the sheds is
running day and night and every man is working unusual hours; the
next, everything is changed. Short time is declared; only half the output
will be needed and about half the time worked. Similarly, after a period
of short weeks, a full-time notice is posted, and by the next night all the
men are pell-mell on overtime, working as though they had but a few
hours to live. Whether it is necessary or not is never ascertained; there is
apparently an astounding want of order and foresight on the part of the
managing staff.

It is remarkable that, notwithstanding the terrific nature of the
hardships endured, the majority of the men at the factory do not show
themselves seriously averse to the working of overtime. There is even
satisfaction evinced at the prospect of putting in an extra day and a half,
a week, and drawing a few shillings more in wages. The few who
dislike it from principle and on other grounds must swallow their
objections and join in with the rest; whether they like it or not they are
forced to follow the crowd. If a man refuses point-blank to work after
the usual hours he is punished either with suspension from the shed or
instant dismissal. Unfortunately for the good of the working classes
generally, those who are satisfied with the ordinary rate of hours are
insignificant in number. The highly-paid workmen and journeymen are
about as unreasonable in the matter as are the lowest paid labourers.

Very often they are the more insatiable of the two; they will put in any number of hours provided an opportunity is given them for so doing. The trade unionists are usually as well agreed as the others to work extra time; there is but very little difference discovered between them. No matter how loudly they declaim against the system and advocate the abolition of overtime, should the order be issued they commonly obey it with alacrity.

Occasionally, though not often, it is announced that the working of overtime may be optional. In the extreme heat of summer, when overtime at the fires is prevalent, the overseer may relax a little and cause it to be known that any who wish it may go home at the ordinary hour, but few take advantage of the offer. I have known those who were highly paid, on the hottest days of summer, to be so severely punished with the heat that they could scarcely stand at their posts, almost incapable of further effort and exhausted with the toil, yet though it was free for them to leave at the usual hour they would not go home. They cling to the shed as long as they possibly can; they have an unnatural fondness of the stench and smoke. Such as these are often teased and twitted and told to 'bring their beds' with them, or an outspoken workman will tell them they ought to die and be buried on the premises.

A great part of the overtime, moreover, is not always genuinely necessary, but is artificially engineered in order to please this or that one and to provide someone or other with additional pocket-money. A few chargemen in every shed systematically nurse the overseer and entreat, or influence him, directly or otherwise, to allow them to work a few quarters, a Saturday afternoon, or a Sunday.

Very often, too, some of the men live in houses owned by their foreman. In this case a little overtime will expedite payment of the rent; it will not then be amiss to allow them to work a few quarters. The putting on a few new hands and the addition of a night shift would obviate much overtime and give the unemployed a chance, but the daymen are offended should that proposition be made. I have actually heard men volunteer to work double-handed at the fires and promise to turn out considerably increased quantities of work on their turn rather than for the foreman to run a night shift and so prevent them from working overtime.

The men's takings at such times as these are fairly high. Some of the new hands are astonished when they receive their wages, with the piecework 'balance' added, on a full week. One of them, in the days of the old foreman of the frame shed, was so aghast at the amount he had to draw he could not believe it was all intended for him; he thought there must be a mistake somewhere. Accordingly, holding the money in his hand, he went back to the foreman, and, in front of all the other men cried – 'Be this all mine, sir?' The foreman, who happened to be in an ill-temper, cursed him for an idiot and promptly told him to 'clear out.'

At another time, when the men were being paid on breaking up for Christmas holidays, a good-natured country lad, whose earnings were small, chanced by mistake to draw the wages of another, much more highly rated than himself, and, thinking the extras were intended for a Christmas-box, promptly went and laid out the money in presents for his mother and dad. He was quickly called to account, however, and had to refund the cash at once, and he furthermore received the imputation of being a sly rogue and a thief. Without doubt money is plentiful during overtime, though the extras are far from being all profit. It costs more to live. The workman requires more to eat and drink, more clothes, firing, light, and other sundries, to say nothing of the sacrifice of freedom and life.

It is little real gain to the workman, even though he have a trifle better food and clothing, a finer house and costlier furniture, while he has to work excessively long hours in order to pay for it. The more expensively he lives the more time he must spend in the smoke and stench of the shed and the greater must be his dependence upon his employer. He that lives simply in a modest cottage is much nearer to freedom than the other can ever hope to be, for he is bound down to life-long servitude. Every hour spent outside the factory walls is a precious addition to life; whoever willingly throws away the opportunity of enjoying it is guilty of the highest folly and negligence. He is the curtailer of his dearest rights and liberties, the forger of fetters for himself and his children after him, and the sooner the working classes can be brought to see this the better it will be for them.

There is a great deal of talk, chiefly with a political bias, about the sheds, of getting back to the land. Many of the men tell you they are sick of town life and conditions and would like to see themselves established upon a dozen acres of land far away from the noise of the factory, but they never make the slightest effort towards the consummation of the wish. The fact is that, notwithstanding all the punishments and hardships endured in the workshop, they are still strongly attached to it or to the life they are enabled to live by reason of it. They have no intention whatever at heart of changing their occupation. They are content to mix with the crowd, and are unable to withstand the novelty and excitement of the town existence.

During the many years I have spent in the works I have known of but one case in which a man left the shed to go back to the land as a small working farmer. He had always been careful and thrifty, and seemed to be well fitted for the agricultural life, but he could not succeed in it. After five or six years of hard labour, trying in vain to prosper, he returned to the shed, a disappointed and ruined man: he had spent his savings and lost the whole of his small capital. He is still working in the shed, and he has no intention of repeating the experiment. The wages at the works, though low as compared with those obtainable at other towns, are much higher than what the farm labourer receives. Youths of eighteen years of age in the sheds often draw more than the carter or cowman, who may have to maintain big families.

Consequently, while the cry of 'Back to the land' is heard on all sides, there is at the same time a most passionate desire to get away from it and to come into the town to work and live; whoever is of the requisite age will be certain to appear at the factory gates to try and obtain admission there. The whole countryside, within a radius of six or eight miles of the town, is almost destitute of good strong workmen. Only the feeble and decrepit are left behind to work on the farms – those who cannot pass the physical tests and those who formerly worked in the factory and were discharged through old age or other causes of unfitness. Once a man becomes settled in the factory he is very reluctant to leave it. Notwithstanding the rigour of the system imposed, he usually remains there till the end of his working days, unless he happens to meet with an accident or dismissal. He soon loses his self-confidence and independent spirit. The world is considerably narrowed down in his view; he feels bound to the life with indissoluble fetters.

As for the work itself, men do that in the factory they would scorn to do outside or upon the farm. They would not be seen milking or 'clod-hopping,' or carrying a yoke and pails, a truss of hay on their head, or a little pig in their arms, or driving cattle to market. At the same time they are not ashamed to scour down filthy roofs and windows, to do white-washing, to clean black and greasy engines, to wheel coal and ashes up or down the stage, to tar the axles and wheels of waggons and vehicles, to stand at the furnace or machine all day in a half-fainting condition choked with the smoke and dust of the shed; as though it were not more wholesome to have to do with cattle and crops than to be for ever penned up within four walls!

Although perhaps not as keen intellectually as are some of those who get their living in the town, and not receiving as much in wages, the best of the farm-hands are healthier, happier, and generally more well-to-do than are the factory labourers. At the same time, it is but natural that a man should desire to leave the country to come into the town. Though the work is much sharper and infinitely more painful while it lasts, the shorter hours and higher pay are powerful inducements for him to make the change. He will be free on Saturday afternoons, and there is no Sunday labour, while his wages will often be half as much again as what he would get on the farm. It is idle to say that the desertion of the countryside is a modern symptom; that has very little force, for it was always the same among highly civilised communities. The Greek husbandman left the soil and flocked to Athens to sit in the Agora, the Egyptians thronged the streets of Alexandria, and the Italians deserted the plough and sickle and crowded in Rome to see the circus games and other diversions of the '*Urbs Terrarum.*'

Those who, most of all, use the cry of 'Back to the land' are they that obtain the highest wages in the sheds, and who are themselves the least likely to set the example. Men with families enlarge upon the blessings and privileges of agricultural life, but they take great care to get their sons started in the shed at the very earliest opportunity. As soon as they leave school they are brought along in knickerbockers and presented to the overseer, with the earnest hope of a speedy admission to work on the premises. I know of several cases in which workmen have been offered financial help in order to instal them in small-holdings, and they have refused point-blank. When I asked them the reason they replied that they 'would rather go home at half-past five, if it made no difference,' and that is the crux of the whole matter. Not only this, there is the football match, the railway 'Trip,' the privilege fares, the theatre, the cinematograph, the skating-rink, and the trams, all which must be sacrificed if the workman determines in favour of the simple life on the farm or small-holding. The class of men to secure for the land is the pick of the agricultural labourers, those who are uncontaminated with the life of the town; it is useless to think of reclaiming those who have once entered the factory and become established there.

Even very many of those who dwell outside the town are not content to spend their leisure in the village; in the evening and at week-ends they wash and dress and flock back to the street corners or parade up and down the thoroughfares. Innovations such as the cinematograph and the skating-rink, though harmless enough in some respects, are of little real value to the workman; with all their claims to be 'educational' and 'health-giving' the town could very well afford to dispense with them.

Overleaf: The Rink, 1911. 'Fast Skating Not Allowed'. Musicians' gallery, top right, above sales' counter. Gentlemen were requested not to wear hats

There is little that is really manly and vigorous in roller-skating, and many of the cinematograph pictures serve only to indulge the craving for the novel and sensational. Half the boys of the shed, and even the infants of the town, can think of little but those ridiculously stupid and often debasing entertainments, of blood and thunder, crime, and mawkish love dramas; their minds are rendered quite incapable of imbibing sound and useful knowledge.

Even the trams, useful as they are, prove in several ways detrimental to

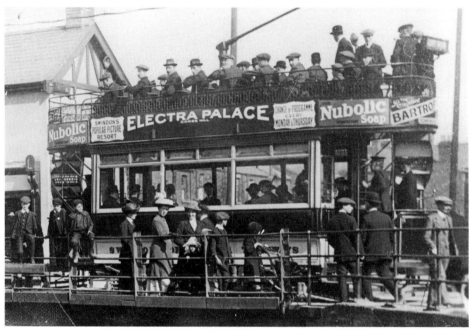

Advertisement for 'Cinematograph': Electra Palace, Gorse Hill, change of film twice weekly, about 1910. Crowded tram on Fleet Street Bridge over canal. Films were first shown in Swindon, 1907

the toiler and contribute to the restriction of his liberty. Scores of workmen I know wait at their doors or at street corners for five, and very often for ten minutes, in order to ride a distance of about a quarter of a mile. I have nothing to say against the habit provided the man can afford twopence or threepence a day for fares. At the same time, considered from the point of view of health, walking the distance would often be much better, and every copper needlessly spent by the worker tends to make him more and more dependent upon the shed. Where a man is engaged upon very hot and laborious work he is often too tired to walk home. The wages of such a one ought to be sufficiently high to enable him to make the journey in a taxicab, if he desired it.

Very different from this, however, is the lot of the small-holder. He must rise early all the year round – in summer and winter, light or dark, hot or cold weather. His work is not of five-and-a-half, but of six or seven days. Where cattle are kept there can be no such thing as a day off; dumb mouths must be fed and their needs ministered to. He has no trams to take him to work, very often no shelter from the storms and showers, no shade in summer and no steam-heated refuge in winter. His leisure is short, his companions few, his whole life laborious. But he is happy and strong, healthy, and vigorous in body and mind; he is in many ways a better man than is his *confrère* of the town. Considerably more skill, knowledge, and human feeling are also required on the part of the carter, cowman, and shepherd in dealing with their teams, flocks, and herds, than in the case of those who merely superintend mechanical processes and have to do with lifeless blocks of iron and steel, yet the countrymen are more or less despised by the factory workers and are greatly deficient in wages. Low wages are given on the farm simply because it is the custom so to do; if the Government were to intervene and fix a higher rate the extra money would be paid as a matter of course. This is the only kind of reform that would really popularise work on the land from the point of view of the poor man and help to check the wholesale migration to the towns. Not until such improvements have been made will the labourer be willing heartily to respond to the cry of 'Back to the land.'

One thing is especially to be deplored in the factory and that is the serious lack of recognition and appreciation of the skilful and conscientious workman; there is very little inducement for anyone to make efforts in order to obtain better results at the steam-hammer or other machine. If a workman proves himself to be possessed of unusual skill and originality, instead of being rewarded for it he is boycotted and held in check. Even the managers are not above exhibiting the same petty feeling where they find their ideas have been eclipsed by those of less authority. It is their habit to think that anything they suggest is the best possible of its kind.

Whatever inventions are produced by the workmen, whether in leisure time or at the shed, become the property of the railway company; they claim the right of free and unrestricted use of all patents applied for by their employees. Consequently, if a workman discovers means by which he might assist the firm with a new process he holds his peace and

Overleaf: New trams at the Centre, 22 September 1904. This was the opening day, when electricity came to the town. Globe gaslights over shop-fronts, right

troubles no more about it. He knows that he would not be thanked for the information, and he is also aware that if the scheme were adopted his prices would consequently be reduced. In more up to date sheds, and particularly in America, bonuses are given for the best work made and every man is induced, by all reasonable means, to think out new methods. An 'idea box' is kept on the premises; every 'happy thought' is written upon a form and slipped into this. The managers alone inspect the sheets and any suggestion considered worthy of being adopted is paid for.

Bonuses are paid to firemen and engine-drivers on the line for economy in fuel. The same plan might profitably be adopted in the factory. It is well-known that certain men invariably produce the best work. One furnaceman will waste as much again fuel as another. One machineman breaks no end of drills and tools. The work of this or that smith always looks rough and shoddy. One stamper spoils more dies in a year than another will in ten and often gets his work sent back, while the other does never. If the best men were the most highly paid there would be no just cause for complaint, but they are not. They are all classed the same. The incompetent receives as much as the competent and is usually held higher in esteem.

That great changes have taken place in regard to everything connected with the factory of late years is not to be disputed. Different schemes of work and other methods of dealing with the men have everywhere been introduced. New machinery has revolutionised many branches of the labour and it usually happens that where an appliance that saves 50 per cent. to the firm is adopted the men are hustled into double activity; the great delight of the managers is to boast of the large amount of work produced by a machine, and to add that 'one man does it all.' In addition, prices all round are continually being sharpened; 'balance' is earned with greater difficulty and only by increased effort. The officials declare openly that piecework balance is merely given to the men when they earn it without strenuous efforts; they will not admit the reasonableness of working with any degree of sanity and comfort.

As well as new machinery, which has revolutionised many branches of work in the factory, there are such things as fresh laws and regulations touching accidents and compensation for injuries, which have helped considerably to modify the tone and character of the sheds. Only those in perfect health are now admitted to the works; those possessed of flaws of any kind are rejected. The tests are almost as severe as are those used for recruiting for the Army and Navy, and young men are refused on account of the most trivial ailments and infirmities.

When a man shows signs of being subject to recurrent spells of sickness he is marked out as an undesirable; as soon as any opportunity comes he will be quietly shifted off the premises. If a workman falls ill he must not only satisfy the medical authorities at the works' infirmary, and notify his foreman of the fact, but, after passing the doctor's examination and clearing off the funds, he must present himself at one of the manager's offices and be further interrogated before he is allowed to start again. This last-named examination is deeply resented by the rank and file, and many, though ill, continue at work when they ought to be at home because they do not like the irritating process of passing the test and the certainty of having something or other recorded against them.

In reality this is a system of espionage, a cowardly inquisition, but one that is in high favour with the foreman because it gives him the chance of getting rid of a man on so-called medical grounds without his suspecting that he has been discharged for other reasons. By this means the shed foreman may remove anyone against whom he has a grudge and he cannot well be blamed himself; the victim is told that he is 'medically unfit,' and there is an end of it. The game is played by putting a private pen mark upon the official slip to be presented at the office. If the foreman desires to retain the workman he puts a private mark upon the paper, and if he wants to get rid of him and has not the courage to tell him so to his face the mark is omitted. This is so arranged in order that if the workman suspects that the paper contains something to his detriment and demands to see it, there shall be nothing that he can cavil at. The damaging thing is in that there is no sign upon it. Honest Mark Fell, who was one of the finest smiths that ever worked at a forge, an excellent time-keeper, and who was possessed of a grand character, died rather than go out on the sick list and be forced to pass the dreaded inquisition. He was run down with over-work, and was badly in need of a rest, but he did not like the idea of going to the offices. Accordingly he kept coming to work day after day, and grew weaker and weaker. When at last he did stay out it was too late; his strength and vitality were gone and he died within a week or two afterwards.

A decade and a half ago one could come to the shed fearlessly, and with perfect complacence; work was a pleasure in comparison with what it is now. It was not that the toil was easy, though, as a matter of fact, it was not so exhausting as it is at present, but there was an entirely different feeling prevalent. The workman was not watched and timed at every little operation, and he knew that as the job had been one day so it would be the next. Now, however, every day brings fresh troubles from some quarter or other. The supervisory staff has been doubled or trebled, and they must do something to justify their existence. Before the workman can recover from one shock he is visited with another; he is kept in a state of continual agitation and suspense which, in time, operate on his mind and temper and transform his whole character.

At one time old and experienced hands were trusted and respected, both by reason of their great knowledge of the work, acquired through many years, and as a kind of tacit recognition of their long connection with the firm, but now, when a man has been in the shed for twenty years, however young he may be, he is no longer wanted. There is now a very real desire to be rid of him. For one thing, his wages are high. In addition to this, he knows too much; he is not pliable. It is time he was shifted to make room for someone lower paid, more plastic and more ignorant of the inner working of things.

If a workman has a grievance it is useless for him to complain to the overseer, who is usually the cause of it, and if he takes it upon himself to go and see the manager he gets no redress. The manager always supports the foreman whether he has acted rightly or wrongly, and the man is remembered and branded as a malcontent; he will be carefully watched ever after. The safest way to quell a man is to keep him hard at work. While his nose is firm upon the grindstone there is no danger of his indulging in speculations of any kind; he could no more realise himself than he could hope to see the stars at midday.

While the men are inside the walls of the factory, they are under the most severe laws and restrictions, many of which are utterly ridiculous, and out of all reason considering the general circumstances of the toil and the conditions in vogue; they are indeed prisoners in every sense of the term. In the midst of the busiest period of hay-making and harvest-cart, ploughing or threshing, a short stop is always made for refreshment, or the labourer takes a crust of bread and cheese from his pocket and eats it at his work and is strengthened with it, but in the factory one must not be seen to crack a nut, or eat an apple or biscuit, much less to partake of any other food. If he should break the rule and be seen eating, he will be marked for it and told to 'get a pass out and go home.' Four or five hours is a long time to keep up a strenuous pace at the fires. A half-way relaxation of ten minutes would be good for everyone; the workman would more than make up for it afterwards.

A regrettable dulness is discovered by very many of the men, which may be bred of the labour itself and the extremely monotonous conditions of the factory. There is little or no thought taken for the future, no knowledge of the value of life, and not much desire to know, either. The workmen do not think for themselves, and if you should be at the pains of pointing out anything for their benefit they will tell you that you are mad, or curse you for a Socialist. Anyone at the works who holds a view different from that expressed by the crowd is called a Socialist, rightly or wrongly; it would need an earthquake to rouse many of the men out of their apathy and indifference. It is more than education at fault. There is something wrong at the very roots of the tree. The whole system of life requires overhauling and revolutionising; the national character is become flat and stale.

I have already, in the first chapter, referred to labour unrest. That is the perfectly natural outcome of modern conditions of labour, the long spell of commercial prosperity, and of the spread of knowledge among the working classes. It is not to be viewed with misgiving at all, at any rate, not by those who can look intelligently into the future and brush aside the paltry prejudices that are common everywhere today. The very fact that working-men are rousing themselves and showing a masterly interest in problems of the hour, and are prepared to fight fairly and bravely for better conditions should be a source of satisfaction to everyone. It proves, at least, that they are awake and alive; that they have cast off torpor and stagnation and put on power and virility, and that is surely a good omen both for the future of democracy and for the nation at large. The extent of the riches of this country is so great as to be inconceivable to the workers; if they knew how much wealth there really is they would need to have no scruples in pressing with all their might for a fairer share in the profits of their labours. Where the pace is so much faster and the output considerably increased it is natural that there should be a demand for higher wages and shorter hours. More leisure and rest are absolutely indispensable in order properly to recuperate for the increased demands made upon the workmen's physical powers. The difficulties of forming agreements with the men are not nearly as great as they are represented to be. Drastic changes could be made with but very little inconvenience or loss to the firm; the transition would be almost imperceptible.

The idea that the general factory week should be completed in five turns, the day shifts to finish working by Friday night, and the night shifts to complete their toils by Saturday morning, has long been in my mind. The having two clear days of leisure would give the worker an opportunity of entirely shaking off the effects of confinement in the shed at the week-end, and of starting work a new man on the Monday morning. It is impossible for one to recuperate sufficiently in the short space of time at present allowed; he is never free from the effects of the hurry and speed of the machinery. There is, moreover, no time to get away from the shadow and ugliness of the factory walls and to make the acquaintance of other scenes in the country round about. When the sheds are closed on Saturdays for short time, crowds of workers either leave the town on foot and walk around the adjacent villages, enjoying the fresh, pure air, or take short trips by the train and come back streng-

Men leaving work by main tunnel entrance, about 1908–10

thened with the change; you hear many a one say, during the following week, that he feels extra fit and well.

If a week of forty-eight hours were divided out and completed in five turns, instead of six, it would be both popular with the men and economical for the employers. The fuel and light, the cost of steaming up the boilers and the general wear and tear of machinery on the sixth turn and for several hours a day besides would be saved, and there would be about an equivalent amount of work produced. It is useless for critics and calculators to come forward with figures and quotations to disprove the statement and show its impossibility; I have worked in the shed long enough to understand the true significance of things. What is more, the workman is not, and never will be a mathematical machine; his efforts and powers are not to be calculated by the set rules of arithmetic.

The whole trend of things in the industrial world is towards shorter hours, better wages, and a greater proportion of liberty for the workman; all the objections that can be raised and schemes devised will not stop the progressive movement. Sooner or later the barriers must give way, and the goal will have been reached; the wonder then will be that the change was not effected earlier. I would bid all toilers and moilers, in and out of factories, to be of good hope and cheer, to fight on and press steadily forward; victory will be certain to follow. At the same time, one must not expect to arrive at an utter immunity from hardships, nor, perhaps, will the whole of the differences between capital and labour ever be absolutely removed and every problem solved. Many conditions, however, will most certainly have been bettered, many disputes settled and evils overcome, and this, it will be confessed, is worth living and hoping for.

Beginning vast extensions to the erecting shop (ahead, right) May 1914.
Within four months, Alfred quitted service of GWR, left his
steam-hammer for ever

APPENDIX

Table of average day wages per week of fifty-four hours paid to men employed at Swindon Railway Works, July 1914:–

Foremen	70s.	Coppersmiths	30s.
Foremen, Assistant	50s.	Tinsmiths	30s.
Draughtsmen	35s.	Moulders	26s.
Clerks, Monthly Staff	30s.	Wheel Turners	24s.
Clerks, Shop	25s.	Machinemen, General	24s.
Forgemen	33s.	Carriage Body-makers	30s.
Smiths	33s.	Carriage Finishers	28s.
Rolling Mills Men	30s.	Waggon-builders	28s.
Furnacemen	28s.	Road-Waggon Builders	28s.
Stampers	28s.	Carpenters	28s.
Stampers' Assistants	22s.	Painters	26s.
Smiths' Strikers	22s.	Saw Mills, Timber	24s.
Pattern-makers	35s.	Riveters	26s.
Boilermakers	34s.	Bricklayers	28s.
Fitters and Turners	34s.	Labourers, Skilled	22s.
Fitters, Engine	34s.	Labourers, Unskilled	20s.
Fitters, Carriage	28s.	Labourers, Fitters'	21s.
Die-sinkers	34s.	Storekeepers	23s.

INDEX

Numbers in italic indicate photographs